War with Iran

War with Iran

Political, Military, and Economic Consequences

Geoffrey Kemp and John Allen Gay

PUBLISHED IN PARTNERSHIP WITH THE
CENTER FOR THE NATIONAL INTEREST

ROWMAN & LITTLEFIELD PUBLISHERS, INC.
Lanham • Boulder • New York • Toronto • Plymouth, UK

Published in partnership with the Center for the National Interest

Published by Rowman & Littlefield Publishers, Inc.
A wholly owned subsidiary of The Rowman & Littlefield Publishing Group, Inc.
4501 Forbes Boulevard, Suite 200, Lanham, Maryland 20706
www.rowman.com

10 Thornbury Road, Plymouth PL6 7PP, United Kingdom

British Library Cataloguing in Publication Information Available

Library of Congress Cataloging-in-Publication Data

Kemp, Geoffrey.
War with Iran : political, military, and economic consequences / Geoffrey Kemp and John Allen.
pages cm.
Includes bibliographical references.
ISBN 978-1-4422-2199-4 (cloth : alk. paper)—ISBN 978-1-4422-2197-0 (pbk. : alk. paper)—ISBN 978-1-4422-2198-7 (electronic)
1. United States—Foreign relations—Iran. 2. United States—Military relations—Iran. 3. Iran—Foreign relations—United States. 4. Iran—Strategic aspects. 5. Iran—Military policy. 6. Nuclear weapons—Iran. I. Title.
E183.8.I55K425 2013
327.73055—dc23
2012050659

∞ ™ The paper used in this publication meets the minimum requirements of American National Standard for Information Sciences Permanence of Paper for Printed Library Materials, ANSI/NISO Z39.48-1992.

Printed in the United States of America

Contents

Prologue

For many years there has been speculation about the possibility of a war between the United States and Iran, perhaps precipitated by an Israeli decision to strike Iran's nuclear facilities. In the worst case, a war could trigger a conflagration with untold costs for regional stability and the global economy. On the other hand, a brief military encounter might be far less painful for the United States and its allies than an Iranian bomb. Between these two extremes, a number of other scenarios are plausible. But all involve troublesome unknowns and provide no certainty that military action alone will end Iran's nuclear program or topple its regime. In the case of a small Israeli strike, delay is the only gain—the hope would be that the longer Iran's nuclear program is delayed, the more likely the regime will fall or be taken down before a bomb can be constructed. But a more pessimistic scenario would suggest that an Israeli strike would unite many Iranians behind the regime, and guarantee that Iran continues with its nuclear program, which would virtually assure the need for another confrontation every time Iran rebuilds its program—in other words, it could be a recipe for an endless war.

Needless to say, none of these options is appealing, and the impact on the global economic recovery could be devastating. It is therefore important to review the political, military, and economic factors that need to be taken into account in contemplating a war with Iran. The first section of this book covers the geopolitical setting, paying particular attention to Iran, the United States, Russia, the European countries, and the major players in the Middle East. The second section looks in some detail at various military scenarios, including both Israeli and American strikes, and what the Iranian response might be. The third section deals primarily with the economic consequences of a war, particularly its impact upon world oil markets, and the ability of Iran to interfere with traffic through the Strait of Hormuz. We have also included a set of appendixes that provide more details of a confrontation.

Acknowledgments

In 2010, the Center for the National Interest (then known as the Nixon Center) was given a small grant by the Ploughshares Fund to host a number of meetings to discuss alternative strategies for stopping the Iranian nuclear weapons program. A further grant was awarded by Ploughshares in 2011 to prepare three papers on the political, military, and economic consequences of a war with Iran. This book is the result of that work, for which we owe many people thanks for their encouragement, their support, and their careful review of sections of the manuscript. In particular, we would like to thank Deana Arsenian and Steve Del Rosso of the Carnegie Corporation; Joe Cirincione, Naila Bolus, and Haleh Hatemi, the Ploughshares Fund; Janne Nolan, the George Washington University; Patrick Clawson, the Washington Institute; Amy Myers Jaffe, the Baker Institute; Suzanne Maloney, the Brookings Institution; and James Placke (formerly with Cambridge Energy), John Adams, and Shlomo Brom, the Institute for National Security Studies. Valuable contributions were also made by Kristen Gehringer, Rajiv Mehta, Noah Benjamin, Stephanie Tietz, Jessica Pealer, Arthur Shinabargar, Hiba Abdulrazzak, Whit Miller, Jyothi Pocha, and R. Christopher Farrar.

Early drafts of this manuscript were presented to members of Congress and the "Wednesday group" at Americans for Tax Reform. At a meeting at Wye in November 2011, the economic section of the paper was circulated and discussed, and at a second Wye meeting in November 2012, jointly hosted by the Center for the National Interest and George Washington University and supported by the Ploughshares Fund and the Carnegie Corporation of New York, further reviews and comments on the themes of the manuscript were sought. We would also like to thank our colleagues here at the Center who have been most supportive, including Dimitri Simes, Paul Saunders, Robert Merry, and Charles Boyd.

Introduction

> Iran's leaders should understand that I do not have a policy of containment; I have a policy to prevent Iran from obtaining a nuclear weapon.
>
> —President Barack Obama speaking at the AIPAC Policy Conference, March 2012[1]

The United States has consistently, across different presidential administrations, stated that it does not accept Iran's nuclear weapons aspirations. The rhetoric, however, has grown increasingly stern and unequivocal, as evidenced by the quote above. In an interview given in late 1995, President Bill Clinton said that his (and the United States government's) problem with Iran was directed at the "unacceptable behavior" of Iran's government and its "acquisition of weapons and technologies of mass destruction—including nuclear."[2] President George W. Bush, in an April 2006 news conference, echoed this sentiment, though with a more direct tone: "And we've agreed on the goal, and that is the Iranians should not have a nuclear weapon, the capacity to make a nuclear weapon, or the knowledge as to how to make a nuclear weapon."[3] And just before he gave remarks at the 2012 AIPAC conference, President Obama stated that "I think both the Iranian and Israeli governments recognize that when the United States says it is unacceptable for Iran to have a nuclear weapon, we mean what we say."[4] Statements to this end are not limited to current and former presidents, but have also been made by former administration officials discussing the views of President Obama.[5]

American leaders have a deep distaste for Iran's foreign policy. Iranian violations of embassies, support for radical movements, and acts of terror and assassination have violated basic norms of international conduct. Iran has also staunchly opposed peace between the Arabs and Israelis, and in recent years some Iranian leaders have used viciously anti-Semitic rhetoric, even in prominent international forums. The acquisition of nuclear weapons by any state would be cause for concern, but the concerns are far greater when the state has a foreign policy like Iran's. Will it use a nuclear deterrent to cover an even more outlandish foreign policy? Would leaders given to revolutionary and even apocalyptic rhetoric respond to nuclear deterrence in a stable manner?

In some respects, however, the roots of this confrontation are much older and deeper, stemming from long-held strategic aims of Iran and the United States. The United States sees the Gulf as an area of vital strategic importance, and itself as the Gulf's ultimate protector. Jimmy Carter, in his 1980 State of the Union, stated that "an attempt by any outside force to gain control of the Persian Gulf region will be regarded as an assault on the vital interests of the United States of America, and such an assault will be repelled by any means necessary, including military force." Carter was, of course, referring to the Soviet Union following its invasion of Afghanistan, but the thrust of his stance, known as the Carter Doctrine, has been upheld and developed by successive American administrations: Reagan ordered a range of military countermeasures to the insecurity of the Iran-Iraq War; Clinton and both Bushes launched major military operations against Iraq. Any president who allowed the rise of a hegemon on the Gulf would have to reverse decades of policy and make significant changes to American strategic culture—a tall order, to say the least.

For even longer, Iran has aimed to the Gulf's dominant power. Under the shah, Iran amassed a large and technologically advanced arsenal, and began laying the groundwork for a nuclear program. The United States tolerated this because the shah was an ally; with his fall in the 1979 revolution, the dynamics changed. The Islamic Republic is not, as some have suggested, an irrational regime willing to risk its own destruction in order to "wipe Israel off the map." It has, however, a revisionist streak—understandable given that it is an isolated but proud country, but also rooted in the ideological context of the regime's founding. Iran's leaders can be cowed by sanctions, threats, and their own limitations, but they ultimately wish to see their nation serve as a fulcrum for a regional transformation in which other Muslim peoples follow their lead—throwing off "Western-aligned" rulers and creating an independent, Islamic power in the region, centered on Tehran. Strong opposition by a range of forces makes this an essentially infeasible aim, at least in the medium term, and Iran's leaders recognize this. They instead aim for a more limited set of goals: regime security, increased roles for non-Western sources of influence (like the Non-Aligned Movement), reduced Western influence in their region, strong links to movements which also aim for a new order, and a stake in key regional issues like the Arab-Israeli peace process or debates on the role of Islam in society. Many of these goals require a reduction of America's role in the region and an increase of their own. Iran's intense rivalry with Saddam Hussein's Iraq hid this, as Iran was forced to devote much energy to countering its neighbor rather than aiming for higher goals. The American invasion of Iraq in 2003 removed the check on Iranian aims, and tensions between Tehran and Washington grew. Some in American neoconservative circles began to talk of taking action against Iran and its government. Possessing a nuclear device is one way for Iran to advance its interests and secure its regime by deterring American threats.

Because both Presidents Bush and Obama have repeated the mantra that Iran cannot be allowed to develop nuclear weapons, the options to prevent this happening can be narrowed to three: diplomacy to engage with Iran to reach a mutually acceptable outcome, economic sanctions to put pressure on the Iranian regime to negotiate an agreement, and the threat and possible use of force to delay Iran's capacity to build and deploy a nuclear weapon.

IRAN'S NUCLEAR PROGRAM

Iran is a fully fledged member of the Nuclear Non-Proliferation Treaty, and as such is subject to inspection by the International Atomic Energy Agency. Iran has been developing nuclear technologies since before the 1979 Islamic Revolution. While the potential for an Iranian bomb was a cause of concern, it never became a source of regular international headlines. Even though the aftershocks of the fall of the shah saw Iran swiftly transformed into an international pariah, the revolutionary regime was not feared for nuclear ambitions, and it did not initially embrace its nuclear inheritance, freezing development at several sites, including a nuclear reactor at Bushehr which had been earlier developed by West Germany. However, its leaders eventually restarted the nuclear program after Iraq used chemical weapons against Iranian forces during the 1980–1988 Iran-Iraq War. Worries about an Iranian bomb have reached a crescendo with the fall of Iran's rival Iraq and the attendant attrition of U.S. military power. Iran's nuclear program has expanded, and inspections by the IAEA have put much of this expansion in the public view. Iran appears intent on establishing, at minimum, a self-sufficient peaceful nuclear program with a capacity to "break out" of international safeguards; at maximum, Iran could be on a path, slow and difficult, to a bomb.

This is unsettling to many states in the international community. From taking U.S. embassy personnel hostage in 1979, to international assassinations and terror sponsorships, to aggressive, anti-Semitic, and even apocalyptic public rhetoric, Iran has repeatedly ignored international norms. Actions by powerful cliques within and close to the government, like the "chain murders" of opposition leaders, the 2007 seizure of Royal Navy personnel, coup threats against the reformist Khatami government, and the growing economic power of hardliners, suggest that Iran is not merely unwilling, but structurally unable to behave predictably and remain within norms of international conduct—as one U.S. official said in early 2012, "Nothing surprises us anymore with Iran."[6] There are worries that a nuclear Iran might thus be far more likely to brandish its arsenal than other nuclear powers in history,[7] or that it might supply nuclear assets to one of its many militant affiliates.

There are also broader concerns about a nuclear Iran. Could Tehran use the bomb to gain new regional leverage, expanding its influence in Iraq while subordinating Saudi Arabia? Could it endanger the world's oil supply, driving up prices to flood its coffers with bigger revenues? Would Turkey's aspirations to regional leadership be counterbalanced by an ascendant Islamic Republic? Could Israel maintain freedom of action in its neighborhood, or would it become an embattled garrison state? Would regional concerns like the Palestine issue be taken over by Iran-backed radicals? Would Iran promote Shia uprisings? These difficult questions become more urgent with each turn of Iran's centrifuges.

This growing concern has led to serious consideration of preventing or delaying Iran's acquisition of nuclear weapons. With progress slow on the diplomacy and sanctions front, war talk grows. Could Iran's most capable regional rivals—Israel and the United States—deal Iran's nuclear ambitions a serious blow? What are the risks of a strike, and what obstacles must be overcome? Most importantly, is there a viable exit strategy for a fight with a state that emphasizes asymmetric conflict and the use of proxies?

NOTES

1. The White House, Office of the Press Secretary, "Remarks by the President at AIPAC Policy Conference," press release, March 4, 2012, www.whitehouse.gov/the-press-office/2012/03/04/remarks-president-aipac-policy-conference-0.

2. "Extensions of Remarks," Congressional Record, Feb. 1, 1996, www.gpo.gov/fdsys/pkg/CREC-1996-02-01/pdf/CREC-1996-02-01-pt1-PgE134.pdf.

3. United States Department of State, "Iran's Nuclear Activities," news conference, April 28, 2006, http://2001-2009.state.gov/p/nea/rls/rm/2006/65479.htm.

4. Goldberg, Jeffrey, "Obama to Iran and Israel: 'As President of the United States, I Don't Bluff'," *The Atlantic*, March 2, 2012, www.theatlantic.com/international/archive/2012/03/obama-to-iran-and-israel-as-president-of-the-united-states-i-dont-bluff/253875/.

5. Conan, Neal, "Ahead of Moscow Talks, U.S. Options on Iran," National Public Radio, June 2 2012, www.npr.org/2012/06/12/154853984/ahead-of-moscow-talks-u-s-options-on-iran. Ross, Dennis, "On Iran, Pressure Works," *Wall Street Journal*, Dec. 23, 2011, http://online.wsj.com/article/SB10001424052970204879004577108643499598220.html.

6. Carter, Sara A., "Iran Missile Test Points to Dangerous 2012 in Dealing with Tehran," *Washington Examiner*, Jan. 2, 2012, http://washingtonexaminer.com/iran-missile-test-points-to-dangerous-2012-in-dealing-with-tehran/article/151891.

7. Similar worries attended the nuclear program of the People's Republic of China, which was possessed by a comparable revisionism; these worries did not play out. The potential stabilizing effects of nuclear armaments have already been heavily discussed; see, for example, Robert Rauchhaus, "Evaluating the Nuclear Peace Hypothesis: A Quantitative Approach," *Journal of Conflict Resolution* 53, no. 2 (April 2009): 258–77.

ONE

Positions of Primary Actors

IRAN

Iran maintains that its nuclear program is peaceful and there is no evidence that they are producing nuclear weapons. As a signatory of the Nuclear Non-Proliferation Treaty (NPT), Iran has a legal right to establish a peaceful nuclear program. This treaty requires states developing nuclear technology to submit to IAEA monitoring and report nuclear materials. The IAEA believes that by concealing certain elements of their nuclear program, Iran is not following the rules and the regulations of the NPT.[1] Existence of the Fordow Fuel Enrichment Plant was first disclosed to the IAEA in 2009; when the plant was disclosed it was already near completion.[2] A 2011 IAEA report on Iran's nuclear program highlighted evidence of possible military dimensions including hiding certain elements of the program, obtaining documentation on the development of nuclear weapons, procuring dual use equipment, and testing weapon system components.[3] Secrecy and cover-ups have suggested that there may be more to the nuclear program than meets the eye.

In negotiations, Iran has espoused a different interpretation of its rights under the NPT. It argues that the NPT does not forbid enrichment, and that the controversy as a whole consists of foreign powers attempting to single Iran out for unequal treatment by insisting that Iran meet higher criteria than other states before it is allowed to exercise rights it already has under its interpretation of the NPT. It sees ulterior political motives—a general thwarting of Iranian ambitions at any human cost—behind this unequal treatment. The relationship between this position and the realities of the program is not clear, but it is certainly not the whole truth—evidence of irregular activities is abundant. Thus far diplomacy has yielded little progress in slowing the program.

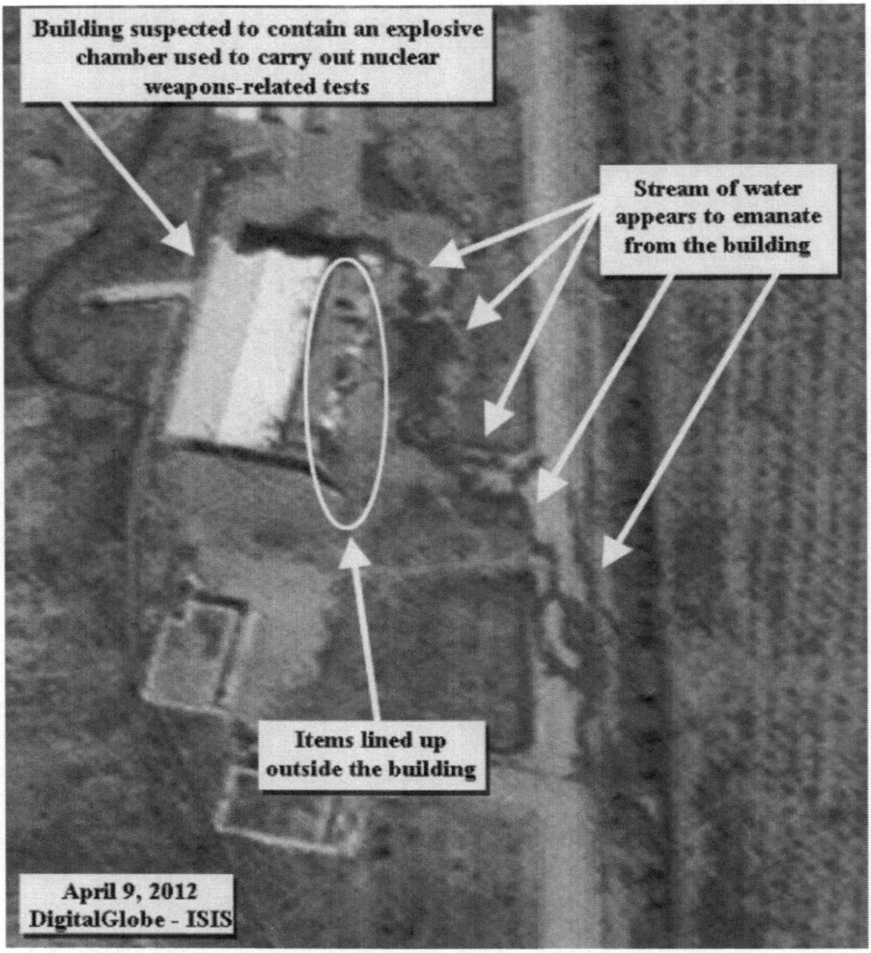

Figure 1.1. A satellite photograph from April 2012 shows cleanup underway at Parchin, suspected of involvement in military-related nuclear development. ***(Institute for Science and International Security.)***

The major actors in the Iranian nuclear development dialogue are known as the P5+1, consisting of the United States, France, the United Kingdom, Russia, China, and Germany (i.e., the five permanent U.N. Security Council members plus Germany. Sometimes the group is called the E3+3, i.e., three European Union powers, and three others.). Most of the P5+1 have supported economic sanctions against Iran. Israel has consistently signaled its willingness to take preventive military action, but the United States has stressed that military action should only be taken as a last resort.

Figure 1.2. The same site shown in May 2012. Several small buildings have been razed and dirt moved around. ***(Institute for Science and International Security.)***

Figure 1.3. A satellite photograph from August 2003 of the Lavizan-Shian site in Tehran, suspected of involvement in military-related nuclear development. ***(Institute for Science and International Security.)***

The Iranian nuclear program began in the late 1950s when Iran signed on to the American Atoms for Peace initiative; in the late 1960s America gave Tehran University a reactor—the Tehran Research Reactor, still in use today—as part of this agreement. This eventually led into the launch of an extensive nuclear program in 1973. By 1976, the Atomic Energy Organization of Iran (AEOI) budget was $1.3 billion, second only to oil. The United States was concerned about Iran's plans for a plutonium enrichment facility and decided to ban sales of nuclear reactors to Iran from American companies. Germany and France, key nuclear exporters, became major contractors of Iran's early nuclear facilities. In 1978 after much back and forth, the shah finally agreed to halt plans for building a plutonium processing plant, and U.S. companies were allowed to sell reactors to Iran.[4] In the 1970s the shah told businessman and confidant Abolfath Mahvi that he ordered the five-megawatt nuclear research reactor for Tehran University "to allow Iran to develop the means to acquire nuclear weapons."[5] The shah also argued to the international media that Iran's nuclear ambitions were subject to a double standard—that nuclear weapons possession by major Western powers was treated as "totally normal" while Iran is condemned even though it is "not automatically protected by any other country."[6]

Iran has consistently stated that it is opposed to nuclear weapons, and Supreme Leader Grand Ayatollah Ali Khamenei condemned the production and use of such weapons on religious grounds.[7] Since the revolution the supreme leader has been the highest authority in the Iranian government, with particular power over national security matters. There are few

Figure 1.4. The same site in August 2004. All buildings have been removed. The site would eventually become a park. *(Institute for Science and International Security.)*

plausible challengers to Khamenei's authority. Any significant decision on the nuclear program will come from the leader's office. However, there are a multitude of power centers that can challenge him. This was most visible during the presidency of Mohammed Khatami, a reformist who it is jokingly said to have listened to Khamenei every day without doing his bidding, but even the Ahmadinejad administration, initially given wary support and kept afloat by the regime via a crackdown after the disputed 2009 elections, has challenged him.

In 2011, the stilettos came out after Ahmadinejad removed a Khamenei ally, Heidar Moslehi, from the Intelligence Ministry; Khamenei refused to accept Moslehi's resignation, and the furious Ahmadinejad vanished from the public eye for days. The struggle continued for several months, with Khamenei allies branding Ahmadinejad's faction a "deviant current," accusing it variously of corruption, seeking relations with Israel and America, secularism, and sorcery. Several Ahmadinejad allies and media outlets faced legal harassment. The former Tehran mayor's power drained away under government pressure and the pending end of his term. In a final blow to Ahmadinejad, Khamenei said publicly that eliminating the position of the presidency altogether would be feasible, citing the former Supreme Leader Ayatollah Khomeini's removal of the position of prime minister as precedent.[8] By July 2012, Ahmadinejad had lost so much power that Khamenei began to tamp down attacks coming from within his own camp in an apparent bid to create conservative unity as sanction pressure grew.[9] The October 2012 collapse in the rial's value ended this period of quiet, and various figures on the right attacked Ahmadinejad with renewed vigor. Ahmadinejad was clearly infuriated, giving a press conference in which he threatened to offer his resignation and leveling accusations at a range of powerful figures, including the state press, the judiciary, and the Revolutionary Guard. Commentators noted that these elements are all under Khamenei.[10] One remark from the press conference, that unlike these institutions, "I am the only person that is accountable before the people," can certainly be interpreted as a veiled jab at the supreme leader.

Though Khamenei's purge has reshaped the top of the political system—many disputes are arguably now mere struggles for power and resources behind a mask of ideological division—there is still much factionalism just below. Historically, the three most influential factions in the Islamic Republic are the radical or hardliner conservatives, the pragmatic conservatives, and the reformists. Hardliners include multiple currents, including both Khamenei and Ahmadinejad; the pragmatic conservatives include former president Hashemi Rafsanjani and Tehran mayor Mohammad Baqer Qalibaf; the reformists are represented by former president Mohammad Khatami and 2009 presidential candidate/Khomeini-era prime minister Mir Hossein Mousavi. All three major groups support Iran's pursuit of nuclear energy, so even if Khamenei dies or returns some power to the lower tiers of the political system, it is unlikely to lead to the halting of the program. However, the groups differ on their willingness to engage and negotiate with the West. Pragmatic conservatives are primarily concerned with economic reform and so favor a measure of international connectedness in order to build the economy. They are also more likely to engage when faced with economic sanctions as they are first and foremost concerned with economic growth unlike the more confrontational conservative groups.[11]

Reformists, unlike their conservative counterparts, advocate social and cultural reform as well as strong dialogue and cooperation with the West. Perhaps if a pragmatic conservative or a reformist was to be elected it could lead to increased engagement and compromise with the United States, but it is unlikely to lead to the permanent cessation of the nuclear program.[12] In a 2009 interview with *Time,* Mousavi said that while the right to nuclear energy is a given, he considers nuclear weaponization to be negotiable.[13] Mayor of Tehran and popular pragmatic conservative Mohammed Baqer Qalibaf supports Iran's nuclear program, but maintains that it is peaceful. He suggested that Iran could engage with the world in a more productive way on the issue.[14] Reformist thinkers tend to be more ambiguous than others about whether the nuclear program ultimately aims for a weapon—some seem to genuinely believe that the program is entirely peaceful in purpose. (Some other Iranian foreign policy thinkers tip their hand here by noting that Iran's nuclear program will increase national security, which is difficult to interpret as anything other than an admission of weaponization intent.) The reformist camp has consistently supported Iran's right to nuclear power, but views the exercise of this right as just one component of Iran's standing. They are thus more sensitive to worries about international isolation than other groups. Now out of government, they have criticized their successors' hard-line approach for deepening Iranian isolation and allowing the international community to transform the nuclear issue into a security issue.[15]

Radical conservatives like President Ahmadinejad have expressed determination to continue the nuclear program at any cost. They are known for taking a combative stance against engagement attempts by the United States and the Western world. They are not entirely opposed to isolation and portray the West as an ideological enemy in an attempt to unite their base of support.[16] A 2006 poll suggested that the Iranian people are overwhelmingly in favor of having a peaceful nuclear program, but not the development of nuclear weapons.[17] There is evidence that public opinion on nuclear issues has become more flexible since the implementation of the harshest sanctions measures.

One root of the hard-line position is the idea that the moderation of the Rafsanjani and Khatami administrations gained Iran nothing. They point out that after Khatami expanded cooperation with the IAEA, initiated a voluntary suspension of the nuclear program, cooperated with America in Afghanistan, and pushed for a "dialogue among civilizations," Iran was still branded a member of the "axis of evil" and subjected to further demands.[18] This, they say, is because the West is simply incapable of accepting Iran's independent, Islamic nature and foreign policy. They argued that because of this, Tehran should instead pursue a policy of strictly advancing its own interests without giving such serious consideration to Western objections. The hardliners have sometimes pushed against making any concessions at all, or even negotiating about the nuclear program. More frequently, they have argued that Iran should negotiate on its own terms—without preconditions and with other regional issues relevant to Iran's foreign policy goals on the agenda—and that Iran should not fear sanctions.

The Islamic Revolutionary Guard Corps (IRGC) is one of the most influential institutions in Iranian politics, controlling a wide range of industries, commercial operations, and black market enterprises. The IRGC is composed of roughly 125,000 soldiers and also controls the Basij paramilitary force of up to one million volunteer fighters. Although the IRGC answers directly to Khamenei, supporting his rule, and was created as a "people's army," it is speculated that it may be growing more powerful than the supreme leader himself—an unsettling possibility, given the Guards' financial interests in continued isolation. Yet, there is fracturing within the IRGC; they are divided in their support to the three political factions and in their economic views, which could limit their ability to consolidate power.[19] However, in recent years the IRGC has become increasingly involved in the political affairs of the state both by fielding more candidates to run in parliamentary elections and exercising increased control over the system itself. Between 2000 and 2008 the IRGC doubled the number of seats held in parliament by former officers. In 2004 they held at least 16 percent of the seats.[20] Khamenei also appointed Ali Reza Afshar, a former IRGC official, to oversee the 2008 elections, an important duty which includes appointing officials to run.[21] Mohsen Rezaei, who headed the IRGC for a decade and a half, has become a major figure among the anti-Ahmadinejad conservatives and is considered a potential president.[22]

Members of the Iranian government continue to insist it is in good standing as a signatory to the Nuclear Non-Proliferation Treaty (NPT) and member of the IAEA. Esmaiel Kosari, deputy chairman of the Iranian Parliament's National Security and Foreign Policy Commission, said "We do not have the slightest concern because we have not infringed on the [International Atomic Energy] Agency's regulations and if the other side has a question or [feels there are] ambiguities, we will not leave any question or ambiguity without a response."[23] Despite continuous claims that the nuclear program is peaceful, Iran has not always been forthcoming with the details of the program. Recently released documents showing correspondence between Iran's nuclear researchers and European companies show Iran using deceptive techniques to acquire nuclear components.[24]

Hassan Rowhani, a top negotiator for Iran's nuclear program and close ally of Khamenei, told a group of Islamic clerics and scholars that while Iran was "negotiating with the Europeans in Tehran we were still installing some of the equipment at the Isfahan site. . . . In reality, by creating a tame situation, we could finish Isfahan," implying that Iran was making use of time spent negotiating with the West to advance its nuclear program without disturbance.[25] Iran's nuclear chief Fereydoun Abbasi (who is a survivor of one of several motorcycle attacks on Iranian nuclear scientists) stated in October 2011 that Iran would continue to enrich its uranium to 20 percent unless a nuclear swap agreement was made.[26] The swap deal never took place: although an agreement was made with Turkey and Brazil to provide fuel needed for medical reactors in exchange for uranium stockpiles, the United States rejected the deal because it would have allowed Iran to continue enriching uranium.[27] Iran says the uranium is for a medical research reactor, but uranium already at 20 percent enrichment can be enriched to a much higher level relatively easily—the amount of work required to enrich natural uranium to a given level of purity is initially a steep curve, but rapidly tapers off at higher level.[28] Iran is producing 20 percent uranium at a far higher rate than is required to support its current needs, which it justifies with reference to research reactors it plans to build at some future date. Some political figures have threatened to enrich to higher levels if negotiations break down, saying the enrichment would be for nuclear submarines, some of which indeed use uranium enriched to this level, but none of which Iran has acquired or built.

In addition, the IAEA released a report in November 2011 that provided evidence that Iran's nuclear program showed signs of military ambitions; Iran responded to this report with a threat to take legal action, claiming the report was subject to pressure by the United States.[29] Iran also strongly objected to a U.N. condemnation of the alleged attempt to assassinate the Saudi ambassador to the United States, for which the United States believes Iran is responsible.[30]

Iran has faced many setbacks in recent years. In addition to the use of magnetic explosives by motorcyclists to target nuclear scientists, various other forms of interference have arisen. The Stuxnet virus, believed to be linked to Israel and the United States, slowed Iran's nuclear advancement, as did the broader cyberwarfare program it was part of, code-named "Olympic Games." There have also been unexplained explosions at nuclear facilities and military bases. Israeli officials said that the explosions were not the result of an accident, but stopped short of claiming responsibility. Iran denied that these explosions were due to strategic military strikes on their facilities, instead claiming that they were accidents.[31] While Israel has not publicly admitted responsibility for these attacks, it is widely speculated that they are behind this range of incidents on Iranian soil.[32]

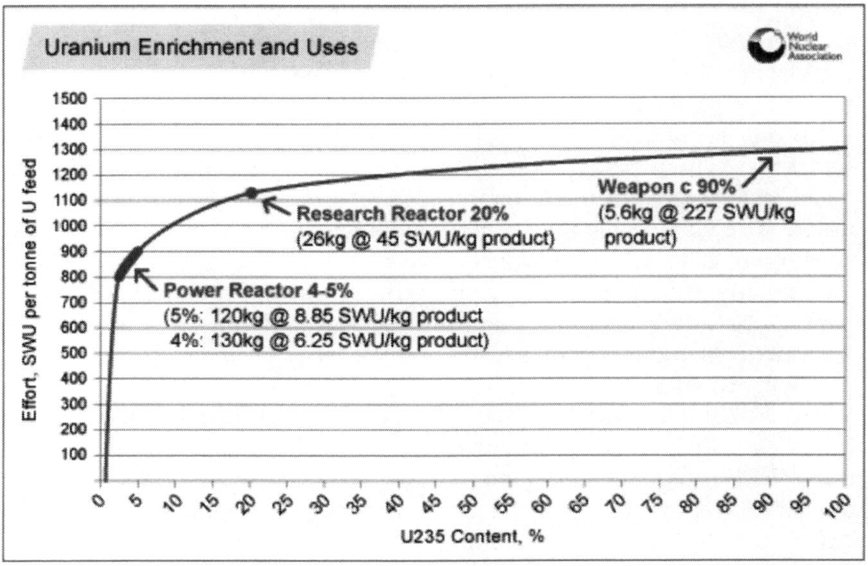

Figure 1.5. Uranium enrichment and uses. ***(World Nuclear Association.)***

KEY OPPONENTS OF THE IRANIAN NUCLEAR PROGRAM

The United States

Though the United States was the first nation to provide nuclear fuel and equipment to Iran to assist with nuclear energy development, officials became worried that the shah had potentially radical ideas for nuclear weapons development.[33] When the shah was forced out of power in the 1979 revolution, Iran halted the nuclear program. When Iran restarted its nuclear program after suffering chemical attacks, there were again suspicions that Iran might be interested in building nuclear weapons. The United States attempted to hinder Iran's nuclear progress by blocking it from obtaining technology and aid from other countries, including China and Russia.[34]

The United States remains suspicious of Iran's intentions and has called for Iran to suspend its uranium enrichment program as a central component of any settlement. In response to Iran's refusal to cooperate with its demands, the United States has pursued both multilateral sanctions through the United Nations Security Council, and unilateral sanctions against Iran's energy sector, banking, military sales, and trade.[35] The United States has a long history of issuing sanctions against Iran, beginning with Carter's November 1979 Executive Order 12170, which froze Iranian assets in the United States in reaction to the American embassy hostage situation. Furthermore, in subsequent years the United States added Iran to the list of states sponsoring terrorism and implemented several more executive orders on Iran. Executive Order 12613, issued in 1987, banned the import of Iranian goods and services. Executive Orders 12957 and 12959, issued in 1995, prohibited U.S. trade with Iran, including its oil industry.

In June 1996, the U.S. Congress passed the Iran and Libya Sanctions Act (ILSA), which called for secondary sanctions on foreign corporations investing more than $20 million in Iran's oil sector within a one-year time period. The Comprehensive Iran Sanctions, Accountability, and Divestment Act of 2010 (CISADA) was passed to modify the ILSA law. CISADA "did not alter this [ILSA] trigger but it did amend the definition of investment to include pipelines to or through Iran and contracts to lead the construction, upgrading, or expansions of energy projects."[36] These sanctions were further expanded upon with additional executive orders.

The FY2012 National Defense Authorization Act requires the imposition of penalties on corporations and foreign banks if they engage with Iran's Central Bank (also known as Bank Merkazi). It "requires the President to prevent a foreign bank from opening an account in the United States—or impose strict limitations on existing U.S. accounts—if that bank processes payments through Iran's Central Bank."[37] Another executive order was issued in February 2012 to impound any Iranian assets still in U.S. financial institutions. The United States has also tried to use its leverage to push other countries to either enact their own sanctions on Iran or reduce the amount of business they do with Iran. In January 2012 the European Union, a major consumer of Iranian oil, initiated sanctions that banned all oil imports from Iran starting in July of the same year.[38]

Speaking generally, the executive branch retains a measure of authority over the sanctions process even though Congress has increasingly codified it. For example, the president is able to grant waivers to individuals and states from CISADA sanctions if he certifies that they are cooperating with efforts against Iranian weapons programs and that waivers are vital to American national security interests. Hypothetically, then, if the United States were able to reach some agreement with Iran, the president would have an ability to offer sanction relief as a component of the agreement—and it would certainly have to be a component of any agreement the Iranians would accept. However, the problem of making certification to an understandably skeptical Congress would be a substantive domestic hurdle to an international agreement, especially since Congressional hearings and the like could allow for a drawn out and high-profile airing of elite and public criticism that will follow a deal.

The Political Trajectory

During the Bush administration, Vice President Dick Cheney stated officially that they wanted to keep the military option against Iran's nuclear program on the table, but informal reports suggest that Cheney pushed for short-term U.S. military action against Iran. Others in government spoke out against the possibility of an attack, particularly after President Bush gave an "amber light" to Israel's plans to attack Iran in the event that they do not comply with the NPT, meaning that Israel could prepare itself to attack as soon as the time was right.[39] It was rumored in 2007 that a handful of senior military officials allegedly threatened to resign in the event of a strike on Iran. Robert Gates, whose view was thought to be representative of upper commanders, strongly advised against using military force against Iran.[40]

The Obama administration has been more inclined to pursue sanctions and dialogue without taking the military option off the table. In April 2009, President Obama stated:

> My administration will seek engagement with Iran based on mutual interests and mutual respect. We believe in dialogue. But in that dialogue we will present a clear choice. We want Iran to take its rightful place in the community of nations, politically and economically. We will support Iran's right to peaceful nuclear energy with rigorous inspections. That's a path that the Islamic Republic can take. Or the government can choose increased isolation, international pressure, and a potential nuclear arms race in the region that will increase insecurity

for all. So let me be clear: Iran's nuclear and ballistic missile activity poses a real threat, not just to the United States, but to Iran's neighbors and our allies.[41]

Early in his administration, President Obama signaled his openness to unprecedented engagement with Iran. Both sides made attempts to reach out but it proved untenable when they were unable to reach any agreements and were unwilling to make big concessions. Following the contested 2009 elections, the Obama administration took a tougher stance on Iran and began implementing tougher sanctions.[42] In December 2011, Obama backtracked slightly in his support for sanctions, asking Congress to ease sanctions against Iran's Central Bank citing a fear that it would cause a boost in oil prices that would benefit Iran.[43] However, in January 2012, the Obama administration reversed their stance and began working with Saudi Arabia and other regional oil producers to increase output of oil in order to act as an alternative to the Iranian oil and compensate for increased demand from Japan, South Korea, and China. Experts said that Saudi Arabia and other suppliers could only temporarily compensate for the shortage in oil to keep prices from rising, which would nevertheless rise eventually when the demand for oil exceeds the supply of oil.[44] However, when the sanctions were finally rolled out, oil prices settled for a time at a significantly lower price level, in large part due to reduced tensions on the Gulf; a slow global economy helped suppress demand for oil.

The relationship with Israel began to sour in this period, as the Israeli government repeatedly urged the United States to take a tougher stance and to make the military threats more credible and the U.S. government attempted to reassure the Israeli government without taking this step. Washington also wished to avoid a unilateral Israeli action against Iran—for just one example, in October 2011, Secretary of Defense Leon Panetta urged Israel to act "responsibly" concerning Iran, reiterating that the United States will defend Israel, but that America does not want a regional war to spark in the Middle East.[45] Washington accordingly sent streams of envoys to Jerusalem, but tension remained, eventually reaching such a level that some American and Israeli commentators began to accuse the Netanyahu government of attempting to stoke public trouble with Obama to make him feel vulnerable to attacks from his right during the 2012 elections. The crisis then quieted at the 2012 General Assembly, after Obama gave a particularly strong reiteration of his prevention policy and Netanyahu tamed his rhetoric somewhat, arguing for a "red line" to be drawn near Iran's present level of nuclear attainment.[46]

The 2012 Republican presidential candidates highlighted the breadth of views in American politics about the Iran problem. Republican contender Mitt Romney had maintained a tough stance against Iran since he ran in the 2008 election. He drew attention to the progress Iran's nuclear program has made during the Obama administration, and argues that Obama's foreign policy was generally weak, "apologetic," and not in keeping with American global leadership. Romney promised to reverse defense cuts and use that money to "retain military supremacy to deter would-be aggressors," and to increase aircraft carrier task force presence in the Middle East.[47]

However, it is also fair to say that Romney's explicit plans for Iran more clearly diverged from Obama's in style, not in substance: Romney repeatedly emphasized the importance of maintaining a credible military option and strengthening ties to regional allies, but Obama refused to rule out force and has worked with American allies in the Gulf region. Romney backed aggressive sanctions, yet so has the Obama administration. Romney was notably more enthusiastic about support for Iran's reformists, but as we argue above the reformists are at best an incomplete solution to the nuclear problem. Even if we are incorrect in this point, a policy of support for the reformists would still have to be pursued in a very aggressive manner in order to by itself be a policy against the nuclear program. The current sanctions regime is having a severe impact on the Iranian economy, although it is not stopping the nuclear program. If the United States shows the right amount of aggression, the international community may fear war and grant still deeper sanctions, possibly hitting a nerve in Tehran. But if Washington is too aggressive, nations may feel blackmailed or seek to balance American influence, shredding the sanctions regime. The only two remaining approaches in this case would be war and acquiescence.

Former Speaker of the House Newt Gingrich, another candidate for the Republican nomination, was extremely vocal about the need to confront Iran over the nuclear issue. He noted that while he was Speaker he publicly pushed for and passed a bill that added "$18 million to the CIA covert action program on Iran, to be used specifically to overthrow the government."[48] Commentators were bemused by his overt advocacy of covert activity. One of the Gingrich campaign's foreign policy advisors has advocated strongly against engagement with the Iranian state, which would leave only confrontational courses of action.[49]

The only candidate to openly rule out the use of preemptive force in Iran was Ron Paul, a stridently libertarian Republican congressman from Texas. Paul expressed no belief that Iran is a threat to American national security.[50] Paul stated that "acting as the world's policeman . . . weakens our country, puts our troops in harm's way, and sends precious resources to other nations in the midst of an historic economic crisis."[51] Paul has also said that U.S. sanctions on Iran should be considered an act of war, arguing that if a country attempted to apply sanctions against the United States in the same fashion as U.S. sanctions against Iran, the United States would regard it as such. While Paul never commanded an impressive position in the polls, his views are a bellwether of increasingly salient isolationist and noninterventionist currents in the GOP, currents powerful enough to be backed by multiple voices in Congress.

Direct Relations

America's bilateral relationship with Iran is defined by a long and turbulent string of adversarial interactions. The United States does not currently have diplomatic relations with Iran, instead conducting their relations through the Swiss embassy in Tehran. Bad relations and Iran's history of disregard for the inviolability of embassies mean this is not likely to change any time soon. Needless to say, the lack of direct and sustained contact limits the ability of each country to glean mutually beneficial information from the other, and hinders cooperation.[52]

U.S. policy so far has been based on a combination of containment, sanctions, and offers for engagement. One major component of U.S. containment strategy is the Gulf Security Dialogue (GSD) intended to keep regional powers from acquiescing to Iranian interests through arms trade, offers of military protection, and improved security.[53]

After a brace of Iranian rhetoric in January 2012 about sealing the Strait of Hormuz in response to sanctions, the United States warned Iran via a back channel—the two states' U.N. missions[54] —that attempts to shut down the strait would cross a red line. This appeared to quiet tensions for a time. Later, in March 2012, the United States warned Iran via Russia that further negotiation delays by Iran would not be tolerated. The message reportedly stated that Israel might attack within months if there are no credible negotiations.[55] Negotiations picked up for a time. Still, Iran has responded to recent demands by the United States regarding inspections of Iran's Parchin military complex with demands of its own. Mohammad Larijani, a top advisor to the supreme leader, responded to these inspection demands by saying, "If the Western community is asking us for more transparency, then we should expect more cooperation."[56]

Israel

Israel is opposed to Iran obtaining nuclear weapons and supports sanctions as well as military options if necessary. Having been the target of many Iranian threats and many attacks by militias with ties to Tehran, Jerusalem is deeply uncomfortable with the prospect of an Iranian bomb. Accordingly, it has generally taken a harder line than even the United States. The charge has been led by Prime Minister Benjamin Netanyahu and his recently departed defense minister, Ehud Barak. Netanyahu has attempted to goad the international community into action—for instance, in November 2010, he asserted that "if the international community . . . hopes to stop Iran's nuclear program without resorting to military action, it will have to convince Iran that it is prepared to take such action."[57] Israel has expressed a willingness to use military force itself if the international community does not act.[58] However, different powers within the Israeli government have shown varying levels of willingness to use military force. The Israeli left, though it has long been out of power, tends to see an Iran war as a potentially serious distraction from the domestic reforms it favors; much of the security establishment is as concerned about Hamas and Hezbollah as it is with Iran. In 2011, freshly retired Mossad chief Meir Dagan called an attack on Iran "foolish," a headline-grabbing breach of the traditional silence of former Mossad heads.[59] Barak was critical of Dagan's comment, and stated that taking the military threat off the table would reduce the effectiveness of deterrence.[60] Dagan continued to insist that there are better ways to stop Iran's nuclear intentions than a military strike and that Iran's nuclear program is not yet close to making a bomb, allowing Israel time to try other options.[61]

However, Barak stated that any decision by Israel to launch an attack on Iran was not in the near future but instead "very far off."[62] Barak was not the only one criticized for pushing for an attack on Iran: Netanyahu has also been accused by current and former Israeli government officials of misleading the Israelis over Iran. Ehud Olmert, former prime minister of Israel, lashed harsh criticism on Netanyahu in a recent conference in New York, describing him and his defense minister, Barak, as excessive and loud talkers, who "are creating an atmosphere and a momentum that may go out of their control."[63] Yuval Diskin, former head of the Shin Bet, stated that the prime minister and his defense minister "make decisions out of messianic feelings" and are not trustworthy to set Israel's Iran policy.[64] Israel's military chief of staff, Lt. Gen. Benny Gantz, stated that Iran has not made a decision to build a nuclear weapon yet and that it is "composed of very rational people" unlikely to make the "huge mistake" of manufacturing a nuclear weapon.[65] And in August 2012, Israeli president Shimon Peres added his opposition to a unilateral strike on Iran by Israel, to which unnamed individuals close to Netanyahu quickly responded with critiques of Peres's past security decisions and reminders of "know your place."[66]

Another opponent, prior to his fall from power amid a scandal, was Avigdor Lieberman, foreign minister of Israel and the head of the secular rightist Yisrael Beiteinu Party. Lieberman is typically known as a hardliner unafraid of controversial stances—most famously, the notion that Israeli Arabs should ultimately be reintegrated into Palestine.[67] However, Lieberman stated during a visit to China that the international community must work together to pressure Iran to give up its nuclear dreams and that a war with Iran would be a "nightmare," leaving no one unaffected by the consequences.[68]

The other significant factions in Israeli politics are the centrist and leftist parties, the Jewish Home Party, and the religious parties. The center-left is fragmentary and troubled, with demographic trends eroding it and with its leaders unable to articulate an appealing alternative to the right's foreign policy and security plans. Divisions about handling Iran do not follow party lines, leaving some Iran hawks on the left and some Iran doves on the right. The stridently rightist Jewish Home Party, headed by the young and charismatic Naftali Bennett, is similarly unclear on Iran. However, Netanyahu reportedly dislikes Bennett and regards him—correctly—as a threat to siphon off right-leaning voters. As the Iran issue heats up and Bennett is forced to clarify his positions, Netanyahu will certainly take notice.

The religious parties have not shown enthusiasm for war with Iran. Interior Minister Eli Yishai, head of Shas and the only member of the religious parties in the security cabinet, has been repeatedly reported to be an opponent of war. The religious parties remain more concerned with the preservation of social welfare, settlements, and their draft exemption. A conflict with Iran could have direct and indirect negative effects in all of these areas. However, given their constituents' minimal contributions to the military that will fight the war and the taxes that will fund it, there is certainly a moral hazard.

The spiritual leader of Shas and former chief rabbi of Israel Ovadia Yosef has a less clear position on Iran. The Baghdad-born cleric has been a sometime advocate of the peace process, ruling that land for peace deals were acceptable if lives were otherwise at risk. In spite of this, his pronouncements on the Palestinians—including wishes for a divine plague against them—have attracted claims of racism, earning rebuke from American and Israeli leaders.[69] A similar pattern may exist in his views on Iran. In late 2011, Yosef urged Israel not to attack Iran, arguing that renewed spiritual devotion would cause God to "save the people of Israel" and "deal with [Ahmadinejad] and he will go to hell."[70] Yosef suggested that Ahmadinejad may be a reincarnation of Haman, a figure in the rabbinical tradition who had sought to exterminate Persia's Jews but was hung. In 2012, Yosef was briefed by National Security Council head Yaakov Amidror, reportedly in the presence of Yishai and as part of an effort by Netanyahu to win Shas support for an attack on Iran.[71] His next two sermons focused on Iran, reiterating the Ahmadinejad-Haman link and calling for God to "obliterate" Hezbollah and the Iranian regime. He apparently did not repeat his call not to attack Iran, although he quoted a psalm that may point to his opinion: "Some call on chariots and horses, but we will invoke the name of God our Lord, they collapse and fall down but we are risen and gather strength."[72] Yosef does not seem to have reversed his opinion on who should deal with Iran, but he may still have opened the door for Yishai to reverse his. Yosef has also been visited by other senior Israeli politicians, including President Shimon Peres.

Worried by the Iranian program yet lacking the support for war, Israel appears to have engaged in a secret campaign to hinder it. Iran has seen assassination attempts on scientists close to the nuclear program, cyberattacks, and explosions at nuclear and missile facilities, all of which are widely attributed to Israel. Tel Aviv has stopped short of officially taking responsibility for the attacks, but the former national security chief Major General Giora Eiland was quoted as saying "There are so many events, there is probably some sort of guiding hand." Intelligence Minister Dan Meridor added that "the guiding hand might be closer to home." Meridor had also said that "there are countries that impose economic sanctions and there are countries who act in other ways in dealing with the Iranian nuclear threat."[73]

Israel's willingness to take action, in spite of the many difficulties the Netanyahu government faces, should not be underestimated. Netanyahu may seek to use Israel's upcoming elections to gain a mandate to act decisively. That said, the threat of action can be an end in itself. By creating fear of a war that would destabilize the region and likely create a major shock in oil markets, Israel has forced the international community to keep Iranian proliferation high on its agenda. However, there are no free lunches in politics. On the domestic front, Netanyahu's persistent emphasis on the Iran threat could leave him humiliated if Iran's progress continues unabated and unstruck. He will be hard pressed to find a way to wind down his position. Internationally, Israel's tough stance has fed criticism. The relationship with the United States, in particular, may have suffered. Polls show just 53 percent of Democrats have more sympathy for Israel than the Palestinians, prompting two prominent experts on the U.S.-Israel relationship to worry that Israel could become a partisan issue in U.S. politics.[74] Israel has long sought to retain bipartisan support in Washington, yet Netanyahu has been criticized on the American left as a warmonger and satirized on *The Daily Show*. Perceived attempts to badger Obama have not helped Netanyahu's image. The fallout of an Israeli strike would have significant economic and security consequences for the United States that could hinder the next administration in other areas of its agenda, which could make partisan differences over Israel deeper and more permanent.

The Rest of the World

Aside from the United States and Israel, members of the European Union have taken a very tough line on Iran's program, with France being particularly hard-nosed. Part of this has to do with traditional support within the EU for nuclear nonproliferation, but it also reflects the view—not widely shared in the United States—that if Iran is allowed to proceed with a weapon, it will be the end of the Nuclear Non-Proliferation Treaty, and a whole host of new problems, both in the Middle East and Asia will come to the fore, making life more difficult and dangerous for the Europeans themselves. It must be remembered that thanks to the proximity and increasing economic pressures in the Middle East, more and more migrants are finding their way to European shores, creating difficulties. Therefore any crisis in the Middle East worries Europeans for more than just security reasons.

Within the European Union, differences are primarily nuanced. Those countries that have had active and prosperous trade with Iran—notably Italy and Spain—have been more reluctant to go along with sanctions than others. Germany is an exception here, having the largest trade with Iran while also being one of the toughest critics of its nuclear programs.

Russia and China are, of course, essential to any United Nations Security Council measures against Iran. Both would be adamantly opposed to sanctions that would truly cripple Iran, and both strongly oppose the use of force. Both countries also have a deep distrust of Western proclivities to change regimes, a distrust that was amplified in 2011, when they voted to authorize some form of force against Libya, only to find that NATO essentially provided air support for the rebels as they advanced and overthrew Gaddafi. This led to reluctance to support tough sanctions against Syria and continued backdoor support for Iran on this matter, even though both have voted for sanctions. Working around Russia and China has become one of the key goals of U.S. diplomacy, and in many ways Washington has been remarkably successful, getting measured cooperation from countries like Japan, India, and Turkey that would normally take a more laissez-faire attitude to relations with one of their more important oil suppliers.

In 2010, Brazil and Turkey attempted to broker their own deal with the Iranians and present the P5+1 with a fait accompli. However, like all other negotiations, it came to nothing, and there is presently no great incentive on the part of Brazil or Turkey to reengage. Turkey has its own quarrels with Iran over the Syrian crisis, and is likely to be quiescent on the nuclear front or at least avoid taking leadership. Other states, like South Korea, have opposed the Iranian program due to its relationship to the North Korean program.

For many countries in the Third World, particularly in Africa and Asia, there is an element of support for Iran's nuclear power ambitions within the framework of the NPT. These states do not feel as strongly as many others about the dangers of an Iranian nuclear program—all have other, more pressing needs. Nevertheless, their views are worth taking into account.

Finally, there are the Arab countries in Iran's neighborhood, who espouse different levels of anxiety about the Iranian program. Only Syria has refused to take action—verbally or otherwise—against the Iranians. The most outspoken critics are Saudi Arabia and the United Arab Emirates, with other small Gulf states taking less strident but nevertheless tough positions. Egypt is concerned that Iran could eventually become a major power again, and the Iraqis, though sometimes supportive due to the backing Iran provided during the Saddam years, know that a nuclear-armed Iran ultimately clashes with its interests. Basically speaking, the Arab world would probably be quietly happy if the United States or Israel could rid the world of the Iranian program with no fallout, but very few expect this to happen. Hence they worry about a war, not only due to its direct impact on their own physical security, but also because of the impact on the oil market on which their prosperity depends. There is thus a degree of ambivalence in Arab elites on an Israeli strike—most would publically disapprove, but their private response would depend on the strike's success.

This brief summary does not do justice to the complexities of the Iranian issue as reflected throughout the capitals of the world. Hence, we have provided an appendix at the end of this book outlining the views of specific states, examining such things as the leaked American diplomatic cables which revealed the depth of Gulf fears about Iran or the rumors of an Azeri-Israeli alliance against an Iranian bomb.

NOTES

1. Michael Adler, "Iran and the IAEA," United States Institute of Peace: Iran Primer, Aug. 2010, http://iranprimer.usip.org/resource/iran-and-iaea.

2. Mike Shuster, "Iran Nuke Plant at Advanced Construction Stage," National Public Radio, Nov. 17, 2009, www.npr.org/templates/story/story.php?storyId=120488578.

3. IAEA Director General, "Implementation of the NPT Safeguards Agreement and Relevant Provisions of the Security Council Resolutions in the Islamic Republic of Iran," *Guardian*, Nov. 8, 2011, www.guardian.co.uk/world/interactive/2011/nov/09/iran-nuclear-programme-iaea-report.

4. Milani Abbas, "The Shah's Atomic Dreams," Foreign Policy, Dec. 29, 2010, www.foreignpolicy.com/articles/2010/12/29/the_shahs_atomic_dreams.

5. Nader Entessar, "Iran's Nuclear Decision-Making Calculus," Middle East Policy Council, www.mepc.org/journal/middle-east-policy-archives/irans-nuclear-decision-making-calculus.

6. See "Shah of Iran on Nuclear Weapons," YouTube video of a French-language interview purportedly in 1975 or 1976, at www.youtube.com/watch?v=uiUQO7wgcyw. The parallel between the remarks by the shah and the present position of the Islamic Republic is striking.

7. Robert Collier, "Nuclear Weapons Unholy, Iran Says," *San Francisco Chronicle*, Oct. 31, 2003, http://articles.sfgate.com/2003-10-31/news/17515120_1_nuclear-program-nuclear-weapons-supreme-leader.

8. Robert Worth, "Iran's Power Struggle Goes beyond Personalities to Future of Presidency Itself," *New York Times*, Oct. 26, 2011. www.nytimes.com/2011/10/27/world/middleeast/in-iran-rivalry-khamenei-takes-on-presidency-itself.html.

9. In a major speech to Iranian politicians, Khamenei said "The reality is that there are problems, however you must not blame them on this or that party. Instead you must solve those problems with unity. You should avoid useless disputes and airing these disputes to help preserve the nation's unity . . . and officials should know these actions will not bring them any honor or prestige among the people." This came amid sharp criticism of the government in the Majlis, spurred by inflation and problems with subsidy reforms. Yeganeh Torbati, "Khamenei Tells Iran Politicians to Show

More Unity," Reuters, July 25, 2012, www.reuters.com/article/2012/07/25/iran-khamenei-idUSL6E8IP17C20120725

10. Mehdi Khalaji, "Is Ahmadinejad Scapegoat for Iran's Economy?," *Al Monitor*, Oct. 4, 2012, www.al-monitor.com/pulse/originals/2012/al-monitor/iran-president-supreme-leader.html.

11. It is critical to note that these notions of economic growth and international contact are not necessarily equivalent to a liberal economy. Rafsanjani, in particular, has seen his and his family's wealth increase in a nontransparent fashion.

12. Isem Askar Karakir and Nilufer Karacasulu, "Unlikely Scenario: Halt of Iranian Nuclear Programme," *Ege Academic Review*, 2010, http://eab.ege.edu.tr/pdf/10_1/C10-S1-M19.pdf.

13. Joe Klein and Nahid Siamdoust, "The Man Who Could Beat Ahmadinejad: Mousavi Talks to TIME," *Time*, June 12, 2009, www.time.com/time/world/article/0,8599,1904343-2,00.html.

14. Scott Macleod and Nahid Siamdoust, "Mohammed-Baqer Qalibaf: The Man to See," *Time*, Aug. 13, 2008.

15. This claim is raised by former ambassador Seyed Hossein Mousavian in his book *The Iranian Nuclear Crisis*. Notably, Mousavian also charges the Ahmadinejad administration with claiming credit for nuclear progress that actually occurred in the Khatami era, and says that he left government when he became convinced that the new nuclear negotiating team, then led by Ali Larijani (now Speaker of the Majlis), failed to appreciate the severity of international anger with Iran and would thus soon face Security Council measures. He was quickly proven right.

16. Askar Karakir and Karacasulu, "Unlikely Scenario."

17. "Public Opinion in Iran and America on Key International Issues: Questionnaire," WorldPublicOpinion.org, 2006, www.worldpublicopinion.org/pipa/pdf/jan07/Iran_Jan07_quaire.pdf.

18. For a much deeper discussion of the approach of the Iranian neoconservatives, see Ambassador Seyed Hossein Mousavian's insider account (from a reformist perspective) *The Iranian Nuclear Crisis* or Vahid Noori's article "Status-Seeking and Iranian Foreign Policy: The Speeches of the President at the United Nations" in the Spring 2012 issue of *Iranian Review of Foreign Affairs*, which examines the rhetorical difference between the reformists and President Ahmadinejad.

19. Greg Bruno and Jayshree Bajoria, "Iran's Revolutionary Guards," Council on Foreign Relations, Oct. 12, 2011, www.cfr.org/iran/irans-revolutionary-guards/p14324.

20. Mehrzad Boroujerdi and Kourosh Rahimkhani, "Revolutionary Guards Soar in Parliament," The United States Institute of Peace: The Iran Primer, Sept. 19, 2011, http://iranprimer.usip.org/blog/2011/sep/19/revolutionary-guards-soar-parliament.

21. Ali Alfoneh, "Iran's Parliamentary Elections and the Revolutionary Guard's Creeping Coup d'Etat," American Enterprise Institute, Feb. 21, 2008, www.aei.org/article/foreign-and-defense-policy/regional/middle-east-and-north-africa/irans-parliamentary-elections-and-the-revolutionary-guards-creeping-coup-detat/.

22. An interesting wrinkle to Rezaei's rise is that the son of one of his advisors, Abdolhossein Ruholamini, was killed during the 2009 election protests. Ruholamini has been a vocal critic of the handling of that crisis. So far he has reserved his ire for Saeed Mortazavi, Tehran's former top prosecutor. Mortazavi is an Ahmadinejad associate, so this dispute may resolve itself when Ahmadinejad leaves office, but one must wonder if behind the scenes Rezaei and his advisors think of Khamenei as the guilty party.

23. "Iran Underlines Commitment to IAEA Rules," Fars News Agency, July 26, 2011, http://english.farsnews.com/newstext.php?nn=9005040306.

24. Joby Warrick, "Formerly Secret Telexes Offer Window into Iran's Nuclear Deceit," *Washington Post*, Feb. 22, 2012, www.washingtonpost.com/world/national-security/formerly-secret-telexes-offer-window-into-irans-nuclear-deceit/2012/02/11/gIQAOiBlTR_story.html.

25. Sherwell, Philip, "How We Duped the West, by Iran's Nuclear Negotiator," *Telegraph,* March 5, 2006, www.telegraph.co.uk/news/worldnews/middleeast/iran/1512161/How-we-duped-the-West-by-Irans-nuclear-negotiator.html.

26. Deutsche Presse-Agentur, "Iran Threatens to Expand Uranium Enrichment if Nuclear Swap Deal Falls Through," *Haaretz,* Oct. 4, 2011, www.haaretz.com/news/diplomacy-defense/iran-threatens-to-expand-uranium-enrichment-if-nuclear-swap-deal-falls-through-1.388067.

27. James Reini, "US Rejects Iran Nuclear Deal Brokered by Turkey and Brazil and Sets Up New Sanctions," *The National,* May 20, 2010, www.thenational.ae/news/world/us-rejects-iran-nuclear-deal-brokered-by-turkey-and-brazil-and-sets-up-new-sanctions.

28. Associate Press, "U.N. Confirms Iran Uranium Enrichment Claim," CBS News, Jan. 9, 2012, www.cbsnews.com/8301-202_162-57354948/u.n-confirms-iran-uranium-enrichment-claim/.

29. "Iran Nuclear: UN Voices 'Deep Concern' over Plans," BBC News, Nov. 18, 2011. www.bbc.co.uk/news/world-middle-east-15797177.

30. Iran Nuclear: UN Voices 'Deep Concern' over Plans," BBC News.

31. Sheera Frenkel, "A Second Iranian Nuclear Facility Has Exploded, as Diplomatic Tensions Rise between the West and Tehran," *The Australian,* Nov. 30, 2011, www.theaustralian.com.au/news/world/a-second-iranian-nuclear-facility-has-exploded-as-diplomatic-tensions-rise-between-the-west-and-tehran/story-e6frg6so-1226209996774.

32. Cark Vick and Aaron Klein, "Who Assassinated and Iranian Nuclear Scientist? Israel Isn't Telling," *Time,* Jan. 13, 2012, www.time.com/time/world/article/0,8599,2104372,00.html.

33. Greg Bruno, "Iran's Nuclear Program," Council on Foreign Relations, March 10, 2010, www.cfr.org/iran/irans-nuclear-program/p16811.

34. Bruno, "Iran's Nuclear Program."

35. Kenneth Katzman, "Iran Sanctions," Congressional Research Service, Dec. 2, 2011, 38–41.

36. Katzman, "Iran Sanctions," 2.

37. Katzman, "Iran Sanctions," 23.

38. "EU Iran Sanctions: Ministers Adopt Iran Oil Imports Ban," BBC News, Jan. 23, 2012, www.bbc.co.uk/news/world-europe-16674660.

39. Uzi Mahnaimi, "President George W. Bush Backs Israeli Plan for Strike on Iran," *Sunday Times,* July 13, 2008, www.timesonline.co.uk/tol/news/world/middle_east/article4322508.ece.

40. Michael Smith and Sarah Baxter, "US Generals 'Will Quit' if Bush Orders Iran Attack," *Sunday Times,* Feb. 25, 2007, www.timesonline.co.uk/tol/news/world/iraq/article1434540.ece.

41. The White House, Office of the Press Secretary, "Remarks by President Barack Obama," press release, April 5, 2009, www.whitehouse.gov/the_press_office/Remarks-By-President-Barack-Obama-In-Prague-As-Delivered/.

42. Brian M. Downing, "Decoding Obama's Iran Policy: A Single Roll of the Dice: Obama's Diplomacy with Iran by Trita Parsi," *Asia Times* online, Feb. 11, 2012, www.atimes.com/atimes/Middle_East/NB11Ak01.html.

43. "Obama Administration Urges Congress to Weaken Iran Sanctions Bill," Fox News, Dec. 6, 2011, www.foxnews.com/politics/2011/12/06/obama-administration-urges-congress-to-weaken-iran-sanctions-bill/.

44. Mark Landler and Clifford Krauss, "Gulf Nations Aid U.S. Push to Choke Off Iran Oil Sales," *New York Times,* Jan. 12, 2012, www.nytimes.com/2012/01/13/world/asia/asia-buyers-of-iran-crude-get-assurances-of-alternate-supply.html?pagewanted=1&_r=1.

45. Amos Harel, "Panetta in TA Warns Israel Off Iran Strike," *Haaretz,* Oct. 4, 2011, www.haaretz.com/print-edition/news/panetta-in-ta-warns-israel-off-iran-strike-1.387975.

46. The media did not necessarily recognize the reduction in the tension between Obama and Netanyahu's positions, as Netanyahu's use of a cartoon bomb as a prop drew significant attention.

47. Mitt Romney, "Text of Speech on Foreign Policy at The Citadel," *Wall Street Journal*, Oct. 7, 2011, http://blogs.wsj.com/washwire/2011/10/07/text-of-mitt-romneys-speech-on-foreign-policy-at-the-citadel/?mod=google_news_blog.

48. Kenneth Pollack, *The Persian Puzzle: The Conflict between Iran and America* (New York: Random House, 2004), 273.

49. Ilan Berman, "Why Engaging Iran Is (Still) a Bad Idea," *Forbes*, Nov. 1, 2011, www.forbes.com/sites/ilanberman/2011/11/01/why-engaging-iran-is-still-a-bad-idea/.

50. Jason M. Volack, "Ron Paul: Iran Does Not Threaten Our National Security," ABC News, Dec. 30, 2011, http://abcnews.go.com/blogs/politics/2011/12/ron-paul-iran-does-not-threaten-our-national-security/.

51. William Cooper, "National Defense Resources Preparedness Executive Order," Campaign for Liberty, Apr. 16, 2011, www.ronpaul2012.com/the-issues/national-defense/.

52. James Dobbins et al., "Coping with a Nuclearizing Iran," RAND Corporation, 2011.

53. Kenneth Katzman, "Iran: U.S. Concerns and Policy Responses," Congressional Research Service, Dec. 15, 2011, 64, www.fas.org/sgp/crs/mideast/RL32048.pdf.

54. "Iran Seeks Strategic Accommodation with Washington," Stratfor, Jan. 19, 2012, www.stratfor.com/geopolitical-diary/iran-seeks-strategic-accommodation-washington.

55. "Report: U.S. Asked Russia to Warn Iran of 'Last Chance' to Avoid Military Strike," *Haaretz*, Mar. 14, 2012, www.haaretz.com/news/middle-east/report-u-s-asked-russia-to-warn-iran-of-last-chance-to-avoid-military-strike-1.418613.

56. "Top Iran Official Calls for Cooperation from West in Return for 'Transparency,'" CNN, Mar. 15, 2012, http://articles.cnn.com/2012-03-15/middleeast/world_meast_iran-nuclear-larijani_1_parchin-top-iran-official-nuclear-related-activities?_s=PM:MIDDLEEAST.

57. Jim Lobe, "Washington Urged to Engage Iran," *Asia Times Online*, Nov. 18, 2010, http://blogs.wsj.com/washwire/2011/10/07/text-of-mitt-romneys-speech-on-foreign-policy-at-the-citadel/?mod=google_news_blog.

58. Ian Black and Simon Tisdall, "Saudi Arabia Urges U.S. Attack on Iran to Stop Nuclear Programme," *Guardian*, Nov. 28, 2010, www.guardian.co.uk/world/2010/nov/28/us-embassy-cables-saudis-iran.

59. Jeffrey Goldberg, "Dagan Thinks That Barak Is Crazy Enough to Strike Iran," *The Atlantic*, May 9, 2011, www.theatlantic.com/international/archive/2011/05/dagan-thinks-that-barak-is-crazy-enough-to-strike-iran/238554/.

60. "Barak: Dagan's Comments on Iran Hurt Israel's Ability of Deterrence," *Haaretz*, June 6, 2011, www.haaretz.com/news/diplomacy-defense/barak-dagan-s-comments-on-iran-hurt-israel-s-ability-of-deterrence-1.366295.

61. Amos Harel, "Former Mossad Chief: Iran Far from Achieving Nuclear Bomb," *Haaretz*, Oct. 4, 2011, www.haaretz.com/news/diplomacy-defense/former-mossad-chief-iran-far-from-achieving-nuclear-bomb-1.388090.

62. Isabel Kershner and Rick Gladstone, "Decision to Attack Iran Is 'Far Off,' Israel Says," *New York Times*, Jan. 18, 2012, www.nytimes.com/2012/01/19/world/middleeast/iran-nuclear-program-sanctions-russia-israel-attack.html.

63. Olmert's remarks should be taken with a grain of salt—having been unceremoniously booted from the political establishment over allegations of corruption, he has been in the wilderness desperately seeking attention.

64. Dan Williams, "Israel Ex-Spy Warns against 'Messianic' War on Iran," Reuters, Apr. 28, 2012, www.reuters.com/article/2012/04/28/cnews-us-iran-nuclear-israel-idCABRE83R07N20120428.

65. Jeffrey Heller and Maayan Lubell, "Israel's Top General Says Iran Unlikely to Make Bomb," Reuters, Apr. 25, 2012, www.reuters.com/article/2012/04/25/us-israel-iran-idUSBRE83O0C520120425.

66. Isabel Kershner, "Israel's President Criticizes Talk of Unilateral Strike on Iran," *New York Times*, www.nytimes.com/2012/08/17/world/middleeast/israels-peres-criticizes-talk-of-unilateral-iran-strike.html.

67. Hugh Naylor, "Israel Foreign Minister Calls for Arab Citizens to be Under Palestinian Rule," *The National*, Jan. 10, 2012, www.thenational.ae/news/world/middle-east/israel-foreign-minister-calls-for-arab-citizens-to-be-under-palestinian-rule.

68. "Avigdor Lieberman: Israeli Foreign Minister Says Iran War Would 'Be a Nightmare,'" *Huffington Post*, Apr. 3, 2012, www.huffingtonpost.com/2012/04/03/avigdor-lieberman-iran-war_n_1399854.html.

69. Herb Keinon et al., "PM Pulls Back from Yosef's Words," *Jerusalem Post*, Aug. 29, 2010, www.jpost.com/Israel/Article.aspx?id=186372.

70. Tzvi Ben Gedalyahu, "Rabbi Yosef: G-d Will Send Ahmadinejad to Hell," Israel National News, Feb. 26, 2012, www.israelnationalnews.com/News/News.aspx/153141#.UD4Ym6BLOWg.

71. Yair Ettinger and Barak Ravid, "Israeli Defense Officials Consult with Rabbi Ovadia Yosef over Iran Strike," *Haaretz*, Aug. 21, 2012, www.haaretz.com/news/diplomacy-defense/israeli-defense-officials-consult-with-rabbi-ovadia-yosef-over-iran-strike.premium-1.459547.

72. Jeremy Sharon, "Rabbi Ovadia Yosef: Pray for the Destruction of Iran," *Jerusalem Post*, Aug. 26, 2012, www.jpost.com/JewishWorld/JewishNews/Article.aspx?id=282661.

73. Sheera Frenkel, "A Second Iranian Nuclear Facility Has Exploded, as Diplomatic Tensions Rise between the West and Tehran," *Australian Times*, Nov. 30, 2011, www.theaustralian.com.au/news/world/a-second-iranian-nuclear-facility-has-exploded-as-diplomatic-tensions-rise-between-the-west-and-tehran/story-e6frg6so-1226209996774.

74. Michael Eisenstadt and David Pollock, "Asset Test: How the United States Benefits from Its Alliance with Israel," WINEP, Sept. 2012, 52–53, www.washingtoninstitute.org/policy-analysis/view/asset-test-how-the-united-states-benefits-from-its-alliance-with-israel.

TWO

Choosing to Attack

CONTEXT FOR A STRIKE

Surprise Attack

Most published discussion of military options against the Iranian nuclear program has focused on surprise attacks. In the imagined scenario, Iran receives no direct warnings or threats of imminent attack, and receives only vague indicators until the aircraft and missiles are overhead. The attacking state's leadership has reached the conclusion that military action is necessary to stop Iran's nuclearization, and may have launched a public relations campaign against Iranian proliferation (rather like that against Iraq in late 2002). However, it launches the attack unprovoked and at an unexpected moment.

This type of attack has some merits. Analysts diverge on whether an attack could succeed if Iran anticipated that an attack is coming within days. Some possible targets—like the nuclear scientists who run the program—can be removed from target sites and dispersed in minutes. Other targets, like stores of radioactive material, processing chemicals, and centrifuges, can be moved in hours or days. Some elements, like the physical facilities built to accommodate the program, are immobile and can thus be attacked even if the Iranians had very early warning. The physical facilities, however, are not as crucial as the technologies, materials, and experts they contain. Thus, some of the most critical elements of the program could be saved if Iran gets enough warning and the attacker's intelligence services lose track of the dispersed assets.

However, a surprise attack has noteworthy drawbacks. The attacker is not likely to garner much international support no matter how they sell the attack, but a more open public run-up to war might allow the attack to be carried out from a slightly better international position. If Iran feels that the international community opposed the strike, it may rebuild its program, perhaps even at an accelerated pace and with declared weaponizing intentions. It can use international law as a cover—Article X of the Non-Proliferation Treaty allows states to withdraw if "extraordinary events related to the subject matter [of the NPT] have jeopardized the supreme interests of its country." An international community opposed to action against Iran might acquiesce to this radical step. If, however, Iran feels that the international community supported the strike—say, if the Security Council had recently passed a particularly sharp resolution or even authorized force—it might abandon its program rather than face even more isolation. Israel and the United States have, for their own reasons, made an extensive effort to sculpt an international context that is tougher on Iran, and have enjoyed some success. Iran is more isolated than at any point in recent memory. However, it is difficult to argue that the world also supports the use of force, so even a resounding tactical success may have limited strategic consequences.

It is likely that an international context favoring force would only emerge after an Iranian provocation, a situation discussed below. However, the United States can try to influence international public opinion through extensive media and diplomatic preparation, as was the case prior to the 2003 invasion of Iraq. This approach will not meet with success in the next few years—commentators would quickly pounce on the 2007 National Intelligence Estimate's "high confidence" that Iran halted its nuclear program,[1] and the international community still has fresh memories of erroneous U.S. claims about weapons of mass destruction in Iraq. However, policymakers eager to denuclearize Iran and willing to give up surprise for a measure of legitimacy might recall that the international community was skeptical in 2003, yet still made extensive efforts to accommodate American maneuvers.[2]

War Escalates

A counterproliferation strike on Iran could be launched after the outbreak of a broader war. The United States and Iran have had a tense, highly confrontational relationship since the fall of the shah. There has always been a risk of conflict, and brief struggles have broken out several times, with risk rising due to recent events. The United States is entangled in a conflict on Iran's eastern frontier in Afghanistan, and has a major presence in Iran's neighbors. Shipping lanes just off Iran's coast have ever-increasing strategic value as oil demand grows. Iran has a nuclear program of increasingly threatening capacity, and the regime has gone from bad (assassinating overseas dissidents under Khomeini and Rafsanjani) to worse (using apocalyptic rhetoric under Ahmadinejad) to shocking (torturing and killing protesters in the wake of the disputed 2009 presidential election), all while aiding terrorist activities around the world and underwriting Shiite violence in Iraq's civil war. The United States and Iran each perceive the other as a regional threat, but they are also aware of the immense dangers of a war. An uneasy stability—too peaceful to be war, too warlike to be peace—has thus persisted for several years with both sides showing much restraint. The physical proximity of each side's forces creates a danger of unintentional escalation, as one side may respond aggressively to unfamiliar actions in border areas. (The speedboat incidents, imprisonments of sailors, and the downing of an Iranian airliner in 1988 are consequences of this tension.) In times of crisis, both sets of leaders have usually avoided actions that increase the risk of war. However, further incidents are inevitable, and there is a risk that overzealous local commanders or constrained politicians will make choices that force conflict.[3] There are several key areas in which this is possible.

An incident at sea is a major risk, as the many confrontations off the Iranian coast have shown.[4] The U.S. Navy's long-term involvement in the region, including permanent basing in Bahrain and the typical presence of two carrier groups, is certainly threatening to Iran. Moreover, the IRGC's naval arm cultivates initiative in its commanders—for instance, the decision to hold fifteen British sailors captive in 2007 was reportedly taken at the naval district level, even though it had significant consequences for Iranian foreign policy.[5] However, if past confrontations are a guide, both sides can satisfy desires for revenge when they are slighted without provoking major confrontation. The Iranian navies are not vital to regime survival or to state power, so even devastating attacks on them can be ignored—as was the case during the Tanker War, when several Iranian vessels were destroyed by American forces. Given that the navies, especially the IRGCN, will likely be instigators of future incidents, the United States will be able to execute a very proportionate response against involved vessels without making the regime feel its survival is at stake.[6] The Iranian retaliation can include the capture of small patrol vessels or harassment of larger ships, behavior which history suggests the United States tolerates as long as there is little bloodshed.

Any crisis that emerges at sea will thus be the result of either a deliberate choice or profoundly bad judgment. This is especially true after Iran threatened to close the Strait of Hormuz in early 2012, because the United States quickly communicated grave warnings through multiple channels and Iran backed down. Both sides are presumably now more aware of each others' naval priorities and red lines—a top U.S. Navy official called Iran's naval orientation "professional and courteous"[7]—reducing the likelihood of unthinking provocation.

A war in Lebanon could drag in regional powers, creating potential for conflict with Iran. Tehran openly supports the Lebanese Hezbollah, which sees itself as the key "resistance" to U.S. ally Israel; Hezbollah is also a rival of Lebanese political factions backed by the United States and

Figure 2.1. Speedboats belonging to the IRGC.

its ally Saudi Arabia. Either of these enmities could kindle a war. Hezbollah's ability to attack Israel has improved dramatically since the 2006 war, and there is a chance that Israel would feel the need to return to South Lebanon to stop major rocket attacks. There is also always a potential for renewed civil warfare, and American allies might fare poorly and call for assistance from patron states like Saudi Arabia. This could provoke both Hezbollah and Iranian agitation around the region, with potential to create a broader confrontation.

Like Hezbollah, Syria provides Iran with a window to the Mediterranean and the Levant. Iran has staunchly defended the al Assad government through a bloody crackdown that began in 2011, and has long used Syria as a conduit to other allies. Western actions against the Assad regime might lead to Iranian replies. An open intervention, though it seems increasingly unlikely, could force Iran to take a concrete position or watch its influence disappear. A proxy conflict, with potential to spread, could result.

Iran's extensive ties to terrorism around the world have led to the deaths of many Americans. It is possible that some future Iranian-backed action will push the United States to the limits of its tolerance—or that the United States will mistakenly attribute a serious attack to Iran.[8] However, the United States has shown itself willing to tolerate Iranian terror—what act could provoke a change of course? Attacks on American soil would certainly cross the Rubicon. However, U.S. tolerance might soon shrink so that currently acceptable acts begin to draw replies. The drawdown of U.S. troop presence in the region over the next several years will create more flexibility—there will be more American troops and resources available, and fewer of them will be sitting targets in countries where Iran has a strong presence—making all Iranian actions slightly more risky. Terrorism, moreover, is a bull in the china shop of American political discourse, so American leaders may find nothing short of regime change satisfactory in the event of a massive Iran-linked attack on American soil; lesser attacks allow a more nuanced response. Given Iran's long history of connections to terror, and its association in the popular consciousness with terror sponsorship, it is possible that a terrorist act of ambiguous provenance could be erroneously pinned on Iran, again yielding conflict.[9] With the February 2012 Iranian attacks in Thailand, Georgia, and India and the July 2012 Hezbollah attack in Bulgaria, this path is more likely than others.

In any of these scenarios, U.S. policymakers will certainly consider attacking Iran's nuclear program.[10] War would remove many of the present barriers to such an attack—the international community would have less cause for anger, Iran's retaliatory forces would be depleted and distracted, and U.S. and allied forces would be in place to mitigate their response. Iran might have attempted to use some of the retaliatory measures we will discuss in this book, and thus shown its strength. Of course, some risks would remain. A counterproliferation attack could still cause Tehran to believe regime change is being attempted, prompting an aggressive response. It could also confirm the hard-line narrative that only a nuclear Iran is safe, particularly if the attack comes early in the war, as it would appear that the United States was trying to remove a key threat to the intervention's strategic success. Unless there were an all-out war in progress, an attack on Iran's nuclear program would be a significant escalation, so American officials would have to consider international perceptions, Iran's ability to react, and their own willingness to expand the conflict before acting; they will likely still find circumstances quite favorable for action.

Response to Nuclear Provocation

Iran's current nuclear policy is ambiguous. It would be bold to claim that Iran's policy elites have a shared understanding of the program's ultimate goal. Iran will soon reach a point at which it must resolve some of these internal disagreements, because some advances will draw international ire regardless of intent. If, at the coming crossroads, Iran chooses to openly build a weapon, it will have to take a number of extremely aggressive actions that make its intentions obvious, like withdrawing from the NPT and expelling IAEA investigators. Actions like these would signal the end of the nuclear negotiations and dangerously undermine the NPT, risking a regional and global nuclear arms race. The United States or Israel will see both an openly defiant nuclear Iran and an arms race as highly unfavorable. Either might choose to reply with a strike. The world, and especially Iran's neighbors, might be silent.

Many of the risks of a surprise attack would remain. An attack could fail to destroy the program, or it could confirm the distorted visions of Iran's most hard-line factions. More seriously, Iran would be more prepared to defend itself against an attack and to initiate retaliation, as its armed forces would have certainly been put on alert before the provocative act. Iran's defenses are weak, though they'd be more troublesome—perhaps troublesome enough to keep the Israelis at bay—if they were on hair-trigger alert. The retaliatory forces would be more dangerous, as they'd be able to disperse, put out to sea, begin infiltrations, identify fleeting attack opportunities, etc. If Iran keeps its retaliatory forces in relatively concentrated areas at fairly low levels of readiness during peacetime, then a prepared Iran could be orders of magnitude more dangerous.

If Iran's provocation is a nuclear test, the implications would be severe. If global intelligence communities failed to predict it, they would face a political hammering unseen since the aftermath of 9/11; if the IAEA failed to predict it, its credibility as a nonproliferation institution would shrink. If the world had known of the test in advance and been unable to dissuade Iran, it would likely have to carry out severe political and economic actions, or it would show by inaction that Iran's nuclear ambitions were quite merited, inspiring other proliferation. Military action to declaw Iran would certainly be worth considering, but the possibility that Iran has other nuclear weapons would deter it, as no power in the world would want to challenge a prepared, nuclear-armed Iran.

The assertion infamously made by the IRGC-affiliated Gerdab news site that the morning after an Iranian nuclear test will bring "a normal day" is quite incorrect. All of Iran's neighbors and rivals would be faced with an unpleasant choice between replying and thus risking nuclear war, offering each other cumbersome strategic assurances, or acquiescing and thus wagering that they have not fired the starting gun of a second nuclear arms race, one that would end with many more nuclear powers, a greater risk of nuclear war, and the severe reduction of major power influence.

On the other hand, Iran might choose to sustain its current level of nuclear ability, ceasing its pattern of stretching the status quo. As of October 2012 it was below the level of capability where it would have a credible "breakout option" where it could assemble a nuclear weapon on short notice in the event of a crisis, but it is not far from that point. The breakout option makes sense for Iran's objective geopolitical situation and would maintain the regime's domestic credibility, though it is not clear that it would be consistent with the regime's long-term foreign policy strategy. Iran's negotiating patterns in 2011–2012 suggest that it is seeking to legitimize the status quo, which is consistent with sustainment or a continuation of a slow push toward some higher level of nuclear ability, including the breakout option. This path has a better chance of avoiding intervention, but Iran would still face the question of the sanctions regime. It could only hope that the United States would be unable to sustain political pressure on countries who have an interest in trading with Iran. This is a reasonable hope.

MERITS AND RISKS OF A STRIKE

Taking all possibilities into consideration, what are the costs and benefits of a strike on Iran? A nuclear Iran is certainly not in the global interest. Iran might behave irrationally—there has always been debate on the rationality of the Iranian regime, but its "less rational" elements, including fanatic elements within the IRGC, are clearly in ascendancy after the crushing of the reformists in the wake of the 2009 election and the undermining of the "deviant current" of anticlerical post-reformist conservatives in 2011. Clericalist hardliners within the elite are sealing off the chambers of power from more moderate rivals. Iran has long expressed a deeply revisionist vision of the Middle East, even though its actions have not always matched its words. Many fear Tehran could use the bomb to provide cover for an aggressive agenda; some are concerned it could even provide nuclear materials to radical allies like Hezbollah. Preventing such a future, all other things being equal, is desirable.

On the other hand, an attack carries with it many risks. It is not a certainty that Iran's nuclear program aims to make weapons—indeed, if the Iranians do have a long-term vision for the nuclear program, they have done an excellent job of keeping it hidden. Attacking might lead Iran to set a course for weaponization. The world benefits from the current nuclear ambiguity—Tehran has been forced to remain party to the NPT and submit to IAEA inspections. These inspections inform the international community and global public of Iran's intransigence. This is good for states opposed to Iranian nuclearization—without the IAEA, they would have to rely on spottier data from their own intelligence services. The collapse of the inspection regime in Iraq was soon followed by inflated intelligence on Iraq's weapons of mass destruction; the loss of international legitimacy and informational accuracy would lead to an erroneous and unpopular war. IAEA safeguarding and reporting put Iran in defiance of a respected international regime rather than merely "the West," and it ensures that Iranian misdeeds are made public by a trusted source. If it ever wishes to develop a weapon, it will have to withdraw from the safeguard regime, which will bring swift global condemnation and possibly war. An attack on Iran before a breakout could remove the safeguards—Article X of the NPT allows nations to withdraw in the event of "extraordinary events . . . [that] have jeopardized [their] supreme interests," and an attack on a nation's nuclear program would surely meet that criterion. Iran would, in the opinion of most experts, see an attack on its nuclear program as proof that it is not safe without a nuclear deterrent. The world would have to either accept a nuclear Iran or repeatedly return in force to prevent it.

There is a risk that an attack wouldn't even be able to slow the nuclear program down. Iran is aware of the debates on attacks within the United States and Israel, so it has taken care to protect its sites—they are typically kept secret until found by foreign intelligence services, and many are in tunnels, bunkers, or urban areas to complicate airstrikes. Secreting away the key elements of a nuclear weapons program would be very difficult, but not impossible. If Iran has accomplished this, a strike would do nothing but ensure that it becomes a nuclear power—and an angry, vengeful one at that.

Perhaps the greatest risk of an attack is Iran's ability to retaliate. Iran has extensive contacts with terrorist groups like Hezbollah and Islamic Jihad (PIJ) that can allow a significant asymmetric response. Iran also has a capable military of its own, and could attempt to trigger an economic nightmare scenario by attacking oil facilities in the Gulf and shutting the Strait of Hormuz—if successful, this combined action would reduce daily global oil production by some 17 million barrels (19.3 percent of global production) for days and perhaps 4 million barrels (4.4 percent of global production) for weeks or months.

An attack on Iran thus has formidable downsides, and this is acknowledged by virtually all attack proponents. However, they maintain that the risks of a nuclear Iran are even greater. As one observer pointed out, both proponents and opponents tend to be largely in agreement on many points; the difference is that opponents stress the risk of acting while proponents stress the risk of doing nothing.[11]

Expert Voices

Expert opinion is divided on the net benefit of an attack. While experts generally believe that even Israel's small air force is capable of physically destroying the Iranian nuclear program's major sites, there is deep division on whether attacks are worth it.

The most technical assessments of the attack were conducted by Whitney Raas and Austin Long at MIT and by Abdullah Toukan and Anthony Cordesman of the Center for Strategic and International Studies. Raas and Long state unequivocally that Israel is capable of striking Iran's nuclear program at its main sites, and that the immediate risks and rewards are more or less the same as those that were in play in Israel's 1981 raid on the Iraqi nuclear reactor at Osirak. However, they note that there is a significant "operational and political risk" associated with action, and that Israeli leaders may change their assessments of the net value of striking over time.

Raas and Long suggest that Israel can accomplish its mission using about fifty aircraft, and that the loss rate to Iran's weak air defenses will not be serious. The most difficult leg of the strike will be hitting the primary enrichment facility at Natanz. Its cavernous underground halls of gas centrifuges would require a large number of successful hits with penetration warheads to be certain of destruction, though that may be serious overkill. The ideal time to carry out a strike, they say, is when the halls are as full of centrifuges as possible, but before they've all been put into operation. This would maximally set back Iran's program by destroying an enormous investment, though it would be crucial to strike before large quantities of weapons-grade highly enriched uranium (HEU) could be produced.[12] Long later wrote a supplementary article to add the newly activated buried enrichment hall outside Qom to the target set, and estimated that twenty-five aircraft would be necessary to destroy it—enough that two raids should be required.[13]

Toukan and Cordesman take a less optimistic view of the IAF. They agree that an attack is possible, but think that it is dangerously "complex and high risk in the operational level." Israeli planners will thus lack "assurances of a high mission success rate" should they order an attack. However, they argue, if Iran has managed to secretly acquire the Antey 2500 (S-300VM/SA-23) surface to air missile, it would be capable of inflicting unacceptably high casualties on the strike package, and Israel would not be able to act.[14] (This scenario is unlikely, as there has not been a serious bid to acquire any S-300V-series missiles, and they do not appear to have the similar S-300P-series, either.)

Patrick Clawson and Michael Eisenstadt, in an analysis published by the Washington Institute, take a more subtle view. They hold deterrence in low regard, suggesting it is a high-risk strategy that merely defers major crisis. However, preemption creates a serious burden, as it will be ineffective unless it is a "sustained policy [rather than] a one-off affair." Carrying out repeated strikes on Iran will require a deep base of global and domestic support, and creating those bases without inadvertently warning Iran of an impending attack would be all but impossible. Political context is key. The international community must feel that there has been a sustained good faith attempt to bring Iran back into good standing in the global counterproliferation regime, and it must feel that Iran has openly rebuffed that attempt. If these criteria are not met and the world is angered by strikes, then the strikes would have only "made matters worse."

According to former Israeli security official Chuck Freilich, Israel's ability to attack known nuclear facilities "does not appear to be in great doubt." There are two salient worries about an attack: first, it will merely delay the program rather than halting it; second, it will be subjected to extensive retaliation from Iranian proxies like Hezbollah. However, Freilich thinks that Israel's strategic culture will still see an attack as justified—a delay is an acceptable end in itself, and the Iranian retaliation will be painful, but hardly devastating. Israel, he argues, "can and should be" willing to bear the costs given the danger of a nuclear Iran.

Gerald Steinberg of Bar Ilan University notes that Israeli deterrence of Iran will be more difficult and riskier than other cases of deterrence, because the lack of Iranian-Israeli contacts and mutual knowledge increases the probability of misunderstandings and spiraling confrontations.[15] A preventive strike is "problematic." Iran witnessed Israel's raid on Osirak and had attempted to attack the site on its own, so its strategists have long been aware of the danger of a raid. They have accordingly separated, hidden, and hardened the elements of their nuclear program, and have favored the more dispersible uranium track to the bomb, making it harder to destroy. However, the United States and Israel have significantly greater capabilities than they did in the early 1980s. Their intelligence systems are better at finding what is hidden, and their air forces are better at hitting what is hardened.[16]

Deputy Secretary of Defense Ashton Carter, in his article "Military Elements in a Strategy to Deal with Iran's Nuclear Program," explains that Iran's dispersed nuclear program will require any attacker to hit hundreds of aimpoints, but that the United States can "easily" hit all these targets "in a few nights." However, even hitting all targets may not be sufficient, as Iran is suspected to have a covert program. If this program is extensive enough and Iran accelerates it after a strike, there will be no net effect on Iranian progress.

Former Defense Intelligence Agency analyst Jeffrey White, in "What Would War with Iran Look Like?," emphasizes Iran's greatly underestimated ability to retaliate by escalating any conflict in asymmetric and multidimensional fashions. Thus, while the United States is "far superior" to Iran in traditional military capabilities, Iran's responses will still require the United States to take defensive actions that its government and intelligence are improperly structured to effect. Thus, a limited conflict aimed only at Iran's nuclear program would be very risky. In order to reduce the threat of Iranian retaliation, the United States would have to warn Iran that any retaliation will be met with an all-out attempt to change the regime. It would be difficult to make such a threat credible, and difficult to communicate it without straining international and domestic tolerance. However, living with a nuclear Iran is also high risk and "open-ended," so "the fear of potentially negative consequences from a war should not necessarily rule one out."

The Preventive Defense Project's star-studded 2006 WMD Workshop suggested that an attack could cause Iran to make an all-out rush for the bomb instead of moving at a slow, secretive pace. An Iranian bomb could then arrive on the scene sooner than it otherwise would have—in other words, if an attack can only delay Iran's nuclear program and not stop it, talks are preferable because they may be more effective at creating delay. Either way, the consequences of an attack would be "severe," as the United States would be isolated internationally and subjected to extensive retaliation to which it cannot respond effectively without expending its only bargaining chip with the regime—its ability to widen the conflict.

Paul Rogers of the University of Bradford wrote two major studies of the military option against Iran, one in 2006 and the other in 2010, with the former focusing primarily on the United States and the latter on Israel. He takes a negative view in each, suggesting that escalation would be very likely and that success would be almost impossible: regardless of the damage to its facilities, Iran would now be determined to get the bomb and would be unwilling to communicate with the United States, except through violence. He is explicit in his opposition to the use of preemptive strikes, saying that "war is not an option" and that "the consequences . . . are so serious that they should not be encouraged in any shape or form."

Political Voices

Support for strikes on Iran is particularly common among neoconservatives and uncommon in the left's dovish circles, as we would expect. One of the leading neoconservative voices in favor of an attack has been AEI fellow and former CIA operative Reuel Marc Gerecht. Gerecht's assessments, presented in the *Weekly Standard* in 2006 and 2010, are strikingly different from many of the others, in that he believes Iran's capacity to retaliate has been significantly overhyped—for instance, the growing investment of the Iraqi Shia in their government will make them unwilling to destabilize their own country to do favors for Iran. Like most other authors, he thinks attacks will be the beginning of a long confrontation—"a decade or more"—with Iran. He does not believe that an attack will certainly be successful, but regardless of its impact on Iran's program, it will show Iran and the world that the United States has red lines.

His assessment of an attack by Israel is surprisingly guarded. He notes that Israel has a comparatively high likelihood of striking due to the vital role that preemption has played in the state's survival (the Six-Day War and the Osirak raid are but two examples). However, he worries that this time the Israelis are overestimating the capabilities of their air force given the distance and complexity of the mission.

Outside of these settings, views are much more varied. In the United States, neither left nor right has advanced a clear program for dealing effectively with Iran's nuclear program, and diversity of opinion is thus tolerated in each. There is a notable tendency for all but the most hawkish members of Congress to advocate the use of congressional powers—that is, sanctions—as the primary means of dealing with Iran. Some members advocate very broad sanctions regimes and justify their position by speaking of the urgency of dealing with Iran's program, yet make no mention of any nonfinancial measures.

Within the Obama administration, there are no vocal Iran hawks. Because Iran can retaliate by destabilizing Iraq and Afghanistan, the Department of Defense and military voices tend to be against strikes, and tend to speak of stability as the key worry preventing intervention (and not, for instance, physical and technical capacities). There is speculation that their statements were subtly coordinated by ex–secretary of defense Robert Gates, who has become a strong public critic of attacks. While senators, both Joe Biden and Hillary Clinton voted for legislation that suggested their opposition to strikes, though Clinton attacked Obama's suggestions of engagement with Iran when the two were rivals on the campaign trail.

Then senator Obama's views were more ambiguous. He was one of two senators who abstained from the vote on 2007's Lieberman-Kyl Amendment to the defense budget, which designated the IRGC as a terrorist organization and, in its initial form, suggested that military force should be used to "roll back" Iranian influence and support for terror in Iraq. (The other abstaining senator was John McCain, so this may have been a case of pre-electoral caution, as both candidates had announced their intention to run several months earlier.) During the 2008 campaign, he staked out a very hazy position on Iran, suggesting that significant American concessions and shifts in tone could result in significant improvements in Iranian behavior (a point that was extremely controversial) while simultaneously refusing to keep military measures off of the table. At some points, Obama used wordings that suggested he was resigned to a nuclear Iran; at others, he suggested the United States might "take action."[17] It seems safe to say that the candidate Obama did not have a straightforward Iran policy, or that if he did, he kept it hidden in order to avoid providing ammunition to political rivals.

As president, Obama's views remained opaque for a time. The early days of his administration featured an attempt to "engage" Iran with the carrot-based approach that he had proposed in his campaign; remarks avoided discussion of the military option. The brutal crackdown following the 2009 elections forced Obama to take a less conciliatory approach. Though Obama told reporters in July of that year (a month after the elections) that he would not give a green light for an Israeli attack, the administration's tone became appreciably more critical of Iran, with regular State Department statements on Iran's nuclear program and human rights issues. Rhetoric has since become more militaristic.

The year 2012 witnessed a dramatic increase in government attention to the Iran crisis. American policymakers have repeatedly increased sanctions against Iran, and have drawn the cooperation of many states around the world. American and Israeli officials have entered into regular high-level consultations to clarify positions, with American officials arguing that the sanctions need time to work and Israelis arguing that the nuclear program will soon enter a "zone of immunity" safe from attack. It remains unclear whether the United States believes that Israel is capable of an effective strike—some sectors of the intelligence community are allegedly very skeptical. Washington has also not stated explicitly under what conditions it would take military action against Iran, or what Iran could do to avoid being attacked.

NOTES

1. The NIE uses the term "high confidence" technically—it "generally means that [their] judgments are based on high-quality information, and/or that the nature of the issue makes it possible to render a solid judgment." Notably, the 2005 NIE assigns "high confidence" to its claim that Iran "is determined to develop nuclear weapons." 2010 testimony by the director of national intelligence to the Senate Select Committee on Intelligence did not make an explicit claim about Iran's intentions, and instead merely noted Iran's growing capabilities (a distinction that is troublingly glossed over in many discussions of Iran's security state). See "Iran: Nuclear Intentions and Capabilities," Office of the Director of National Intelligence, Nov. 2007, www.dni.gov/press_releases/20071203_release.pdf, and Dennis C. Blair, "Annual Threat Assessment of the U.S. Intelligence Community for the Senate Select Committee on Intelligence," Feb. 2010.

2. The accommodation efforts were so extensive that they contributed to political crises in places like the Netherlands and the United Kingdom.

3. Bad luck is also possible—recall the key role of chance in Clausewitz's famous "fascinating trinity" of warfare. During the January 2008 speedboat incident, as Iranian boats approached the USS *Hopper*, a voice told the Americans by radio "I am coming to you. You will explode in a few minutes." The navy later stated it was unsure where this voice had come from; some sailors familiar with the area stated it may have been a local radio prankster known as the "Filipino Monkey." Had the crew of the *Hopper* treated the message as a credible threat, a mutually unintended clash of arms could have resulted, without poor judgment on either side. Since chance events like this have some slight probability of occurring on any given day, with enough time they are inevitable—a worrisome conclusion. (c.f. Scutro and Brown, "'Filipino Monkey' Behind Threats?," *Navy Times*, Jan. 11, 2008, www.navytimes.com/news/2008/01/navy_hormuz_iran_radio_080111.)

4. Many of these incidents have not gotten major media attention, but they are regular, and the United States and Iran do not yet have hotlines or explicitly shared understandings of behavior in the Gulf. For a slightly dated list of incidents, see Henderson, "Energy in Danger: Iran, Oil, and the West," Washington Institute, 2008, 3. The withdrawal from Iraq will ease some tension, as contentious patrols on the Shatt al Arab are no longer conducted by Western forces.

5. See Haghshenass, "Iran's Asymmetric Naval Warfare," Washington Institute Policy Focus #87, Sept. 2008, and Crist, "Gulf of Conflict: A History of U.S.-Iranian Confrontation at Sea," Washington Institute Policy Focus #95, June 2009, 26.

6. As the IRGC deepens its role in the regime, this may not hold, although the IRGCN remains a minor player.

7. Associated Press, "US Navy Chief: Provocative in the Past, Iranian Navy in Gulf Quiet Lately," *Times of Israel*, June 28, 2012, www.timesofisrael.com/us-navy-chief-provocative-in-the-past-iranian-navy-in-gulf-quiet-lately/.

8. The ongoing controversies about Iranian responsibility for the 1996 Khobar Towers bombing are an example of the difficulties of attribution. It may be unclear

who is responsible for an attack, and investigators and sympathizers may lend credence to alternative theories even if evidence is abundant.

9. Virtually any act of Shiite terror, for example, might be misattributed to Iran, though American intelligence officers are surely used to the tendency of the more paranoid Sunni leaders to see an Iranian hand behind every Shiite action.

10. A study of various attacks on nuclear programs found that warfare makes both consideration and execution of counterproliferation strikes significantly more likely. See Fuhrmann and Kreps, "Targeting Nuclear Programs in Times of War and Peace."

11. Perkovich, "Five Scenarios for the Iranian Crisis," 2006. There is, however, significant variation among experts on the details of Iranian retaliation, for one example.

12. Centrifuges are operated in semi-discrete "cascades" of 164, meaning enrichment can still be conducted at dangerous levels without completely filling the halls. Iran also claims to be developing several more advanced centrifuge models that can conduct enrichment faster. If a hall full of 50,000 basic centrifuges merits a strike, there would be some smaller number of more advanced centrifuges that would equally merit a strike even if the halls have not been filled. This number could be less than 10,000, given how inefficient Iran's first-generation centrifuges are in comparison to proposed later models.

13. Austin Long, "Can They?," *Tablet Magazine*, Nov. 18, 2011, www.tabletmag.com/news-and-politics/83631/can-they/.

14. It is not clear how Toukan and Cordesman determined Iran was close to acquiring any S-300V-series weapons, especially the VM, as these are very advanced weapons that the Russians are wary of exporting. Iran and Russia had been negotiating the purchase of smaller, cheaper, less capable (but still very dangerous) weapons from the S-300P family. This deal has, according to open sources, fallen through due to pressure from the United States, and Iran claims—very dubiously—to have produced an equally capable indigenous version. (There are rumors that Iran acquired P-family missiles from Russia or Belarus in the mid-1990s, but these are hotly disputed.)

15. This may be slightly inaccurate, as there are many Israelis of Iranian extraction. Disgraced former president Moshe Katzav, for instance, was born in Yazd and speaks fluent Farsi; his Iranian counterpart Mohammed Khatami was born two years earlier in the same province. However, as the major aliyot and the Islamic Revolution fade into the past, the number of Israelis with personal familiarity with Iran will decline, and Steinberg's worry will become more of a concern; a deterrence perspective must by nature take the long view.

16. Recall, for example, that the Osirak raid was conducted without the use of guided munitions.

17. See "Barack Obama on War & Peace," On the Issues, www.ontheissues.org/2012/Barack_Obama_War_+_Peace.htm#Trouble_Spots, especially Obama's remarks in response to a direct question during the Drexel University Democratic debates.

THREE

How an Attack Might Work

TARGETING

Any successful attack on Iran's nuclear program would require the destruction of four main targets: the uranium conversion facility at Esfahan, the heavy water plant at Arak, and especially the enrichment facilities at Natanz and Fordow. These facilities form the backbone of the Iranian nuclear program, with Esfahan crucial for Iran's possession of a complete fuel cycle and Natanz and Fordow, should Iran build enough centrifuges, capable of producing enough highly enriched uranium for multiple bombs each year. Arak could be used to reprocess plutonium, a different track for a bomb. Each target presents particular challenges, with tunneling activity present at Esfahan and the centrifuge halls at Natanz and Fordow buried underground. However, experts are in agreement that all of these targets, except perhaps Fordow, can be destroyed by an Israeli or American air raid.

In addition, there are numerous sites around the country that are involved in the manufacture of centrifuge components. While these are not nearly as hard to hit as the buried centrifuge halls, they are scattered across a large area, including in the city of Mashhad, some 2,300 km from Israel.

There are also several locations associated with potential weaponization, including missile development areas and the military base at Parchin (near Tehran) suspected to have been used to develop explosive arrays used in nuclear bombs. These would also be likely targets.

The most difficult target is Fordow, revealed in 2009, in tunnels near Qom. The site is a fraction of the size of Natanz, but it has been assigned to take the lead in enriching to nearly 20 percent, a key next step in Iran's program that will make breakout time much shorter. The site is reported-

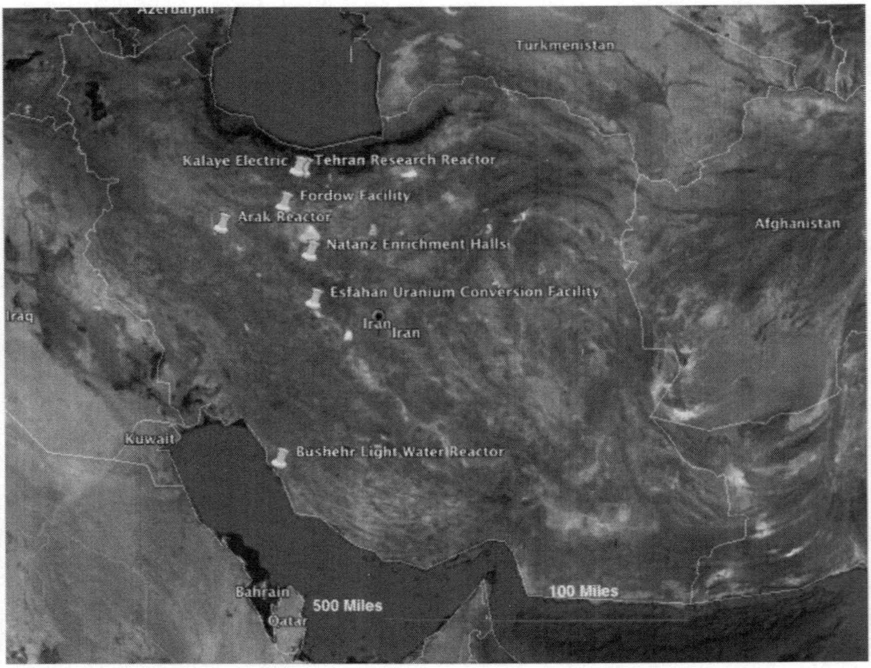

Figure 3.1. Map of key Iranian nuclear sites. ***(Produced with Google Earth.)***

ly at a depth of 70–90 meters inside a small mountain. This is at the edge of known bunker-buster capabilities. If Iran is able to successfully deploy advanced centrifuges, Fordow may become the vital center of an Iranian push for high enriched uranium.

Intelligence agencies may be aware of a covert nuclear program,[1] so there may be some targets unknown to open sources. It is reasonable to suspect that Iran has at least some nuclear activities that are unknown to any outside actors, given its history of deception. Attackers will hit the targets they know and hope there is nothing big that they don't know. It is unlikely that there are other major sites on the scale of Natanz, since the Natanz site was itself covert for a time and it would have been wasteful to have multiple large covert nuclear programs.

Other nuclear sites are not likely to be targeted. The most well-known of these is the Russian-built light water reactor at Bushehr. If the Iranians were to nationalize the reactor and remove Russia's controls, it could be a source of plutonium. However, this is considered highly unlikely, and there is a risk of significant regional environmental damage if the reactor core is breached by an attack.

Another unlikely target is the Tehran Research Reactor. The small reactor is located in an urban area, provides materials needed for medical activities, and is not a proliferation risk. Iran could easily score a propaganda victory by noting the many cancer patients dependent on its isotopes for treatment. There is a wrinkle—the TRR uses fuel enriched to the uncommon and relatively high 19.75 percent level. Iran uses this to justify its enrichment of uranium to such levels. Destroying the TRR would remove this justification for enrichment, albeit at the cost of providing another under Article X of the NPT.

Other facilities in Iran without direct roles in the nuclear program have been suggested as potential targets of the campaign associated with an antinuclear strike. Iran's submarines and patrol boats might be a target, as they would play a key role in any attempt to seal the Strait of Hormuz if unmolested. Facilities of the Islamic Revolutionary Guard Corps might also be destroyed, as these are vital to the regime's ability to retaliate—and to its survival.

This target set should be understood as a menu of options available to leaders planning an attack on Iran; carefully selected attacks could still do significant damage to the Iranian nuclear program. The nuclear fuel cycle is complex, requiring a range of facilities. Some of these facilities are choke points within the cycle due to the high cost of their development and constraints on their operation. The Iranian program has three major choke points—Natanz, Fordow, and Esfahan. Destroying some of them—especially the two enrichment halls, would flush massive amounts of Iranian money and labor down the toilet. Other parts within the cycle are far less vulnerable—uranium mines, for instance—to the point that bombing them would be a waste of resources.

AN ISRAELI STRIKE

The current governmental composition of Israel, combined with its military history and strategic interests, make it much more likely to initiate hostilities against Iran than the United States. Major political commentators have suggested that an Israeli strike may be imminent–though they have been suggesting this for perhaps a decade. The limiting factor is Israel's small fleet of twenty-five F-15I Ra'am strike fighters (the Israeli variant of the F-15E Strike Eagle). The F-15I is Israel's only aircraft capable of delivering the 5,000 lb GBU-28, the most powerful penetration weapon in Israel's arsenal. Each F-15I can carry two of these bombs, meaning the Israeli strike package will have up to fifty GBU-28s at its disposal. The vast majority of these will be needed for use against the Natanz facility's two cavernous underground centrifuge halls. This will require many bombs in order to ensure successful penetration and full destruction inside the halls. Planners estimate at least twenty-four GBU-

28s will be needed to assure destruction in Natanz; if more are required, the margin of error for a single-sortie strike on Natanz will become very thin, even without diverting some GBU-28s to the facility at Fordow.[2] It is thus quite likely that the Israelis will launch multiple sorties.

Supporting the F-15Is would be a substantial number of F-16I Sufas (a heavily modified Israeli version of the F-16D Fighting Falcon). Some of these aircraft would be carrying lighter 2,000 lb guided penetration bombs for dealing with less challenging targets than the Natanz enrichment halls. Others would be equipped to suppress Iran's air defenses, and some would likely be armed purely for air-to-air combat to protect the strike package from Iranian interceptors.

The strike force would need aerial refueling to safely travel to and from Iran. Israel is secretive about its tanker capabilities, but the number of aircraft involved in this mission would strain them to their limits. Depending on the location chosen for refueling, they might also be in significant danger—some hypothetical plans have them conducting refueling over the Gulf, where Iranian interceptors and even Iranian SAMs can interfere.

Route selection is the most challenging aspect of an Israeli strike. In flying to Iran, the Israelis simply cannot avoid entering the airspace of a third party for an extended period. There are three potential routes, and all pose difficulties.

First, the Israelis could fly north over Turkey and enter Iran from the northwest. This would strain relations with their only Muslim ally (albeit a fading one) and take the strike package over numerous Iranian airbases. The recent performative anti-Israeli turn of the Erdogan government might make the Turks feel more pressure to interfere with the Israeli effort.

Second, the Israelis could fly south, over the Gulf of Aqaba and through Saudi Arabia's remote north, then across the Gulf and up into Iran. This route would be longest, but possibly safest and least risky, as the Saudis would be quite happy to allow the Israelis to weaken their rival. However, given the political risks for Ankara and Riyadh in these first two cases, it is likely that neither "host" would allow more than one or two raids through their territory. This limits the effectiveness of the strike.

Third, the Israelis could fly over Iraq, a matter worth deeper discussion as it is now by far the most likely approach.

The Central Route: Overflying Iraq

For many years, the possibility that Israel could get into Iran via Iraq was discounted. The United States was responsible for the security of Iraq's airspace, so Israel would have needed to get American permission or risk America's wrath—and America's interference. Washington would

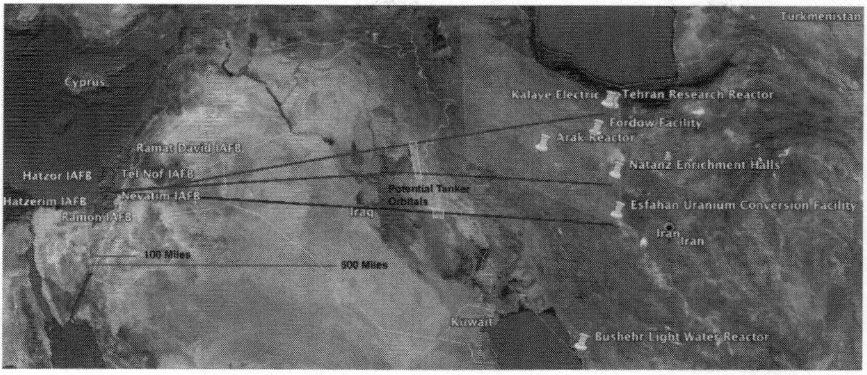

Figure 3.2. Map of Israeli flight paths to Iran through Iraq and Jordan. A possible area for tanker aircraft to refuel is marked in green. Note that in the report we argue that Bushehr is not likely to be targeted by the Israelis, but we include flight and refueling options in case they do. The gray polygon in northwest Iran is referenced in one of the appendices as Iran's "strategic core," an area with many key military facilities that would be the focus of any sustained air campaign by either the United States or Israel. The core area is bounded by Tehran in the northeast, Esfahan in the southeast, Kermanshah in the southwest, and Tabriz in the northwest. ***(Produced with Google Earth.)***

be unlikely to grant that permission—it has never looked kindly on Israeli preemption, and it would suffer major costs for an apparent collusion against Iran. An attack through Iraq would have strained U.S.-Israel relations at a critical moment—a highly counterproductive outcome. However, this situation changed dramatically when Washington and Baghdad could not agree on a new Status of Forces Agreement, forcing American troops to depart Iraq in late 2011. The United States no longer has a direct stake in Israel's selection of attack routes. An Israeli overflight of Iraq is now between those two governments alone.

In practical terms, Israel doesn't need Baghdad's permission to enter Iraqi airspace. Iraq is presently unable to defend its skies. Its air force has no operational fighter aircraft and is dominated by helicopters, transport aircraft, and light trainers. Its air defenses, though supported by powerful radar systems, are not armed with SAMs capable of covering large areas or hitting high-flying aircraft. For Israeli attackers, the airspace over Iraq might as well be over an empty sea; what's more, they may be able to use historical friendliness with Iraqi Kurdistan to obtain search and rescue support for any pilots lost in Iraq. Iraq is so weak, in fact, that its best air defense option is likely to use its long-range radars to warn the Iranians of approaching attackers, and even this option is dubious. Despite media statements that the Iraqi Air Force has a long-range radar site at Taji near Baghdad, right in the middle of the best routes to Iran, reporters that actually visited Taji in late 2011 found personnel struggling to learn how to use basic radar to guide aircraft in for landing and complaining of the difficulty of tracking multiple aircraft. This is hardly a strategic asset; beset by Israeli jammers, the radar site is not likely to pose a serious risk.

The availability of the Iraq route is a game-changer for Israel's military option against Iran. The route is hundreds of kilometers shorter than any alternatives, allowing the strike package significantly more flexibility in refueling, weapons loads, and self-defense. More crucially, because Iraq cannot stop the Israelis from using its airspace, Israel can execute multiple raids, returning to targets it failed to destroy instead of trying to win by knock-out in the first and only round. This significantly increases Israel's airpower against Iran and its odds of success, and allows Israel to respond if Iran retaliates with ballistic missile strikes or terrorism. With Iraq newly "empty," Israel gained significant power relative to Iran.

Of course, there are only two ways to get to Iraq from Israel: through Jordan, and through Syria. Each poses its own challenges. From a tactical standpoint, the Jordanian route is best, as Jordan sits on the shortest path from most IAF bases to Iranian nuclear facilities. Jordan's air defenses are relatively advanced—the kingdom is equipped with modernized F-16s, AMRAAM air-to-air missiles, and Patriot surface-to-air missiles, along with older systems like the F-5, Mirage F1, and Hawk missile. Israel is of course familiar with all of these systems, but even with tailored countermeasures it could expect losses if Jordan offers unexpected resistance. The politics of flying over Jordan are more complicated. Israel and Jordan signed a historic peace in 1994, and the two states have long enjoyed relatively positive relations. Entering Jordanian airspace without Jordanian permission would jeopardize the relationship and could significantly impair the broader peace processes. Jordanian permission is itself a thorny issue. Amman's policies have long been driven by fears of internal instability, whether by Islamists, Palestinian groups, tribes, or cliques in the security services. Tehran is feared throughout the region for its ability to create instability, so Amman is likely very wary of even appearing to have granted Israel permission to attack Iran, especially given the current upheavals within the Hashemite Kingdom. Cursory resistance to an Israeli overflight may occur. It is unlikely that the Israelis will ask permission.

Flying through Syria adds about 40 km round-trip to targets in the north of Iran and about 100 km round-trip to targets in the middle of Iran.[3] The challenge posed by flight through Syria is quite different from that of Jordan. Syria has long taken the hardest line on Israel among the Arab states, so there is no serious peace process that could collapse. However, there is an unsteady truce between the two states that could be endangered by an attack through Syria on its ally Iran. Like Iran, Syria has many potential paths for retaliation, including Hezbollah, Palestinian extremists, and its own missile forces. Syria also has relatively advanced air defense equipment, including the Kub (SA-6), and Buk (SA-11) missile systems,[4] backed by a range of MiG-29s and other Soviet-era aircraft. Syria is certainly more capable of defending its airspace than Iran. An Israeli attack on Iran via Syria would risk alerting Iran to an impending attack.[5]

Current events in Syria may have changed this grim picture. Mass unrest has put the Assad regime on the defensive, with thousands arrested or killed and fears of international intervention. Syria's armed forces have experienced waves of desertion, and insubordinate recruits have reportedly been killed by Syrian intelligence operatives. Rebel forces have launched attacks throughout the country. Syria's armed forces have been significantly weakened, both in numbers and in organization. Their ability to defend their airspace against an Israeli incursion against which they will have only minutes' notice is reduced, and it is plausible that many Syrian air defense assets will not even realize what is happening until the Israelis are gone. However, Assad may still try to beat the drums of war in order to reinvigorate his presidency. This will end in failure, but it will add a new dimension of challenge for Israel.

Logistics of an Israeli Strike

A common criticism of the claim that Israel can credibly threaten Iran's nuclear program is that Israel lacks the materiel and logistical capacity to project sufficient force. Israel is one of the world's major military powers, with advanced technologies, large reserves, and strong traditions. However, it remains a small nation, relatively isolated from its neighbors, with limited capabilities. Without aircraft carriers—or any significant navy[6]—and without open alliances in its neighborhood, Israel can only hit Iran via a long flight. This restricts the capabilities of the powerful Israeli Air Force. An aircraft on a long strike mission must carry additional fuel, and must pay for the space and weight of the fuel by carrying fewer weapons. It is able to hit fewer targets. The time it takes for the aircraft to travel to its destination cuts the time it can spend in the target area and increases pilot fatigue. If the distance is great enough, the aircraft will also need to refuel, which adds time and complexity to the mission and further increases demand at home for airspace, runways, tarmac, fuel, and other components of air operations. A long strike thus requires more aircraft, more time, more fuel, and more support. At some point, the magnitude of the operation and the distance to be covered exceed the capabilities of any air force.

The Israelis have spent perhaps a decade expanding their ability to strike at long distances. Prior to the expansion, their ability was still impressive: in 1985, eight F-15B/Ds, assisted by tankers, bombed a PLO headquarters in Tunisia, more than 2,000 km from home. The modern expansion has focused on two modified aircraft—the F-15I and F-16I.

Figure 3.3. IAF F-16I Sufa of the 107th Squadron ("The Knights of the Orange Tail Squadron") preparing for take-off during Operation Cast Lead. ***(Yosi Yaari, Fresh Military & Security Forum.)***

(The "I" in each stands for "Israel," though some have joked that it stands for "Iran.") Both aircraft have large amounts of additional fuel stored in conformal fuel tanks (CFTs) attached to the fuselage that significantly increase range without a major increase in drag.

The ranges the modified aircraft can reach without refueling are subject to speculation, but common estimates give them a combat radius (the distance at which they can execute a military mission and return) of 1,200–2,000 km. Flying over Jordan and Iraq, Iran's vital nuclear sites are all within 1,700 km of Israel's main air bases. It is thus possible that Israel can conduct a raid with no need to refuel, but either way refueling will be preferred for safety and flexibility. The Israelis have two sorts of tanker aircraft: the KC-707 (a modified Boeing 707 airliner) and the KC-130 (a modified C-130 transport). Only the KC-707s are useful for this mission, as the KC-130 cannot link with Israel's fighter aircraft. This could impose limits on the number of Israeli aircraft that can participate in an attack on Iran—it cannot exceed the ability of the Israeli tanker fleet to provide fuel. This has become a theme in discussion of Israel's military option. However, it may not be accurate. The Israelis have expanded their fleet of KC-707s in recent years, and now have eight. Despite a measure of secrecy, significant information on the aircraft and its capabilities is available to the public, and much more can be estimated from the performance of similar 707 and 707-derived aircraft. We can also create a reasonably accurate portrait of how the tankers and fighters will interact during a strike using public information about other nations' tanker use and an examination of the mission's requirements. We thus can determine just how many aircraft the IAF's tanker force can support over Iran and answer questions about IAF capability.

In all of our calculations and assumptions, we will err on the side of pessimism. Israel's operational planners will likely be doing the same, as it is their duty to make a plan that will not merely succeed, but succeed even when numerous unplanned events interfere.[7] We will assume that the Israelis choose to fly over Jordan and Iraq, because it is the most direct route, the safest, and likely the least controversial. We will also assume that the Israelis will conduct refueling operations over Iraq, even though their tanker doctrine reportedly allows operation inside hostile airspace, as Iraqi airspace is safer from Iranian fighters and adds minimal distance to the operation. A mission for a fighter will thus include two phases: first, transit to a refueling zone in eastern Iraq, 1,000 km from home; second, transit to a target 600–700 km further. The fighters will then return home; conservative estimates of their fuel consumption suggest that they will need to refuel again on the way.

Our calculations, explained at length in the appendix, suggest that the Israelis can support a strike force of all twenty-five of their F-15Is, plus as

Figure 3.4. IAF flight for Israel's 63rd Independence Day. ***(Israel Defense Forces.)***

many as forty F-16Is in support. This is likely enough to hit the major targets in one grand raid; several raids would ensure that Israel gets to attack all the nuclear program assets it is aware of. However, the Israelis do not have the capacity to sustain a dominant air patrol over Iran in the manner that the United States does during its wars. All of its attacks will have to be raids, and as the crisis unfolds the Iranians will have more and more warning and more opportunities to prepare counters. Israel will also have almost no ability against Iranian forces on the Gulf, which could force the United States into the war to attack them. Additionally, if the conflict is sustained and includes action by Iranian proxies in Israel's neighbors, the strain on Israeli fuel reserves could become critical, potentially forcing tough decisions in Jerusalem or an American resupply operation.

The weaknesses of the Israeli military option—uncertainty over targeting and effectiveness, limits on the number of aircraft they can get to Iran, and strains on supply—do not preclude its use. The Israelis, and in particular key elements of their political establishment, have deep concerns about a nuclear Iran that they can mitigate to at least some degree by taking action. They must be cautious, however. Victory in war is a political condition. The IAF can probably do critical damage to Iran's nuclear program, which will increase its costs but might not destroy the underlying political will. They have admitted they may find themselves forced to attack Iran's nuclear infrastructure again in the years after a strike. This pattern could persist indefinitely, creating a permanent crisis.

AN AMERICAN STRIKE

There is a significant chance that Iran would retaliate against the United States and its allies after an Israeli strike. There would be a global perception that the United States had given the Israelis a "green light" to carry out the attack, and Iran would gleefully play up the connection. Israel would not have the option of destroying more than a small portion of Iran's retaliatory assets, and would be likely to focus on those that can reach Israel directly (like long-range missiles) while ignoring those that have more impact on global interests (like antiship missiles and naval posts). There would thus be substantial risks to giving the Israelis a green light should they wish to attack. The United States would have several options for resolving an Israeli request. It could refuse to grant permission, which would anger its ally and risk them attempting it anyway with the knowledge that the United States would find it politically impossible to interfere. It could offer Israel additional security guarantees to deter Iran—for example, a promise that Iran would not be allowed to reach certain milestones on the path to a deliverable nuclear weapon. This might not be believable—given the current strains on U.S. forces, it is difficult to view what is essentially a promise to start a war at an unspecified future date as an ironclad guarantee. Such a promise might cause other regional powers to demand similar protections, or to attempt to outflank planning for such an operation. The United States could allow Israel to act, and "muddle through" the Iranian retaliation as it occurs—a risky approach given the high stakes of conflict in the Strait of Hormuz. The United States might thus decide to attack Iran itself, with the idea that the job, if it is to be done, should be done right.

A U.S. attack on Iran's nuclear program would not be as brief and simple as an Israeli strike. However, with carrier- and land-based tactical aircraft,[8] cruise missiles, long-range bombers, stealth capabilities, and the ability to carry out repeated strikes, an American strike would be much more effective. The attack would proceed in a manner familiar to students of American aerial warfare, with initial strikes by cruise missiles and stealthy aircraft on key command and control and air defense facilities, followed by a general attack by bombers and strike aircraft on a range of targets. Most estimate that the nuclear program's key sites could all be destroyed within a few days. A minimal campaign with the sole objective of counterproliferation would still inflict significant damage on Iranian air defenses and associated systems. However, depending on political context, American leaders may choose to destroy more of the mullahs' assets. The most natural and proportional targets would be the regime's retaliatory capabilities, including its missile facilities and its navies. Only a handful of experts suggest that these sorts of targets should not be attacked, and their reasoning is that leaving the regime's retaliatory capacity alone will make it feel less endangered and leave it with more to lose, thus reducing the likelihood of retaliation. The majority of experts suggest that retaliatory assets should be very high priority targets, as Iran will otherwise doubtless use them.

U.S. policymakers might also attack the facilities of the IRGC. This would hinder the regime's ability to retaliate, especially abroad, and it would be much less risky than an attack on the regular army, which is drawn from the common people. Crippling the IRGC might destabilize the regime, as it is a key tool of repression; an Iranian regime that sees its existence at stake could respond to dangers in aggressive and unpredictable ways, especially given the loose command structures found in some parts of the IRGC—it has been meticulously decentralized to prevent the decapitation attacks America favors.

It is possible that the United States would experience retaliations that demand a reply, creating a vicious cycle that could turn into warfare. Experts are almost universally pessimistic about a war with Iran. The United States has long struggled with asymmetric conflicts, but this war would be particularly difficult. The Iranians can open a multifront war, attacking the United States physically at sites around the Gulf region and the world, economically by destabilizing oil sources, and socially by attempts to activate Islamic and Shiite sympathies around the region.[9] As the cases of Iraq, Afghanistan, Libya, and Kosovo have shown, it is of vital importance for U.S. policymakers to plan the end of the war as much as the beginning. The literature is largely silent on how to disengage Iran, save for the risky approach of leaving various key regime assets untouched and threatening their immediate destruction in the event of warfare, and even this is presented without alternatives. If a sustained confrontation involving even low-level violence were to result, the risks of escalation would be severe. If Iran responds to an attack with terrorism—a likely scenario—the United States will be faced with an unpalatable choice between retaliating and thus potentially entering a long-term conflict or ignoring an act of state-sponsored terrorism. If the United States attacks Iran, Iran will be faced with a similar hard decision—retaliate and risk further pummeling, or ignore the attack and appear to have surrendered to American pressure—an act that would not be merely unthinkable, but a violation of a key element of the regime's raison d'etre.

Bunker Busting

One of the major concerns with an attack on Iran's nuclear program is the ability to hit enrichment chambers buried beneath earth, rock, and reinforced concrete at Natanz and Fordow. Hardened and deeply buried targets (HDBTs), as they are known in military parlance, remain one of the greatest challenges to airpower after the dawn of the precision-guided munition. The need to destroy HDBTs has driven some of the most impressive feats of military innovation and engineering, from the massive Tallboy bomb used against German submarine pens in the Second World War to America's GBU-28, which went from the drawing board to the inside of an Iraqi bunker in just two weeks in 1991. Efforts to create structures invulnerable to advanced weapons have expanded in parallel, with deeper burials and more advanced concretes many times harder than ordinary concrete. There is thus an arms race, one ultimately unwinnable for the offense, as imagination, geology, and cost are the only impediments for those building deep facilities, while weapons engineers can only provide for certain depths of penetration, beyond which the bombs "hit a wall."

The chief challenge in creating penetration munitions is the incredible forces they must survive on impact with the ground—potentially thousands of times the force of gravity. Warhead casings must be made of advanced materials that can withstand these forces, or the bomb will be destroyed.[10] The warhead must be long and narrow to create penetrating "punch," yet if it is too long and too narrow it will break on impact. The warhead must strike its target with utmost precision, for impact at a slight angle will dramatically reduce penetration and could cause the casing to fail. The warhead's fuse must be able to survive initial impact and then determine when it has reached an appropriate depth for detonation. Even if all these problems are successfully addressed, the target may be too deep or too hard to allow for effective penetration. Intelligence must thus provide information about the geology around the target, the materials used in its construction, and the target's exact physical disposition and location, despite the fact that some of this information is literally buried.

Solving these problems of engineering and information acquisition has been an extremely high priority for the national security establishment. Two key innovations have been the GBU-28 and the massive ordnance penetrator (MOP) (GBU-57). The GBU-28 system has been upgraded from its original BLU-113 warhead, which was built from old howitzer barrels, to the BLU-122 warhead, which uses an advanced steel alloy and improved casing design that improved its penetration performance over its predecessor by at least 20 percent, leading to speculation that it could burst through nearly thirty feet of reinforced concrete, or over one hundred feet of earth.[11] The GBU-28's guidance system has also been improved. More public attention has gone to the MOP, which weighs fifteen tons—so large it can only be delivered by a modified B-2A stealth bomber. The MOP can reportedly penetrate 200 ft of 5,000 psi concrete, 125 ft of "moderately hard" rock, and 25 ft of 10,000 psi concrete.[12]

The Natanz facility is reportedly under fifty feet of concrete and earth,[13] and its walls are between six and ten feet thick.[14] It is built in the "cut and cover" style, in which builders dig a pit in the earth, construct a structure inside, and then bury the structure. This method is only cost-effective at shallow depths. The Fordow facility could be much deeper, as it appears to be tunneled into a mountain.[15] Typical estimates of depth range between seventy meters and ninety meters; the compressive strength of the rock overhead is not publicly known but is at least several thousand pounds per square inch. Similar tunnels can be seen in commercial satellite images of Esfahan, and it is plausible that there are similar tunnels in various stages of construction around the country (the Fordow facility, for instance, had existed for many years before it was discovered in 2009, and may have initially been intended for military use).

The Natanz facility is probably vulnerable to the GBU-28 and almost certainly vulnerable to the GBU-57. The only caveat is that the employment of superhard concrete—perhaps of 20,000 to 30,000 psi—in large mass over the facility could still protect it.[16] The Fordow facility might not be vulnerable to either type of bomb, though there are other ways of dealing with such facilities regardless of their depth.

If Natanz, Fordow, or some future facility yet to be discovered is in fact too deep or hardened for conventional bunker busters, one of the most straightforward ways of reducing the facility's usefulness to Iran's nuclear program would be to collapse its entrances, though it is difficult

Figure 3.5. A U.S. Air Force (USAF) F-15E Strike Eagle aircraft from the 492nd Fighter Squadron, Royal Air Force (RAF) Lakenheath, United Kingdom, releases a GBU-38 "bunker buster" 5,000-pound laster-guided bomb over the Utah Test and Training Range during a weapons evaluation test. ***(TSGT Michael Ammons, USAF.)***

to imagine this setting Iran back even as much as a relatively ineffective strike. It could also be possible to drop a penetrating munition into the soil immediately adjacent to the hardened facility and then detonate it near one of its subsurface walls or beneath its floor. This is a known technique that has been employed in the past, however, so savvy Iranian engineers could extend the superhardened concrete shield beyond the edges of the underground structure, protecting not just the bunker but its immediate surroundings.

Emerging technologies may provide new ways to destroy deeply buried targets. There have been research projects on bombs that gently land on the surface, drill into the rock or concrete below, and array themselves in a carefully calculated formation that, upon detonation, allows them to send massive shockwaves through their immediate area that can devastate underground bunkers. It is not known to the public that devices like this exist in a usable form. Given the high vulnerability of operating centrifuges to disruptions, a shockwave is certainly still worth considering.

Of course, the United States has developed options against bunkers other than high-quality conventional penetrator weapons. The most obvious way to destroy a deeply buried target is with a nuclear weapon. A

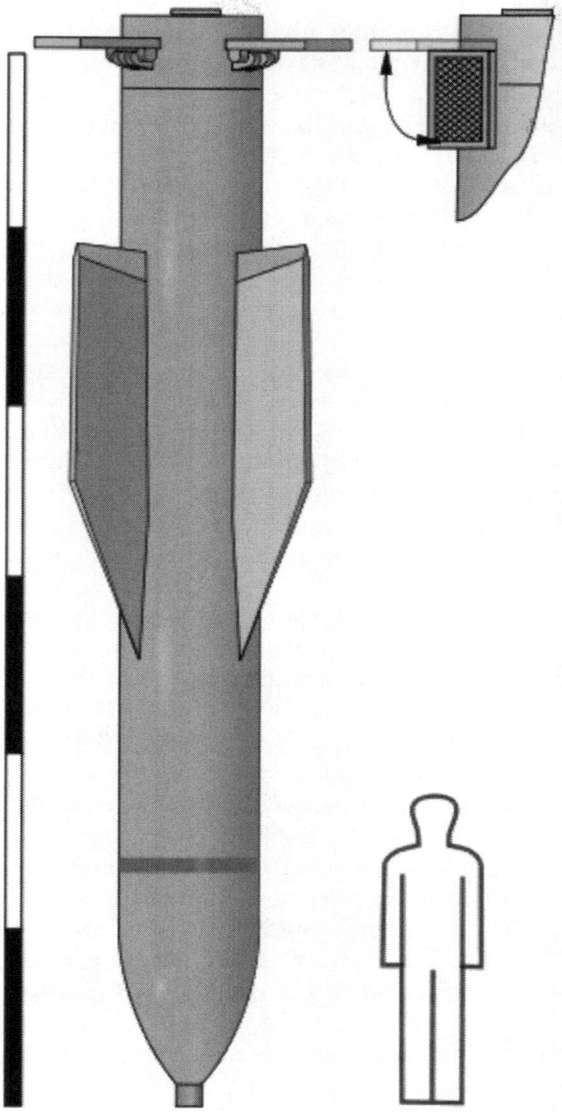

Figure 3.6. Massive Ordnance Penetrator GBU-57

massive warhead detonated above the facility could do the job, as could a penetrator with a nuclear warhead, along the lines of the cancelled Robust Nuclear Earth Penetrator. However, there are major drawbacks to this option. Facilities can always be built deeper, so that even nuclear devices cannot threaten them. The development of a nuclear bunker buster would require the United States to violate many of its treaty obligations with Russia and the international community. Though the project may be possible without violating the treaties, increasing international and especially Russian and Chinese distrust of American strategic responsibility could be very destabilizing. Violation of nonproliferation treaties would seriously reduce U.S. credibility on nuclear issues, precisely the opposite of what the United States would want when confronted with an Iran on the brink of nuclear arms. Nuclear bunker-busters also create enormous amounts of fallout because of the earth they kick up and irradiate; it is technically infeasible to detonate them deep enough that fallout will be contained within a cavern created by the bomb's detonation.[17] Iran's major nuclear facilities are not located in the immediate area of cities, so attacking them conventionally does not create a realistic risk of mass casualties; with nuclear weapons, this may not be the case.

Regardless of justification, the use of strategic weapons against another country, particularly one without advanced weapons of mass destruction, would be an extraordinary and aggressive step. America's allies would be under enormous domestic pressure to condemn America's actions, and some may be forced to take more independent paths. Some states may try to accommodate the new American tendency and become friendlier, but many would be forced into the arms of rival great powers like China, an effect which could create another era of WMD-backed geopolitical confrontation. This would be a strategic disaster.

However, a nuclear Iran poses its own challenges to the nuclear posture of the United States. The 2010 *Nuclear Posture Review* stated an intention to reduce reliance on nuclear weapons, including within the American nuclear umbrella (the nuclear role being supplanted by conventional capabilities), and to "support continued progress toward a world free of nuclear weapons." This position could become obsolete with a nuclear Iran, as Iran's neighbors would seek American assurances against a nuclear attack. There would be a parallel worry that the neighbors would seek a nuclear deterrent of their own (the Saudis, for instance, have made hints to that effect[18]). The United States may feel compelled to extend its nuclear umbrella over a highly volatile region of the world; it may alternatively be pushed to deploy more troops into the Middle East, which has in the past been very contentious.[19]

Israel also has a nuclear arsenal, deliverable by missile, by aircraft, and probably by submarine. Israeli leaders may find that these weapons' marginally better abilities against buried targets will make the military option viable even if more Fordows emerge. They are less constrained by fears of international isolation and are more afraid of Iran's bomb. These factors make them more likely than the United States to seriously consider a nuclear attack. However, they would experience many of the same drawbacks. European support for Israel—which is far greater than the popular imagination suggests—would end, and American support would be seriously strained. Anti-Israeli measures such as the Boycott, Divestment, and Sanctions campaign may gain new life. States with interests in Iran, or in a stable Middle East,[20] may interpret an Israeli nuclear attack as a sign of an extremely aggressive national tendency and accordingly seek balance and stability by beefing up the militaries of Israel's neighbors. This could reduce Israel's freedom of action in its neighborhood far more than even the vastest Iranian nuclear arsenal.

All this said, there have been no revelations that governments are considering a nuclear first strike on Iran, and it is likely that at least rumors of such a discussion would have leaked due to their inflammatory subject. Public talk of such an option would have a malign influence on both Iranian propaganda and Iran's strategic calculus, and could also hurt many of America's relationships. However, if the Israelis genuinely perceive an existential threat from Iran and Iran enters Barak's "zone of immunity," some hawkish voices might start calling for this new option to be put on the table. If the United States defense establishment also believes in a zone of immunity (there is not real evidence that they do), then they might similarly consider extending that zone artificially. Of course, if Iran does develop a nuclear weapon, both states will develop plans for responding to a nuclear attack by Iran, and these will likely (especially in the case of Israel) involve the use of nuclear weapons.

IRAN'S AIR DEFENSES

Iran's air defenses do not pose a serious threat to an American strike, and would also be hard pressed to threaten an Israeli attack.

Any strike force would be using large numbers of guided bombs. These can be delivered at impressive distances from their targets via lofting (i.e., releasing the bomb on an upward trajectory) or higher-altitude level and dive bombing. Thus, Iran's short-ranged air defense systems (SHORADS) like anti-aircraft guns and light surface-to-air missiles pose no substantive threat to the strike package.

Iran's aircraft are also a minor threat to a modern air force. The most modern aircraft in their arsenal are early model MIG-29s and F-14As, both of which are very outdated; these aircraft are supported by even older F-4s and F-5s; everything other than the MIGs was acquired under the shah. Many suspect that the operational readiness of these aircraft is low, given their age and increasing rarity around the world. Iran must use covert channels to acquire parts for some of these aircraft. There is a similar challenge in arming them—the F-14A is capable of carrying the long range AIM-54 air-to-air missile, yet due to its age the Iranians have been replacing it with a homebuilt modification of the surface-to-air I-HAWK missile.

Iran's surface-to-air missile forces have attracted the most attention in speculation about attacks. Familiarity is key in defense against surface-to-air missiles—knowledge of the electromagnetic frequencies they use and the manner in which they use them allows the construction of electronic countermeasures that can confuse the missile—for instance, when Israel attacked a suspected Syrian nuclear reactor in 2007, Syrian radar screens reportedly showed hundreds of attacking aircraft. Many Iranian missile systems are quite familiar to Iran's enemies. The backbone of Iran's air defense is the MIM-23B Improved HAWK, which was invented by the United States and used extensively by Israel. The force is supplemented by the SA-6 Gainful, a threat familiar to the United States after the two Gulf Wars, the Kosovo intervention, and the 2011 Libya conflict; it was largely ineffective. The United States has also encountered Iran's long-range SA-5 (S-200) Gammon, which was unable to repel American aircraft during the 1986 raids on Libya. One doubts that either of these technologies, after decades of failure, can suddenly pose a serious threat to American or Israeli aircraft equipped with advanced electronic countermeasures. Indeed, some commentators have speculated that the most dangerous SAM in Iran's arsenal might be the HQ-2, a reverse-engineered Chinese model of the SA-2 Guideline (S-75), simply because it is most unfamiliar.[21] We must note, however, that the SA-2 system is ancient, having been first deployed against an American aircraft in 1960 (with the downing of Gary Powers's U-2); no kills by SA-2 systems have been reported in nearly two decades.

There is a hitch in the Iranian defense question. Iran has long been attempting to acquire more advanced surface-to-air missile systems like those in Russia's S-300 family (SA-10/SA-12/SA-20/SA-23). These missiles are greatly superior to those currently in Iran's arsenal, and their effectiveness is unknown—they have never been fired in anger,[22] but NATO forces have had at least some access to them through former Warsaw Pact states. There have been rumors swirling for decades about Iran's possession of the system. However, Russia publicly decided against selling S-300s to Iran in 2010 after years of negotiations, which should incline us to doubt that Iran has the missile or that whatever missiles it may have are up to date. If Iran, against all evidence, does turn out to have the S-300, the impact on a strike force may be dire, especially if it is a smaller Israeli attack. Russia or China could certainly play spoiler to Israeli plans by supplying advanced air defense systems to Iran, though Israel can still likely defeat the system.

Some members of nationalist factions within the Russian government advocate selling Iran the S-400 (SA-21) missile system, Russia's most advanced long-range system.[23] This would dramatically change regional dynamics. An airstrike would be less likely as long as the system remained in place, for it could inflict hefty losses against intruding aircraft. If Iran were provided with enough S-400s, it might even place some of them beyond the geographic core where the nuclear facilities are concentrated. The system's 250-mile range when equipped with the 40N6 missile would allow a system on Abu Musa to engage aircraft anywhere over the United Arab Emirates and over much of Oman and Qatar. A system placed in Iran's northeast could cover Armenia, Azerbaijan, eastern Turkey, and parts of Georgia and Russia. A system in the west could cover the Iraqi core; a system in the east, restive Helmand Province and even the approaches to Kandahar. A system at Bushehr could cover Bahrain and the Saudi oil centers. This coverage would allow Iran to hold under threat military and civilian aircraft in its neighbors' airspace, and would constitute a general advance in Iran's air defense readiness.

A key challenge for Iran's air defenses as they presently exist is their lack of effective integration. Modern militaries use integrated air defense systems (IADS) to harmonize the actions of all elements of the air defense. Without this, interceptors operating within the range of ground-based defenses could find themselves receiving friendly fire—a nightmare scenario, given that they would already be under attack from the enemy. Incidents have already been reported, with a leaked U.S. military report from 2008 mentioning interceptions of airliners and shots fired at both civilian and military aircraft.[24]

In spite of these weaknesses, the Iranian defense industry exhibits a certain bravado about its many "inventions." When the S-300 negotiations with Russia broke down, Iran announced that it had developed its own indigenous version of the system that it would use instead.[25] The Saeqeh fighter aircraft project is an excellent case study of Iran's military manufacturing. Iranian media asserted that the Saeqeh was comparable to America's modern F/A-18 Hornet, but when photographs of the aircraft emerged, it became clear that the Saeqeh is an F-5 (a significantly older and less capable aircraft first developed in the 1950s by Northrop) with two angled tails, giving it a merely superficial resemblance to the F/A-18. Iran announced a plan to form a unit of Saeqeh fighters, but it is not clear that enough have been manufactured. This pattern has been repeated time and again—copy an obsolete foreign technology, claim it was indigenously developed, claim its capabilities match those of even the most modern militaries, manufacture a few prototypes or mockups, parade them before the press, and then forget about it. Thus, Iran's claims to have S-300s, precision-guided ballistic missiles capable of hitting ships, or to be developing its own fifth-generation stealth fighter should be taken with a grain—no, a full shaker—of salt. If Iran hasn't procured the S-300 from Russia, then it has no air defense systems that are capable of preventing U.S. or Israeli incursion.

Iran's low-altitude air defenses include the relatively advanced Russian Tor-M1 missile system. The Tor-M1 was designed to protect valuable targets—like S-300s—against precision-guided weapons by detecting them and shooting them out of the sky. Tor-M1 systems are believed to be deployed around Natanz; because they are highly mobile, they could be prepositioned at any key site if Iran's leaders anticipate an attack. These systems, assisted by radar-guided anti-aircraft artillery, would attempt to prevent falling bombs from reaching their targets. Their effectiveness in this role is ambiguous. Several American allies, including Egypt and Greece, operate the Tor-M1. American forces may have information on how the Tor-M1 works. Both the United States and Israel have advanced electronic warfare capabilities that could be calibrated to confound the missile system and prevent it from effectively engaging actual munitions. Such a result against the Tor-M1, and against the older AAA systems Iran deploys, may be attainable.[26]

FOLLOW-ON STRIKES

There is a consensus among experts that even a completely successful attack on Iran's nuclear program would not prevent them from continuing; indeed, many think it would prompt their withdrawal from the NPT and possibly even their open pursuit of the bomb. It is thus nearly certain that an attack would need to be repeated several years later in order to provide continued assurance of a nonnuclear Iran. It is even possible that this cycle of violence will repeat itself multiple times, leading Israeli thinkers to refer to repeated attacks on Iran's program as "mowing the lawn."

The need for follow-on strikes has largely not penetrated the public discourse on war with Iran. Repeated strikes would add substantial costs. There would be many similar risks of Iranian retaliation. However, if Iran had engaged in minor retaliations the first time, its leaders would be forced to rethink their position in the days before a second attack, as the threat of another attack would show that the West had clearly not been adequately injured by the first response. The temptation to extreme action—whether brutal retaliation or a settlement—would increase. Follow-on strikes could also reinforce Iranian perceptions that nuclear weapons are the only path to true security.

THE IMPACT ON IRAN'S NUCLEAR PROGRAM

If the attack is a success—Iran's nuclear facilities, both covert and overt, are destroyed, and the scientists and engineers that operate them are either killed or intimidated into nonparticipation—what will the long-term impact on Iran's nuclear program be? There are three main possibilities. First, Iran could simply continue its current policy of ambiguity, in which there is clearly a trend towards either a weapon or an improved breakout capability, but in which the program is carried out under some international observation and in a vaguely legal fashion. Second, Iran could have a realization that its nuclear weapons program makes it no safer—after all, it was just the cause of an international intervention in Iran on a scale unseen since the Soviet occupation or the fall of Mossadeq—and abandon it. Third, Iran could expel international observers and pursue nuclear weapons in an all-out rush.

There is a general consensus among experts that Iran would not choose the third option, and that the attacks would confirm fears that Iran will only be safe from outside involvement when it gets nuclear weapons. However, the loss of key program assets in the raid will significantly slow acquisition—unless Iran has unfathomably massive secret enrichment halls, the loss of facilities like Natanz and Fordow will be a major delay to the program. Iran has still been unable to fill Natanz with basic IR-1 centrifuges, so the loss of the several thousand it has in operation now would be a substantial setback; waiting a few years for the halls to be filled with centrifuges would slow the process even more. Expert estimates of how much a strike would delay an Iranian bomb do not exceed five years. A three-year delay is the most common figure, and a handful of pessimists think that the program will not be delayed at all, especially if Iran accelerates its program in response to the attacks.

This path of delaying action would seem to have little to recommend it. *Ceteris paribus* it would be preferable for Iran to get the bomb later rather than sooner, but in the real world the risks of an attack and of angering Iran seriously challenge that preference. However, some authors suggest that a delay can still be worthwhile, as unexpected events can aid in the delaying effect. The planners of the 1981 Israeli raid on Iraq's Osirak nuclear reactor, for example, could not have known that the 1991 and 2003 wars would end up playing the role of follow-up strikes at virtually no cost to Israel, with the end result being the complete termination of Iraq's nuclear program.[27] Syria, too, is unlikely to have the stability and resources needed for a substantive nuclear program due to the current uprisings, a change that the 2007 attackers could not have anticipated with any certainty.

If policymakers suspect that an attack will provoke an Iranian nuclear rush and are pessimistic about the length of the delay, they may wish to consider prolonging talks. This could produce a net delay comparable to that caused by a physical attack,[28] and the only loss (i.e., in addition to the losses incurred by allowing Iran to get the bomb regardless of timing) would be a little diplomatic credibility.

The international context in which the strike occurs could determine its final effect on the Iranian nuclear program.[29] If Israel or the United States were to launch a strike out of the blue, world condemnation would be certain, and Iran would feel it has cover to rebuild its program in earnest. A strike when the world and the major players in nuclear diplomacy feel they have been rebuffed would reduce condemnation and offers the most realistic chance of a post-strike Iran voluntarily ending its nuclear weapons project. The international climate is mixed. States are very eager to prevent an Israeli strike, but they have also displayed an unprecedented willingness to sanction Iran or reduce trade. If Iranian intransigence continues even after the sanctions—and the PR—have had several months to work, countries may soften their opposition to an Israeli strike. However, Iran is adept at diplomatic subterfuge, and will try to create enough confusion and misperception to fragment collective efforts before they leave the drawing board.

ALTERNATIVE MEANS OF DESTRUCTION

The facilities' electronics and electricity may be a chink in their armor. With most underground military facilities—command centers, and so on—the destruction of the nearby power plants that supply them would only be a temporary setback, as they almost always have their own generators as a backup power source. This is not likely to be the case for hidden enrichment halls. Nuclear enrichment is an extremely energy-intensive activity. It may be prohibitively difficult to provide full backup power for thousands of centrifuges while adequately protecting the backup power source. A late 2012 explosion damaging power lines leading to Fordow suggests some actors believe this to be the case.

Electronics are also vulnerable to electromagnetic radiation. A facility that is carefully shielded with Faraday caging and the like could still be vulnerable, as it may have communications cables, antennae, and power lines extending out of the facility, and these can all transmit the electromagnetic burst into the facility and damage electronics connected to them.[30] Given the very fine tuning required to keep nuclear centrifuges functioning, an electromagnetic burst could be particularly devastating against an Iranian enrichment facility like Natanz. However, the simplest way to create a militarily useful electromagnetic pulse is with a nuclear weapon, giving it many of the same drawbacks as a more direct nuclear attack without the benefit of certain physical destruction of the target. Additionally, hitting an Iranian facility with an EMP would either require the use of a small bomb at lower altitude—an act scarcely less aggressive than a straightforward nuclear attack—or the use of a larger bomb at higher altitude, which would create a radiation burst with serious effects not just at the target site, but throughout the region.

There are ways to create an EMP without using a nuclear weapon, though they are less effective and must be much closer to their target. Large electronic arrays can generate electromagnetic pulses, though it is difficult to envision a scenario in which these can be applied against Iranian nuclear facilities. Standard explosives can also be detonated within a special set of electronics to create a directed EMP burst. The availability and effectiveness of such weapons for Iran's enemies is not publicly known, though if effective conventional explosive EMP devices are available, policymakers should certainly consider them as an option, and they could pose the lowest risk of collateral damage of any military option.[31] Another option is the use of high-powered aircraft radar—the most modern active electronically scanned array (AESA) radars may be powerful enough to use as an electronic weapon at short ranges, so the possibility of damaging facilities should be evaluated for technical feasibility. If Iran has not shielded its facilities adequately from electromagnetic radiation, there may be a vulnerability; such an attack would be a great embarrassment to the regime, yet would retain an element of deniability. It may be the best hope within the spectrum of military options for a relatively quiet Iranian response.

It is also possible to merely render an underground fortification uninhabitable, which against some targets may be a desirable outcome.[32] Underground facilities need an environmental control system (ECS) to remain accessible to humans.[33] Compromising this control system could make work within the facility extremely unpleasant or difficult. Most options have only short-term effects—elimination of lighting, introduction of toxic or narcotic chemicals, and so on—but a few have longer-term effectiveness. A deliberate reduction in ECS effectiveness might lead to increases in temperature and humidity that would wear down sensitive equipment. Perhaps the most outside-the-box idea is the impregnation of the facility with extremely foul smells.[34]

Sabotage

The wave of mysterious blasts at sites associated with the Iranian nuclear program suggests that Iran's opponents may have settled on a different method of attacking Iran's nuclear program: sabotage. The program relies on advanced technologies and materials, and Iran has not demonstrated mastery over them. The first-generation IR-1 centrifuges currently in mass use are based on a Pakistani design known for being finicky; IAEA reports have shown a steady decline in their separative efficiency.[35] Saboteurs might thus be able to bleed off Iran's effectiveness without giving the program's leaders clear evidence that something malicious is afoot. They could also engage in more catastrophic attacks, from mass cyber warfare attacks like Stuxnet, motorcycle assassinations, to bombings.

The most basic and hard-to-detect form of sabotage is deliberate incompetence by staff. Applied to Iran's nuclear program, this could include actions like the following:

Iranian bureaucracies are known to exhibit several of these tendencies without outside inducement. However, Iran's nuclear workers may be less susceptible to influence than others, as they have seen colleagues assassinated and yet continued to work. Many of these tactics would

Table 3.1.

Mishandling of radioactive materials, leading to contamination	Corruption
Use of equipment at improper settings[1]	Tardiness
Intentionally slow work	Destruction of key equipment
Bureaucratization of work processes	Theft
Micromanagement	Faulty maintenance
Misdirection and mislabeling of materials	Calling needless meetings[2]
Payroll and cost inflation	Lax safety procedures
Discouraging interdepartmental communication and cooperation	Tolerance of substance abuse[3]

[1] This was Stuxnet's mechanism for destruction of centrifuges. It can also be used on less advanced equipment—for instance, habitually driving an official vehicle in the wrong gear.
[2] The U.S. Department of Defense may find it useful to teach Iran's nuclear engineers its approach to Microsoft PowerPoint; Iran's nuclear negotiators have already adopted PowerPoint, but have not yet demonstrated mastery of the technology and its destructive potential.
[3] The wide availability of opium in Iran has had negative impacts on other sectors of the economy; there are even reports that some factories grant employees drug breaks.

need to be implemented by relatively large numbers of employees in order to have major effects, yet these large numbers would increase the odds that Iranian counterintelligence forces would get wind of the operation. It may be more effective to target key personnel for transformation into sources of snafus and confusion. Junior personnel such as secretaries could misdirect shipments—a tactic so effective that two sabotage researchers said that "the most hazardous of all weapons" is the ballpoint pen.[36] Senior administrators could encourage the organization to become stovepiped, ossified, and ineffective; they could deliberately hire poor personnel and damage institutional relationships to ensure that their legacy survives their own retirement.

Harder options include more obviously nonaccidental destruction of key equipment—from inducement of catastrophic mechanical failures in centrifuges to small explosions—and massive demolition like that which apparently occurred in the al Ghadir missile base blast. Whether conducted by disloyal employees or merely with their aid, these events will have more impact on the program but will almost certainly provoke security backlashes that will make them harder to replicate. (Those security backlashes, if they interfere with the program's work or create resentment among its staff, could be an added bonus.) Iranian media and government figures have responded in an inconsistent manner to the al Ghadir and Esfahan blasts; the official narratives that ultimately emerge tend towards the cover-up. This makes it clear that Tehran is both confused and embarrassed by the attacks. Damage to the nuclear facilities suggests that the regime is incapable of securing Iran from outside intervention. The regime could be seen as vulnerable and a poor custodian of Iran's proud heritage. Fearing collapse, it might lash out.

Case studies of saboteurs have shown patterns in their behavior and priorities.[37] Saboteurs are typically employees or others with insider knowledge of an organization. This knowledge can allow them to inflict serious damage with minimal use of weapons or explosives. Saboteurs typically work alone or in small groups, and their actions are often isolated rather than part of a campaign. Motivation varies widely. The most serious acts were perpetrated by disgruntled employees, whose actions make up about one third of all sabotage cases. One quarter of cases involved political radicals. The remainder consists of foreign agents and unidentified persons. Some sabotage is spontaneous; other acts are the product of extensive planning. Saboteurs rarely risk their own lives or those of others. There are many people in the Iranian nuclear program; though they are doubtless screened for loyalty, it is reasonable to believe that some can be compromised or convinced to take action against their employer. Both disgruntlement and ideology may be fruitful. The nuclear program attracts highly talented individuals with technical skills that may have a very lean set of political allegiances (for instance, former representative to the IAEA Ali Akbar Salehi has served in very senior posts in both the Khatami and Ahmadinejad administrations despite deep ideological differences between the two). These individuals work for an organization that is overseen by the deeply political IRGC—a classic opportunity for conflicts of personal style. Additionally, some of these individuals may become angry with the political leadership if the accidents, attacks, and assassinations continue. Others may be politicized and may, for instance, be caught up in the political and religious conflicts within the conservative factions; this could make them open to influence.[38]

McGeorge and Ketcham suggest that the saboteur identifies worthy targets based on six factors: the target's criticality, accessibility, recuperability, and vulnerability, the effect of the attack on the local population, and the risk to the attacker. Using these criteria, are Iran's facilities susceptible to sabotage?

The Iranian nuclear program is thus susceptible to sabotage, but many types of attacks carry significant risks to both the attacker and fellow employees. This means that larger-scale sabotage might best be conducted by outside agents (either from foreign intelligence services or, as some have speculated, from dissident groups like the Mojahedin-e Khalq [MEK]). Given the risks they face, internal saboteurs would be most effective against Iran's more fragile equipment and rarer materials, destroying them by misuse and misplacement and thus increasing the friction on Iran's capacity to enrich uranium.

The more subtle forms of sabotage are not likely to provoke an Iranian nuclear reversal—in the eyes of experts, they can only provide extra time

Table 3.2.

Factor	*Description*	*Application to Iran*
Criticality	Is the target a key node of enemy operations, or is its function unimportant or redundant?	Both. Some elements of Iran's nuclear program, like its uranium mines, are heavily redundant. Others, like the uranium conversion facility at Esfahan, are not.
Accessibility	Can the saboteur get easy access to the target?	Access to critical areas is likely highly regulated, even for essential personnel. These individuals likely have the best chance of getting to targets, with the next best chance being someone aided by them.[1]
Recuperability	Can the target be easily restored to normal working order, or does it rely on hard-to-replace components?	Some elements of the program use fairly basic chemical industry equipment that would not be excruciatingly difficult to replace. However, the slow growth in centrifuge numbers and decline in their quality shows that Iran has difficulty acquiring, manufacturing, and maintaining its complement of centrifuges. Sabotage of existing centrifuges, or the supply of defective components, could be productive.
Vulnerability	How much damage is possible with the materials available to the saboteur?	Some components of the program would require explosives to do maximum damage; these are likely available through foreign intelligence agencies. Other elements are highly vulnerable and may require nothing more than technical know-how to damage. Stuxnet damaged centrifuges by running them above or below normal operating speeds. Releases of toxic chemical compounds, radioactive dusts, or flammable vapors could also cause serious damage.
Effect on Local Population	Will the attack or its effects produce a backlash by the local population?	The release of radiation could certainly produce a backlash (especially if it is at one of the facilities near the holy city of Qom, or one of the smaller projects in the middle of Tehran). Assuming that the saboteur is wary of creating lethal danger, they will likely avoid massive radiation leaks. Damage to the nuclear program could also produce a nationalistic backlash, although this backlash may be against the government for failing to protect the program. Of course, this criterion applies more to guerrilla movements than individuals, as the latter are not attempting to win their support.
Risk to Saboteur	Is the saboteur likely to be killed or captured?	Someone caught carrying out these acts, especially if they catch the public eye, is quite likely to face lengthy imprisonment, torture, or execution. Saboteurs will have to be willing to brave this danger (as discussed, this is uncommon among saboteurs) or believe they can avoid blame.

[1] Note, however, that other sensitive Iranian areas have shown surprisingly lax security—consider Iranian American writer Hooman Majd's account of visits to the Iranian Foreign Ministry and presidential offices in his 2008 book *The Ayatollah Begs to Differ*.

for diplomats to reach a solution.[39] The more aggressive options might do enough damage to cause severe delays through mass destruction of equipment, contamination of work areas, or destruction of facilities. However, with the Islamic Republic under financial strain, small cost increases through subtle measures like inefficiency might push the program's overall expenditures above comfortable levels. Loss of key raw materials that the sanctions program has made difficult to obtain (like maraging steel) could have a serious effect on productivity. Military theorists do not typically regard sabotage as a matter of strategic consequence, so we must bound our expectations for what can be accomplished, but most targets of military sabotage are not highly complicated, bottlenecked production systems. A full spectrum sabotage campaign, if Iran's nuclear organizations can be penetrated, might be almost as effective as a successful air campaign (followed by aggressive Iranian reconstruction) in terms of the delay it causes the program.[40] However, it is not clear that this full spectrum can be implemented.

Many in the Israeli leadership appear to believe that the path of sabotage is already approaching exhaustion. In recent years, interference with the Iranian program has been a major Mossad priority. In addition to the headline-grabbing assassinations and Stuxnet, they have reportedly created fake black marketers to supply bad centrifuge parts, and their involvement is suspected in explosions at key facilities and crashes of airplanes carrying senior figures. All these actions, however, have only slowed—not stopped—Iran's enrichment of uranium in greater quantities and higher levels of purity. It may not be possible for Israel to increase the effectiveness of the campaign to the point that Iranian progress is arrested, in which case this discussion is moot. However, the use of larger-scale sabotage efforts—like those that may have been behind the massive 2011 explosion that destroyed a missile development center near Tehran and killed a senior IRGC general[41]—against the major targets (such as Natanz and Fordow) and against sites storing enriched uranium might still cause a major setback beyond those already seen.

Commando Raid

Another way to damage Iran's nuclear program, if an air raid is not deemed favorable, is a raid by commandos. The U.S. military has already attempted mass infiltration into Iran, with the disastrous *Operation Eagle Claw*, a failed 1980 attempt to rescue the embassy hostages in which eight American servicemen perished in a sandstorm-induced aircraft collision. Iran has more than weather to protect it. Amateur image analysts have identified dozens of apparent anti-aircraft emplacements around key nuclear sites like that at Natanz. The most straightforward way to raid Iran's nuclear program would be with troops inserted by helicopter, with the need for an *Eagle Claw*–style desert rendezvous eliminated by the use of aerial refueling. However, because helicopters are slow (and must slow down further to deposit their troops on the ground), they are highly vulnerable to anti-aircraft guns. An initial strike and continued assistance by American aircraft would be required to deal with this threat. It is also quite likely that Iran has prepositioned a range of short ranged surface-to-air missile systems at key nuclear sites that could be brought out in the event of an attack, further endangering helicopters. Among the most worrisome of these is the Tor-M1 (SA-15 Gauntlet) system, which uses some of Russia's best technology. The system is most effective against targets flying under twenty thousand feet within eight miles. Because it is mounted on a vehicle, the Tor-M1 can move from place to place during an attack to keep enemy anti-air defense patrols at bay; it can even acquire targets while in motion, stopping only to fire.

It is likely that a dedicated effort can prevent these factors from seriously endangering a helicopter assault. After the initial strike on fixed air defenses, multiple drones could be used to monitor the site, spot trouble, and designate targets for loitering attack aircraft.[42]

Entering the sites poses a range of problems. Landing directly in the target site can amplify the surprise—consider the Bin Laden raid. However, it is also risky—the helicopters will draw much fire from the ground, even if major air defenses are destroyed. It is likely possible to find open spaces, either nearby or far away, where troops can be inserted (possibly by parachute instead of helicopter) and approach the sites on the ground, break through their defensive perimeters, and then attack key components. This has two serious risks. First, the raiders will still have to be extracted, which will require either a direct approach by helicopter or an escape to an extraction point after Iran's forces have been alerted to the raid. Second, at the key facility of Natanz they will have to enter the compound over open ground—satellite images and local photos show relatively flat terrain with only light scrub for concealment; the danger of this sparse environment is amplified by elevated guard towers and possible infantry detection radars. If the team is spotted on its approach, it could be wiped out.[43] Even a larger force would risk unpalatably high casualties in a direct assault.

Suppose that the team successfully enters the compound. Where will it go, and what will it do when it gets there? The Natanz compound has several nuclear activities, but the most important target is its two underground enrichment halls. It is difficult to imagine that the raiders will have reached their entrances undetected; it is likely that the entrances are designed to be sealed or barricaded in the event of an emergency. If this cannot be prevented, it might be that the raid would be unable to enter the crucial areas. Suppose, again, that it is successful in entering these areas, that by coincidence or design the doors cannot be sealed when the alarm is raised, or that the raiders open them. What will they do when they enter the enrichment chamber? Enrichment equipment is extremely fragile, especially when running—their rapid movement creates enormous angular momentum that could be released if they are disturbed, creating a cascade of destruction. However, there are also currently a reported eight thousand centrifuges in the halls, more than 6,000 of which are operational. The halls are 25,000 m^2 and 16,000 m^2, and the raiders may meet resistance inside them, as the defenders are certainly aware that the halls would be a focal point of any assault.

The best approach in this case may simply be to damage as many of the centrifuges as is possible, spreading volatile, radioactive UF_6 throughout the plant and making it an unsafe environment for its employees. This could render the plant useless for a period, as UF_6 and the hydrofluoric acid it produces when exposed to water are both harmful to humans. Past accidents involving the release of UF_6 have seen massive, dense clouds of steam and gas, with serious short-term health consequences for those who are exposed and some minor health impacts on nearby communities.

There is one other method that could allow a commando team to do critical damage to a facility like Natanz. There has been work in the past on small nuclear charges that can be deposited by commandos and then detonated once they escape. The U.S. military, for instance, developed the Special Atomic Demolition Munition (SADM), with a small variable yield warhead capable of producing an explosion of one kiloton. The detonation of one of these inside any of Iran's nuclear facilities would have a catastrophic impact, likely destroying the structure, its contents, and pos-

Figure 3.7. The main enrichment halls at Natanz, seen before they were buried. The long rectangle between them is an American football field with endzones, included for scale. *(Produced with Google Earth.)*

Table 3.3. Human Toxicity Estimates for a 1-h Inhalation Exposure to Uranium Hexafluoride[1]

Effect	*Concentration (mg/m³)*	*Concentration (ppm)*	*Equivalent Concentration*
No effect	<9.6	<0.667	Natural atmospheric hydrogen
Mild health effects	9.6–18.5	0.667–1.286	
Renal injury	18.5	1.286	Natural atmospheric krypton
10% lethal	352	24.464	Natural atmospheric neon
50% lethal	862	59.909	15% of atmospheric carbon dioxide

Note: See endnotes for comparative figures.
[1] From Board on Environmental Studies and Technology, *Acute Exposure Guideline Levels for Selected Airborne Chemicals*, vol. 4 (2004). Available online at www.nap.edu/openbook.php?record_id=10902&page=273.

sibly its surroundings. A nuclear weapon deployed in this way might be less inflammatory than one deployed by any of the legs of the nuclear triad.[44] However, it would still produce significant fallout, and it would still be very aggressive; additionally, if the weapon is captured or fails to detonate and is repaired by the Iranians, they would immediately become a nuclear power, and they would have a miniaturized nuclear weapon that would be very easy for a terrorist group to use. Such a mission could thus achieve what it intended to prevent.

Commando operations against the major nuclear facilities do not appear likely to succeed given the many possible ways that they could fail and the multiple defensive perimeters around the key site of Natanz. A successful assault would likely require a large force with heavy air and missile support, and would have a high risk of casualties even if things went well. It would also have difficulty causing severe damage. Commando raids are thus a bad choice against the major sites. However, if Iran has a covert nuclear program with hidden sites, surprise commando raids may be very effective. Case studies of commando raids have found they succeed about 76 percent of the time, and that enemy defenses are able to stop them just 11 percent of the time. If the Iran nuclear crisis eventually comes to military force, policymakers may seriously consider using commando raids rather than airstrikes against smaller and more secretive program assets, especially when these are located in densely populated areas where explosions and radiation releases are to be avoided.

Commandos will likely be used in some aspect in any operation against Iran—and may have already been used. The Israelis are believed to have used commando units extensively in the 2007 Syria raid, collecting environmental samples to establish the role of the suspected reactor, designating targets for attack aircraft, and assessing the impact of the raid. Search and rescue commandos may also play a part.

NOTES

1. We assume here that Iran has one. Both the Natanz and Qom sites were kept secret until exposed by outside forces, so it is quite plausible that there are numerous sites that have still not been discovered. However, these sites are long-term projects, so Iran would have to have had a very large secret program to have major sites still hidden after two had been exposed. Iran has a history of operating covert programs—for instance, ISIS has alleged that the Physics Research Center, an institute active during the 1990s, was in fact a parallel nuclear program that used an Iranian university as a front to acquire sensitive goods. See Albright, Brannan, and Stricker, "The Physics Research Center and Iran's Parallel Military Nuclear Program," ISIS 2012.

2. The high estimates of forces needed come from Toukan and Cordesman's "Study on a Possible Israeli Strike"; the low estimates come from Raas and Long's "Osirak Redux?" Military plans have a way of flying out the window once the first blows are landed, so we will tend to favor the larger strike package estimates, as surplus aircraft would allow the Israelis to adjust in the event of difficulties.

3. Measurements were from the IAF base at Hatzor, outside Ashdod, to the Kalaye Electric site in Tehran and the uranium conversion facility in Esfahan. Note that Hatzor is not a permanent base for the F-16I and F-15I deep-strike aircraft that would be the main tool in an Israeli operation. Israel can easily rebase its aircraft to one of its many airfields in the event of a crisis, and may find this to be a very prudent step to reduce the impact of Iranian retaliation. Hatzor is chosen as representative because it is roughly at the center of the string of major IAF bases. Israel's F-15Is operate out of Hatzerim, 60 km south of Hatzor; F-16Is operate out of Hatzerim near Beersheba, Ramon in the Negev, and Ramat David in Galilee. Flights from the bases further south would have to divert slightly to the north to avoid entering Saudi airspace but would otherwise have a straight path to Iran; flying through Syria would significantly lengthen their mission, though most added distance would be in Israeli airspace. Flights from Ramat David would enjoy a shorter, more direct flight to targets in the north when flying over Syria, but diversion through Jordan does not add significantly to the distance they must cover. However, flying an adjusted course through Syria and Iraqi Kurdistan would allow the strike force the best chance at avoiding identification by the alleged long-range radar site at Taji, just north of Baghdad.

4. There are limited rumors that Syria has also acquired the relatively advanced S-300P (SA-10) system, though these are not highly credible.

5. Researchers with access to classified information may wish to see whether this is precedented—did Iran go on alert when the Israelis entered Syrian airspace to bomb a suspected nuclear site in 2007? Did they alert when the Israelis buzzed the Syrian coastal city of Latakia the same year?

6. The Israelis do have a small fleet of Dolphin-class submarines that may be able to fire cruise missiles against Iranian targets, but they will likely be playing second fiddle to the Israeli Air Force in a major confrontation.

7. Clausewitz famously compared the distinction between planning for war and actually waging it to the distinction between the ease of walking on land and the difficulty of walking in water: "with ordinary powers, one cannot even hold to mediocre standards."

8. We cannot be certain that the United States would be allowed to use its bases in the region for air operations. However, since Iran's retaliation would likely target host countries even if the United States doesn't use its land bases, it is likely that the host countries would then allow the United States full usage rights.

9. Jeffrey White, "What Would War with Iran Look Like?," *American Interest*, July/August 2011, www.the-american-interest.com/article-bd.cfm?piece=982.

10. This is thus an unusual example of the oft-quoted Shiite phrase "victory of the blood over the sword."

11. "Guided Bomb Unit-28 (GBU-28): BLU-113 Penetrator," Global Security, 2011, www.globalsecurity.org/military/systems/munitions/gbu-28-specs.htm, also David

Hambling, "Brawny New Bunker Buster: 'Divine Thunderbolt,'" *Danger Room* (blog), Feb. 4, 2008, www.wired.com/dangerroom/2008/02/bigger-better-b/, and Mike Lauden, "BLU-122 Warhead Program: Precision Strike Technology Symposium," Oct. 19, 2005, www.dtic.mil/ndia/2005psts/lauden.pdf.

12. "GBU-57/B Massive Ordnance Penetrator (MOP)," Global Security, 2011, www.globalsecurity.org/military/systems/munitions/mop.htm.

13. Seth G. Jones, "Striking Iran Is an Option, Not Inevitable," *Christian Science Monitor*, Apr. 11, 2006, www.rand.org/commentary/2006/04/11/CSM.html.

14. David Albright and Corey Hinderstein, "The Iranian Gas Centrifuge Uranium Enrichment Plant at Natanz: Drawing from Commercial Satellite Images," Institute for Science and International Security, Mar. 14, 2003, www.isis-online.org/publications/iran/natanz03_02.html.

15. Various sources, including Long's "Can They?" and articles in popular media, have suggested that Fordow is 90 m deep. For more information on Fordow's construction, see Paul Brannan, "Satellite Imagery Narrows Qom Enrichment Facility Construction Start Date," Institute for Science and International Security, Nov. 5, 2009, isis-online.org/isis-reports/detail/satellite-imagery-narrows-qom-enrichment-facility-construction-start-date/.

16. Note that the ground around Fordow is also relatively hard—the Zagros Mountains and the Bakhtyari formation are composed of dolomites, sandstones (1,000–30,000 psi compressive strength), and limestones (25,600–30,000 psi compressive strength). Depending on the formation and the depth of the tunnels, this could make strikes difficult. One American official has suggested that even the hardest targets are vulnerable to the GBU-57, as repeated drops could chip away at one aimpoint on the target's cover. This might not be a realistic solution—only the B-2 deploys the GBU-57, and only some of them are modified to accept it; the B-2 would be in high demand in the critical early hours of a campaign against Iran, so diverting several to repeatedly hit one target could complicate the mission.

17. The technical term for this is a camouflet, not a cavern.

18. There is reason to be skeptical of these comments, given that they often emerge from the periphery of the royal family's core group. Authors have argued that the Saudis are, in fact, unlikely to pursue a nuclear weapon, but a key element of their decision is a perception that the U.S. protects them. See, for example, Gawdat Bahgat, "Nuclear Proliferation: The Case of Saudi Arabia," *Middle East Journal* 60, no. 3 (Summer 2006): 421–43.

19. Consider, for instance, the role of the U.S. presence in Saudi Arabia in the rise of al Qaeda.

20. Russia and China fit the bill here. Note that their interest in a "stable Middle East" is not a pejorative to the policies of other major powers—it simply notes that the two nations have a preference for the status quo and an aversion to regional changes of any sort, as manifested most clearly in the Syria crisis.

21. Knowledge is crucial to electronic warfare—understanding the way an opposing electronic system works allows for the development of particularly effective countermeasures. Thus, if the HQ-2 variant being used by Iran is unfamiliar, American or Israeli pilots will have to hope that their electronic countermeasures will be effective against the threat (a reasonable, yet not fully certain, proposal). Of course, some elements of Iran's HQ-2 electronics have doubtless been sniffed out by passive monitoring of their radar activity by American electronic intelligence aircraft.

22. S-300 variants have, however, been sold to NATO members Greece and Slovakia, and have reportedly been used in NATO exercises. At least some systems in the S-300 family, then, may be "compromised."

23. From public remarks reported in Iranian media.

24. Michael R. Gordon, "Wary of Israel, Iran Said to Blunder in Strikes," *New York Times*, Oct. 2, 2012, www.nytimes.com/2012/10/03/world/middleeast/wary-of-israel-iran-is-said-to-blunder-in-strikes.html?_r=0. This highly irresponsible behavior by Iranian air defense units is especially shocking when one recalls that Iran itself was once

the victim of a mistaken attack on a civilian aircraft—the USS *Vincennes* shootdown incident.

25. Semiofficial media sources continue to alternate between praising the indigenous S-300's capabilities—it is now, in some of their accounts, superior to the Russian original—and complaining that Russia still refuses to deliver its version; it does not take much reading between the lines to understand what this implies for the quality of the Iranian system.

26. This is of critical importance to the success of the strike, as the Tor-M1 has a reported kill probability against precision weapons of between 0.6 and 0.9; assuming there are, as amateur spotters have suggested, three Tor-M1s (with eight missiles each) deployed at Natanz, this would mean that they would be likely to destroy between fourteen and twenty-one incoming bombs, a result that could lead to the failure of an Israeli attack. See "Tor-M1 9M330 Air Defense System," Defense Update, 2007, http://defense-update.com/products/t/tor.htm.

27. Steven Simon, "Contingency Planning Memorandum No. 5: An Israeli Strike on Iran," Council on Foreign Relations, November 2009, www.cfr.org/israel/israeli-strike-iran/p20637.

28. Ashton B. Carter and William J. Perry, "Plan B for Iran: What If Nuclear Diplomacy Fails?," The Preventive Defense Project, September 2006, www.carnegieendowment.org/static/npp/reports/carter_9-19-06.pdf.

29. Patrick Clawson and Michael Eisenstadt, "The Last Resort: Consequences of Preventive Military Action against Iran," WINEP, June 2008, www.washingtoninstitute.org/policy-analysis/view/the-last-resort-consequences-of-preventive-military-action-against-iran.

30. See Sepp, "Deeply Buried Facilities: Implications for Military Operations," Occasional Paper No. 14, Center for Strategy and Technology, Air War College, May 2000.

31. Unlike other options, there would be virtually no chance of a noteworthy release of radioactive material from the facilities, unless the facilities have been constructed with very inadequate safeguards.

32. Against facilities with high levels of automation and low need for human repair, this might not be effective.

33. Sepp, "Deeply Buried Facilities."

34. See Sepp, "Deeply Buried Facilities." Note that biological efforts against the ECS, such as the introduction of mold spores, would not be very effective provided the ECS keeps the environment reasonably cool and dry.

35. For documentation, see isisnucleariran.org/reports, especially "Performance of the IR-1 Centrifuge at Natanz" and analyses of the regular IAEA Safeguards Reports.

36. Harvey J. McGeorge II and Christine C. Ketcham, "Sabotage: A Strategic Tool for Guerrilla Forces," *World Affairs* 146, no. 3 (Winter 1983–1984): 253.

37. Jenkins DeLeon and Krofcheck Kellen, "Attributes of Potential Criminal Adversaries of U.S. Nuclear Programs," RAND Corporation, February 1978.

38. There is also an outside chance that someone inside the program could become involved in an apocalyptic Mahdist cult, like Iraq's Soldiers of Heaven, that might make them willing to take any number of dangerous and harmful actions.

39. See Vali Nasr's remarks in the "Covert Action" video at the Council on Foreign Relations' Crisis Guide: Iran Multimedia Project, www.cfr.org/interactives/CG_Iran/index.html#/analyzing-the-options/.

40. The primary difference between an effective air attack and sabotage is that the air attack is more likely to destroy or collapse key facilities; most sabotage measures do not offer this possibility even if they might be comparably effective against the nuclear program's human capital and machinery.

41. American sources suggest this was not sabotage, but was an accident during the mixing of the highly volatile chemicals used to power some of Iran's missiles. This is very plausible, but here plausibility is also plausible deniability.

42. Use of the stealthy RQ-170 Sentinel could allow the drones to arrive on target around the time of the initial strike, thus preserving surprise.

43. There is precedent for covert actions being abandoned for this cause: the Clinton administration decided against a raid on Bin Laden's compound at Tarnak Farms in part because of the open terrain surrounding the compound.

44. The United States and likely Israel have nuclear triads. The most inflammatory delivery would be by ICBM, as this would seriously risk an inadvertent nuclear war with China or Russia.

FOUR

Iran's Retaliation

Anyone who follows the Iranian media is aware of the Islamic Republic's frequent threats of severe retaliation if it is attacked. Iran has many domains in which it can retaliate. It can attack Israel or its neighbors on the Gulf. It can engage in terrorism around the world on its own or via allies like Hezbollah or Hamas. It can whip up insurgency against American troops and interests in Afghanistan and Iraq. It can even attempt to interfere with the production and shipment of oil from the region—an action that could pull the rug out from under the global economy with massive increases in oil prices. Experts are divided on whether Iran would go all-out in its riposte—after all, forceful retaliation invites forceful retaliation—but there is a general consensus that some response, if only a small one, is inevitable.

A historical examination of the Islamic Republic's behavior shows a mixed record of retaliation. A study found that in three of seven cases of attacks on Iran, there was no significant response; each of those three nonresponses was in a confrontation with the United States. Iran did retaliate against the United States once, during the Tanker War; the United States responded by destroying a large portion of Iran's navy.[1] Iran knows what it is up against when confronting America, leading some to predict Iran will respond to a strike on its nuclear program in a "calibrated" fashion.[2]

However, many are not so optimistic. The clerics legitimize their rule in part through resistance to the West, so a Western attack would attack their raison d'être. Many plausible plans against the nuclear program include destruction of facilities associated with the IRGC. The IRGC plays a crucial role in supporting the regime against the people and the regular army, so serious damage to its capabilities could be destabilizing. The regime is thus in a two-level game—it must address both the international community and its domestic audiences. If there is a risk of instability, it will feel that the domestic audience is more important and respond in proportion to the threat it feels to its own survival—in other words, the response would be pushed toward more aggressive options.[3]

Intervening powers would thus be wise to consider Iran's ability to retaliate in their initial plans of attack. Many analysts recommend destroying the retaliatory apparatus early on to minimize its effectiveness;[4] this is reasonable given uncertainty about the regime's response and its significant capabilities. Others advise a forcible appeal to the regime's rationality—the initial strike leaves key regime assets untouched, but Tehran is informed in no uncertain terms that retaliation will see those assets swiftly destroyed[5] or even result in direct attacks on key members of the regime.[6] Obviously, this strategy would backfire severely if Iran were to retaliate anyway, and its exposure in the press would yield troubles foreign and domestic.

LEBANESE HEZBOLLAH

One of Iran's most potent and challenging avenues of retaliation is its close ally, the Lebanese militant political group Hezbollah, which can attack Israel or use its many overseas ties to carry out terrorism. Because it is at least semiautonomous, Hezbollah's actions will be difficult to attribute fully to Tehran, so threatening retaliation will not satisfy all audiences (especially since Iran could make peace while Hezbollah fights on[7]). Because a war by any Muslim force against Israel is a political powder keg, American retaliation against Hezbollah would be unlikely. Hezbollah is also much more capable as a military force than one would expect from a paramilitary that makes its home in a weak and sickly state. Hezbollah won accolades for fighting the IDF to a draw in the 2006 war—this was the best result any Arab force had achieved in battle with Israel. The war saw numerous surprising military feats, including the destruction of many Israeli tanks and the lethal use of an antiship missile against an Israeli corvette. Hezbollah also endangered the lives of huge numbers of civilians with rocket launches against areas in northern Israel.

Since the war, Iran has massively upgraded Hezbollah's missile forces. Analysts believe that Hezbollah is now capable of hitting targets anywhere in Israel, and that some of its weapons are accurate enough to target areas of tactical value like military bases. Estimates suggest that Hezbollah can fire up to 600 missiles each day, and that it could potentially gain access to Syria's arsenal of *Yakhont* (SS-N-26) antiship missiles, giving it some capability against ships up to 300 km offshore.[8] There are even worries that Iran could provide Hezbollah with substances for use in chemical, biological, or radiological (CBR) attacks,[9] or that Hezbollah could acquire them through the chaos in Syria (given Syria's possession of especially deadly chemical agents like VX and the limited number of gas masks available to the Israeli public, this could be a very serious threat).[10] Under such heavy attacks, Israel might again need to invade Southern Lebanon.[11]

Of course, an all-out Hezbollah assault on Israel is not guaranteed. Hezbollah would not win the war, and it would surely be subjected to heavy Israeli retaliation. After the damages it suffered in 2006 and the unpleasantness of the Saudi-Syrian rapprochement on Lebanon (prior to the Arab Spring instabilities in Syria), it may be reluctant to take aggressive action.[12] Hezbollah has seen its influence in Lebanon's political system grow since 2006, as the crisis over the Special Tribunal for Lebanon illustrated. Instigating war with Israel would jeopardize its current strong position, so Iran might have trouble convincing the Party of God to do its dirty work.

ISRAELI NATURAL GAS SITES

Another point of vulnerability that will emerge if the crisis lasts for a number of years is Israel's natural gas fields. Israel has made significant discoveries of natural gas off its coasts in the Leviathan and Tamar fields, and is already producing from the Mari-B field off the coast of the Gaza Strip. Successful exploitation of these resources will not only benefit Israel economically—it will also alleviate a severe energy security vulnerability. Natural gas generates 36 percent of Israel's electricity; 40 percent of Israel's natural gas comes from Egypt.[13] Though there are some worries of future instability in the Israeli-Egyptian relationship that could endanger the gas flow, the single pipeline that carries Egypt's natural gas to Ashkelon has proven troublesome enough in the present, with saboteurs having attacked it more than a dozen times since the start of the Egyptian uprisings. Loss of Egyptian gas costs Israel up to $2 million per day.

As Israel begins production from the farther gas fields in coming years, it will create a new vulnerability. Some of the fields are in waters claimed by Lebanon, and Hezbollah has been particularly threatening in pressing the claims.[14] A former Israeli official noted that Hezbollah could attack Israeli rigs in the Mediterranean using "a proximity attack by frogmen, by boats, [or] by terrorists," or by missiles "launch[ed] from tens of kilometers away."[15] During the 2006 war, Hezbollah fired C-802 (CSS-N-8 Saccade) antiship missiles at ships off the coast of Beirut, hitting a Cambodian vessel from 60 km and a *Saar 5*–class Israeli corvette from 30 km.[16] Given the massive size and radar visibility of gas rigs, and the 110 km range of the C-802, they may be vulnerable to missile attack.

Israel regards the threat against the platforms as serious enough to merit increased naval patrols. However, Israel's navy is only beginning to become accustomed to this mission and to operations far from the shore. If Hezbollah can simultaneously threaten the platforms with missiles launched from on and near the shore and with small boats, the IDF's various branches may not be able to keep the platforms safe or effectively coordinate their responses; a simultaneous Hezbollah rocket campaign against Israeli territory might push platform defense to the back burner.

The economic impact of such an attack is difficult to estimate. Estimates of the reserves found in the new fields are not yet at a high degree of certainty, and production has not yet begun. A production facility in the Tamar field will be able to handle up to 1.2 billion cubic feet per day; at recent price levels, this is worth $4.5–$6 million, so the loss of the facility for a few weeks could cost hundreds of millions of dollars before associated expenses are even taken into account.[17]

IRAQ AND AFGHANISTAN

The presence of U.S. troops in Afghanistan and Iraq (in small numbers) is a vulnerability that Iran could exploit in a vengeance campaign. Iran shares long, porous borders with both countries and has supported insurgent groups in each. It also has cultural, linguistic, and religious commonalities with elements in both societies. Many worry that Iran has been pulling its punches, that it can significantly increase its support for anti-American activity and cause the loss of more American lives. However, Iran has its own stake in the outcome of the Iraq and Afghanistan conflicts—unlike the United States, it has to live next door to Afghanistan and Iraq, and it does not want unstable neighbors. There is thus disagreement on the extent to which Iran is willing to act against American interests in these states.

Afghanistan is home to large numbers of Persian-speaking and Shia people. Iran may be able to take significant destructive actions in Afghanistan, creating an additional source of insecurity for the NATO forces there. However, it's doubtful that Iran would take an aggressive path in Afghanistan. Iran's primary interest in Afghanistan has dovetailed rather neatly with America's—Iran fears the violent Sunni fundamentalism of the Taliban, does not want instability, and suffers the brunt of the Afghan opiate trade. Iran nearly went to war with the Taliban in 1998, and then fought them alongside the Americans in 2001. The pending withdrawal of American forces in 2014 might change Iran's calculus somewhat—the regime may find that developing Shia militancy is an appropriate preparation for the possibility of a post-American Taliban ascent—especially as word of expanded Iranian contacts with the Taliban ahead of the withdrawal emerges.[18]

Though the United States has withdrawn its forces from Iraq and reduced its diplomatic presence, it is clear that American policymakers continue to closely watch events in Baghdad, and continue to believe that Iraq is of great importance to American regional interests. Iran can still use Iraq to hurt America. It can support or conduct attacks against America's remaining physical presence in Iraq, or launch political maneuvers to undermine America's remaining influence. It can attempt to promote general chaos to draw America back in—a tall order, given that only a tiny portion of Americans favor a restored military presence. Renewed entanglement in Iraq could be extremely expensive; Iran's more plausible options would hurt but are unlikely to have a strategic impact—and they are just as likely to cause major blowback on Iran.

There is thus reasonable skepticism about Iran's willingness to destabilize its neighbors. Former CIA operative Reuel Marc Gerecht has written that the connections between Iraqi, Afghan, and Iranian societies are too weak, so IRGC personnel would not be able to blend in abroad and Tehran would be limited to the use of proxies.[19] The major Shiite groups in Iraq have never been perfect friends to Iran, and they now have a stake in governing the country—they would be foolish to endanger their standing by launching attacks. Iran's expanded influence in Iraq comes through these groups, so it would also be jeopardizing its own position if it jeopardizes theirs. Attacks in Iraq could even turn the Shia population against Iran due to collateral damage or the anger of Mashhad-born, Najaf-based Grand Ayatollah Ali al Sistani.[20] Given Khamenei's comparatively weak religious credentials, al Sistani's anger could have consequences in Iran.[21] Some scholarly analyses agree with the thrust of Gerecht's argument,[22] though there are also dark warnings that the regime could become less fearful about instability in neighboring countries if it feels its own survival is in the balance.[23]

GENERAL TERRORISM

Iran has extensive ties to terrorist groups. The Qods (Jerusalem) Force of the IRGC liaises with, trains, and supplies terrorists around the region. Iran is arming Lebanon's Hezbollah and has long been accused of arming Palestine's Hamas; Iranian weapons for the Levant are believed to flow through Syria, Egypt, and Sudan.[24] For many years after the dawn of the Islamic Republic, exiled dissidents were killed mysteriously all around the world, highlighting Iranian capabilities.

If attacked, Iran could call in favors and use its own operatives to unleash a campaign of terror. Attacks could range from pinpricks like assassinations of minor figures or acts of sabotage to major incidents like bombings of large buildings and embassies, shooting sprees, or uses of unconventional weapons. One author even worries that Tehran might begin taking diplomatic personnel as hostages.[25] Iranian terror would be a serious challenge for the intervening power. Given that some sectors of the Middle East would be outraged by the intervention, it would be difficult to determine whether a particular act of violence is ordered by Iran or independent, even if it is carried out by an organization with some ties to the Islamic Republic. This deniability will make proportional and timely retaliation difficult and create risks of misunderstandings that could escalate a crisis.

Hezbollah has particularly extensive connections around the world, including a strong presence in South America's lawless Tri-Border region. It uses connections with drug trafficking organizations to raise money;[26] it is plausible that it can use these connections to get personnel and weapons through the porous U.S.-Mexico border.[27] Revenge for an attack on Iran could thus occur against American citizens on American soil.

However, Tehran's use of terror groups as a major instrument of its foreign policy has not necessarily made it good at terrorism. A plot against the Saudi ambassador to Washington was foiled, as was one against the Israeli embassy to Thailand—and both were exposed due to the incompetence of the personnel involved.[28] A bomb planted on an Israeli diplomat's car in Tbilisi, Georgia, was discovered and defused. The only successful attack—on an Israeli embassy employee in India—was not lethal and was likely intended for her husband, the defense attaché. A rumored plot in Azerbaijan resulted in mass arrests. Other alleged Iranian agents were caught before carrying out their mission in Kenya. Iran's greatest successes seem to have been material—the provision of improved weaponry to Shia militias in Iraq or to Hezbollah in Lebanon. The true challenges of terrorist operations are organization, planning, and training, not armament. If Iran's terrorists are truly as incompetent as their recent cock-ups suggest, then they may not be so fearsome. However, it would be unwise to completely discount the capacity of a major state with a large economy to make trouble on the terror front.

THE STRAIT OF HORMUZ

The greatest concern by far is Iran's threat to the flow of oil through the Strait of Hormuz. Iran has repeatedly asserted it will interfere with the strait if it is attacked; the consequences of this action for the global economy could be extreme. Few countries, however, would feel these consequences more than Iran. Experts thus do not agree that Iran would attack Hormuz with all its might. They agree that Iran cannot permanently stop the flow of oil, but they disagree on how long they can make the strait impassable.

An Iranian attack on Hormuz would involve the use of several means. The most eye-catching will be antiship missiles. Iran has a sizeable arsen-

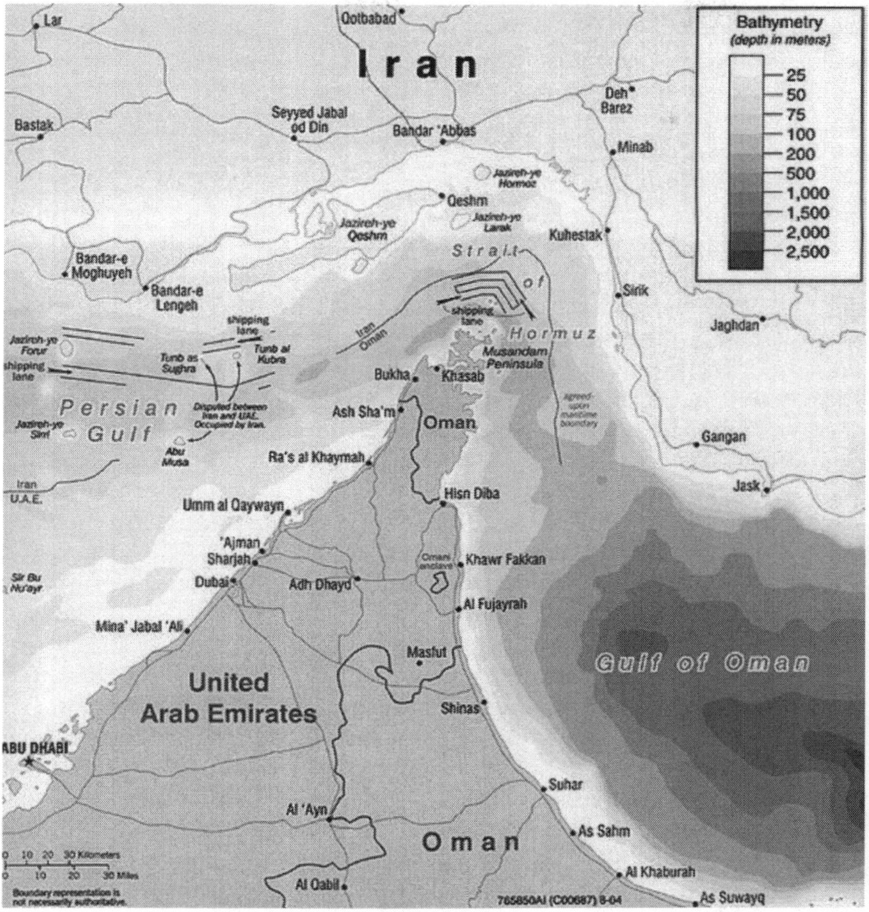

Figure 4.1. Map of Strait of Hormuz with maritime political boundaries. *(Wikipedia.)*

al, but they are not the most modern and effective. Iran's most dangerous capability is its mines, which featured in the Tanker War. It is believed to have acquired modern mines as a part of submarine purchase from Russia; these are supplemented by old-fashioned but still dangerous mines based on early twentieth-century designs. The mines can be placed by dedicated minelaying vessels (which are extremely vulnerable), by Iran's small fleet of *Kilo*-class submarines, or by Iran's diverse set of small boats. The small boats are a much-discussed threat—in addition to their minelaying ability, they can be used in suicide attacks, in targeting and launching antiship missiles, or in lightly armed swarms. The boats are difficult for blue-water navies to engage—they can move quickly, through shallow areas, or among civilian vessels to hinder detection, identification, and engagement, or they can move in groups large enough to ensure that at least some will break through their target's defenses.[29] Estimates suggest that a suicide boat attacking a very large crude carrier (VLCC) oil tanker has about a 20 percent chance of successfully putting it out of commission.[30]

Iran would use these assets in coordination to make the Strait of Hormuz unsafe. Once mines are in place, the small boats and missile forces could harass mine-clearance vessels. If the threat to the mine-clearance vessels is serious enough, navies may choose to keep them at a safe distance until they can make the environment safer; this could add weeks to the crisis. A study using figures from past mine-clearing operations estimated that it would take no more than forty days to clear the strait entirely, but routes of relative safety can be made in less than a week if needed. If Iran chooses to harass mine-clearance operations, however, clearance could take up to 112 days.[31] Mine-clearance off the coast of Kuwait in 1991 occurred at the rate of one mine per vessel per day—while not being harassed by vessels and with known locations of mines.[32] Other estimates are far less pessimistic, suggesting that the closure would last "days"[33] or that, in desperate conditions, tankers could simply sail through even a dense minefield and clear it relatively quickly at the loss of a handful of ships.[34]

Attempting to close the strait carries serious risks for Iran. Eighty-five percent of Iran's imports come through the strait, and the oil exports so crucial to the Iranian government's solvency (60 percent of government revenue, according to Iranian sources[35]) mostly flow out of it. Iran would be cutting off its own lifeline if it closed the strait, and it would have to live on its already dwindling currency reserves.[36] Iran would also be inviting attacks on its own oil facilities by vengeful neighbors, and it would isolate itself internationally.[37] The world would be extremely angry that Iran—and the intervening power, by extension—had taken actions leading to global economic instability. Paradoxically, however, the increasing effectiveness of sanctions on Iran's oil exports gives the regime less to lose from a closure of the strait, and more to gain if an oil-starved world becomes more willing to accept Iranian crude. Additionally, the IRGCN command structure is much more decentralized compared to the Islamic Republic of Iran Navy (IRIN), and has encouraged innovation and "revolutionary élan" amongst its district commanders.[38] Independent initiative by a district commander led to the detention of fifteen British marines in March of 2007 while on routine patrols in the waters between Iraq and Iran.[39]

The planners of any future strike on Iran will surely take the threat to the strait into account and attempt to prevent an Iranian response by seriously damaging Iranian naval and missile forces in the early days of the attack and possibly also by targeting infrastructure in coastal areas.

However, Iran would still retain some capacity to act in Hormuz: laying a mine here, launching a missile there, but never seriously endangering the flow of oil. This would still have an impact on the world's oil markets. Investors would have become very panicky the moment it became clear an intervention was underway in Iran, and they would be watching closely for any signs of Iran's economy-ruining retaliation in Hormuz. The markets cannot be certain that Iran's capacity to act had been fully degraded, and a panic could result. (The market impact of this scenario is examined in more detail in the next chapter.)

In the face of asymmetric threats or actions taken by Iran, common logic might dictate that the United States or whoever respond symmetrically, an eye for an eye. However, a symmetric reaction would not lead to a quick resolution of the conflict, necessary for major oil exports to pass through the strait. In light of this timeline, an overwhelming asymmetric action, taken by the United States and/or its allies and regarded as an escalation, will be the only viable option. While a dispersed and decentralized command-and-control structure is a logical choice for the IRGC (as lines of communication in case of attack cannot be guaranteed), it is a problematic development for those having to deal with the various Revolutionary Guards Corps elements.[40] Should power be consolidated in Tehran under Ayatollah Khamenei, the residual culture of decentralization could prevail long enough for an IRGCN commander to take initiative against American- or other-flagged vessels operating in the region.

In the longer term, the threat to ships traveling through the strait would result in higher shipping insurance rates, whose costs would be passed on to consumers. However, some assert that oil tankers are not as vulnerable to antiship weaponry as one would think. The oil carried in the ships rarely catches fire and helps absorb the force of impacts, so it might take eight to ten hits by antiship missiles to sink a tanker. This rate of usage would deplete missile arsenals rapidly.[41] The Tanker War in the strait during the Iran-Iraq War did not have a serious impact on the global oil market—the oil glut occurred in spite of it—and shippers can spread the costs of insurance across the cargo, resulting in little impact at the pump. It is even possible that regional states will subsidize the passage of their oil to balance prices, as Iran did during the Tanker War.[42]

Iranian attacks on the Strait of Hormuz, whether with or without intent to seal it, would force a response with a serious risk of mission creep. The U.S. intervention would immediately be repurposed: counterproliferation would be replaced by countering action against shipping. This would quickly come to require extensive air patrols over large areas of southern Iran purely for preventing missile launches,[43] efforts to find and destroy Iranian small boats in port, attacks on logistics and command and control facilities, escorts, antisubmarine warfare, mine-clearance, and many other elements. Serious interruptions of oil flows could even provoke some form of ground intervention,[44] an action the United States and everyone else (except perhaps a few IRGC diehards) would like to avoid.

INSURGENCY IN THE GULF

Iran can attempt to activate the Shiite populations in the Gulf region against their Sunni rulers. The Shia of Bahrain and Saudi Arabia are of particular interest. In Saudi Arabia, they are a small minority, but they are heavily concentrated in the oil-rich Eastern Province. Their position in Saudi society is not as bad as it has been in the past, with reforms in the 1990s and 2000s giving them more rights, but they are still subject to incitement and discrimination, and most of the few shoots of the Arab Spring that appeared in the kingdom were in their communities. The Al Saud have long worried about Shia unrest, and there were sympathizers of the Islamic Revolution all over the region in the 1980s. Iran's reputation in Shiite communities, however, has long been declining. The excesses of the Revolution quickly became apparent to the world, and Iran is Persian, not Arab, limiting its cultural reach. With the death of Khomeini and his replacement by the poorly credentialed Khamenei, even the regime's religious legitimacy fell away.

Iran's ability to use international Shiite communities as its pawns is thus limited. A 2009 RAND Corporation analysis of the Saudi Shia suggested that an attack on Iran would provoke only minor acts of sabotage, not a widespread revolt.[45] In the wake of the Arab Spring, we cannot be certain that this assessment is still sound. However, a mass Shia uprising should not be a vital challenge to the Saudi state. For political reasons, the Saudi military has a compartmentalized structure, so the Defense Ministry being at war with Iran wouldn't keep the National Guard or Interior Ministry from cracking down domestically. The government tolerates extensive Shiite-baiting, and the National Guard recruits from conservative Sunni tribes, so orders to massacre protestors might be obeyed—when in the Shiite communities, the Arab Spring protest slogan "the army and the people are one hand" will not apply.

The risk of sympathy rebellion is greater in Bahrain. The tiny island kingdom is estimated to be about 70 percent Shiite, yet it is ruled by the Sunni Al Khalifa clan. Sectarian tension emerged during the nation's Arab Spring protests, as the government killed Shiite protestors and bulldozed many Shiite mosques.[46] The Gulf Cooperation Council sent in troops to assist the regime, and relative quiet has followed. However, one must wonder what would happen if an attack on Iran provoked outrage and then Iranian operatives attempted to incite and arm angry Bahrainis. The presence of the U.S. Navy's Fifth Fleet at Manama would help fan the flames of discontent, and it would be at risk of expulsion. The presence of a GCC security force on Bahrain would likely contain this threat, for as above there is little reason to believe that Saudi troops would be particularly merciful to crowds of rioters. Bahrain's Shia opposition would be foolish to aggressively change tack immediately after an attack on Iran, as they would be confirming the regime's narrative that the Shia are an Iranian fifth column. The best Iran can realistically do is cause a few terrorist incidents and hope the regime replies with a self-defeating brutality that further alienates it from its people.

THE MISSILE THREAT

Iran can also strike its neighbors using its ballistic missile forces. Iran's missile capability was demonstrated during the War of the Cities phase of the Iran-Iraq War, and Tehran has continued to develop its missile forces. Military exercises regularly show off new missiles and tout them as "cutting edge," while semi-official media provide the world with abundant photographs and videos of demonstrations. Iran is still far from developing any missiles that can threaten Western Europe, let alone North America. However, it can hit closer targets like nearby cities or oil refineries. Much ink has been spilled arguing against the political and psychological merits of strategic bombardment, so we will not assert that Iranian missiles would provoke uprisings or surrenders. However, missiles can carry chemical, biological, or radiological weaponry, and this would put immense pressure on the United States to provide its allies missile shielding with its PAC-3 missile systems. There would be a serious risk that the United States, finding its missile shields inadequate, would renew its intervention in Iran, escalating the crisis.

Estimates by Joshua Shifrinson and Miranda Priebe suggest that Iran's current arsenal of missiles is totally inadequate to the task of degrading Saudi oil production, even if there were no Saudi missile defenses. To have 75 percent confidence in destroying the crucial elements of the processing facility at Abqaiq, Iran would need to launch more than 1,300 Shahab-1 missiles, while it likely has no more than 400.[47] (Launching its full complement of missiles would give Tehran a 60 percent chance of taking out one of Abqaiq's eight stabilization towers; since the plant operates below capacity, this should have no impact on output.[48]) Many other potential targets would also require hundreds, if not thousands, of missiles (for instance, the Red Sea oil terminal at Yanbu would require more than *35,000* Shahab-3A missiles for Iran to have 75 percent confidence in its destruction). In order to realistically threaten Saudi oil, Iran would need to dramatically improve the accuracy of its missiles.[49]

Shifrinson and Priebe assume that the Shahab-1 has an estimated circular error probable (or CEP, the radius around the target within which the missile has a 50 percent chance of landing) of between 450 and 610 meters.[50] The Abqaiq stabilization facility is about 3 km^2, or 3,000,000

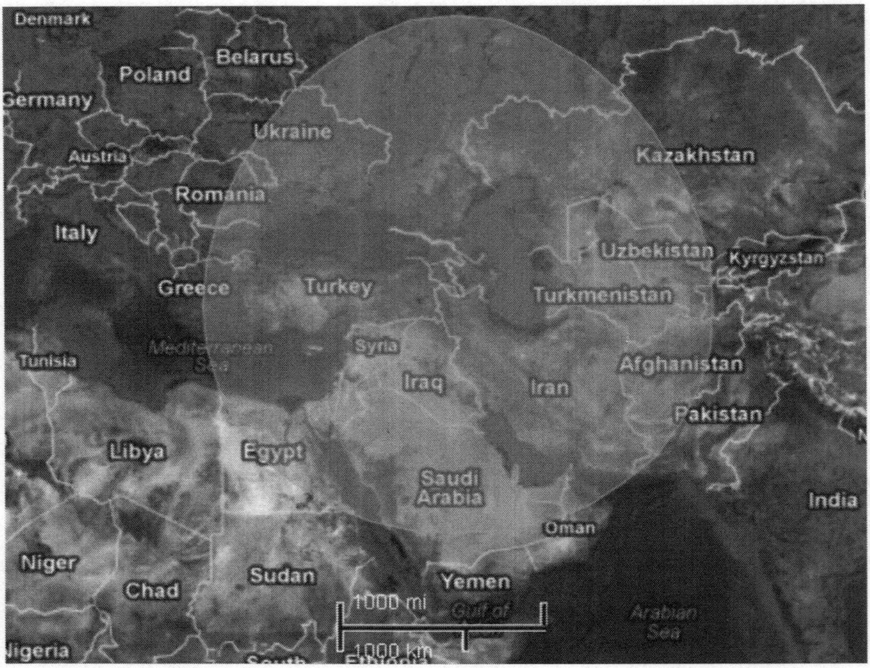

Figure 4.2. Approximate range of Iran's Shahab-3A missile. *(Created with Google Maps using Carlos Labs' Missile Range Map Tool.)*

m^2,[51] an area about 2.5 times the size of the Shahab-1's CEP. The facility is actually roughly circular, so we will say it is essentially a circle with a radius of 977 m. A given Shahab fired at the center of the facility would have a 65–85.4 percent chance of landing within its bounds, assuming it does not fail or get destroyed en route by missile defenses.[52]

However, Shifrinson and Priebe note that improved guidance systems could significantly improve the accuracy of Iran's missile forces. It is quite reasonable to assume that Iran has, in fact, made some improvements—for instance, the Federation of American Scientists estimates that the long-range Shahab-3 missile can achieve a CEP of just 190 meters—a fraction of what their prior estimates had suggested.[53] If they could also achieve this with their shorter-ranged Shahab-1, the calculus may change—each missile would now have a 99.7 percent chance of landing within the facility.[54] However, aimed at a particular stabilization tower, a missile would only have a 0.75 percent chance of an effective impact.

This may be optimistic. Shifrinson and Priebe assess the effectiveness of Iranian attacks based on hits scored on a small portion of the facility, but that is likely not the only way to do major damage—the facility also needs a vast network of pipes to move oil and chemicals from point to

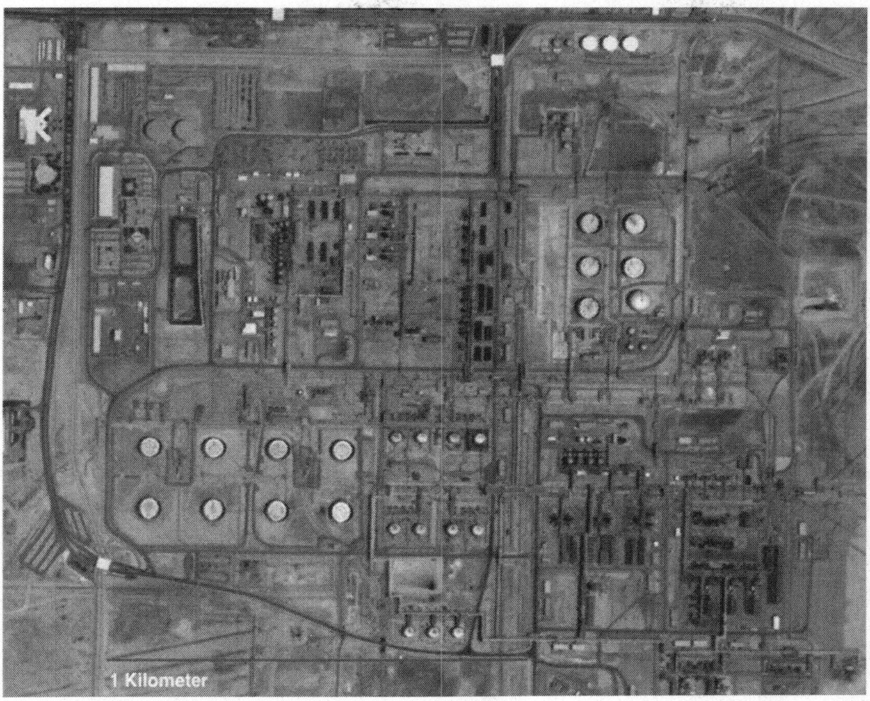

Figure 4.3. Satellite image of oil stabilization facility at Abqaiq, Saudi Arabia. *(Produced with Google Earth.)*

point, tanks for storage, and control facilities. Damage to these would also impair operations, though not as much as hits to the stabilization towers. Several hits within the facility would likely have significant implications for its operations, especially in the short term.

Still, we might be justly accused of pessimism here. Both we and Shifrinson and Priebe use the figure that petroleum fractionating towers take 15 psi of overpressure to rupture, a pressure delivered at a distance of about 30 m by a Shahab-1 with a high-explosive warhead with its hundreds of kilograms of TNT. It's possible, however, that a close-in hit from a full-size high-explosive warhead won't be as devastating to the Abqaiq plant as we think. Most open sources derive their estimates of vulnerability to conventional explosions from research on vulnerability to nuclear explosions (the U.S. Defense Intelligence Agency's *Physical Vulnerability Handbook—Nuclear Weapons* is heavily cited), and these do not scale down perfectly to model vulnerability to conventional explosions. The shockwave from an explosion creates two types of force on objects it hits, peak overpressure and drag loading. The blast wave is not instantaneous—it rapidly builds to the peak and then declines in pressure over time—simplified, it is a sudden gust of wind that fades to a breeze. Some structures are more vulnerable to the sustained drag loading after the peak overpressure. However, nuclear explosions produce more sustained blast waves with more drag loading than conventional explosives:

> It is the effect of the duration of the drag loading on structures which constitutes an important difference between nuclear and high-explosive detonations. For the same peak overpressure in the blast wave, a nuclear weapon will prove to be more destructive than a conventional one, especially for buildings which respond to drag loading.[55]

This distinction is highly relevant to our current discussion. Hydrocarbon processing facilities contain many cylindrical structures—pipes, storage tanks, distillation towers, and so on. Cylindrical structures can be highly resilient against initial overpressures, but vulnerable to sustained drag loading. Smokestacks, for example, "because of their shape . . . are subject essentially to drag loading only" and are resistant to vibration, giving them "considerable blast resistance."[56]

Liquid petroleum gas installations, including large and small tanks connected to appropriate piping, display even more incredible solidity. For example, a 100-pound capacity cylinder was exposed to a 25 psi peak overpressure in a nuclear test. Found "2,000 feet from its original position [and] badly dented," it was "still usable."[57] A small storage plant with an 18,000 gal tank, exposed to 5 psi, "could have been readily put back into operation."[58]

POL (petroleum, oil, lubricant) storage tanks like those found at Abqaiq can also be quite sturdy if they are not completely empty (perhaps due to an effect similar to the one which protects oil tankers from antiship missiles). Many of the tanks at Abqaiq are over 100 feet in diameter, corresponding to resistance to damage at pressures in excess of 12 psi when full.[59] Given that this figure is for a nuclear blast of at least 1 kt, we can expect higher resilience against a briefer conventional shockwave.

Another major disanalogy between nuclear weapons and the smaller conventional blasts we are dealing with here is the nature of the peak overpressure wave that arrives at the object in question. The wave dissipates much sooner with smaller explosions. Imagine a 1 kt nuclear explosion 200 ft from a 100 ft diameter POL storage tank. The near side of the tank will be exposed to 300 psi; the far side will be exposed to about 100 psi. Despite the significant loss of pressure, the tank will still be exposed to an incredible force on all sides. This gives the blast additional destructive power—the shockwave can implode sealed containers by completely enveloping them in high pressures. It also produces immense lateral forces on structures when they are partially surrounded by the blast wave, as the near side experiences massive pressure while the far side does not.[60] Smaller blasts lack this property. Suppose we detonated 1 kg of TNT 4 m from the same 100 ft (30.5 m) diameter tank. The closest area of the tank would be exposed to about 8 psi. The farthest part of the tank would be exposed to about 0.4 psi, roughly equivalent to a 160 mph gust of wind. The tank would surely be more likely to survive than if it were exposed to an 8 psi pressure on the near side from a 1 kt explosion, because that explosion would not drop to 0.4 psi more than a mile away. The far side of the tank would instead be exposed to at least 5 psi, a much more worrisome level of pressure.

Similarly, a 1,000 kg conventional warhead that produces 15 psi of overpressure on a tank 30 m away produces only 3 psi on its far side, while a 1 kt nuclear weapon far enough away to produce 15 psi on one side would produce about 12 psi on the other. The damage done by large conventional warheads, while substantial, simply cannot be estimated using damage assessments from warheads that are literally thousands of times larger.

Taking all these disanalogies into account, the effects of individual conventional warheads on Saudi oil facilities may be even less than those predicted in Shifrinson and Priebe's analysis. Large structures like POL tanks don't experience the same high peak overpressures on all sides, while smaller structures like fractionating towers and pipes don't experience the same sustained drag forces. In both cases, higher overpressures are likely needed to achieve an equivalent level of destruction; given the remarkable survivability of hydrocarbon industry materiel under even nuclear blasts, the increase might have to be substantial. This amplifies Shifrinson and Priebe's argument that Iran's missile forces are woefully inadequate to the task of knocking out Abqaiq's stabilization towers using conventional warheads. Iran should still be capable of doing substantial damage to the facility as a whole, though it will be a far quicker fix than a set of ruptured stabilization towers.

OTHER IRANIAN THREATS TO OIL

Iran has other means of threatening the world oil market. Analysts often do not devote extensive discussion to the impact of Iranian sabotage on oil facilities around the Gulf—they typically merely note that it is possible, and on occasion identify a specific site that could be targeted. However, the potential for interference is significant. Oil refineries are extraordinarily complex, and serious damage to key choke points within the facility could seriously hinder its operations and release dangerous chemicals into the environment. Past attacks on oil facilities have been sufficient to keep them below capacity for months (though most attacks have little effect and result in no more than a few hours of trouble). Large refineries are more capable of absorbing damage, as flows within the refinery can be routed around damaged units, though localized damage can still significantly reduce the refinery's production capacity. Major oil facilities like those found in Saudi Arabia would require fairly large attacks to take them offline. Follow-up attacks could sustain what effects are achieved. The much-attacked gas pipeline in the Sinai has sometimes been kept offline for weeks. The long struggle to restore Iraq's oil production after the 2003 war is even more worrying. Not all of its characteristics would apply to an effort to restore production in Saudi Arabia or Qatar—Iraq's oil facilities were in poor shape before the war due to sanctions—but their reconstruction was repeatedly set back by militant attacks. Iraq reached its prewar production capacity in late 2007, four years and nine months after the beginning of the conflict.

The Gulf's oil production may not be the only target. Iran could punish the world for tolerating an American attack by shutting off its own oil production, depriving global markets of about two million barrels per day. This could also happen if the United States attacks Iran's oil facilities in response to Iranian retaliation, or the growing militaries of the various GCC states might seek revenge for Iranian strikes on their own oil facilities. As of 2008, Iran's hard currency reserves would have been able to fill the economic role of oil for a year and a half; by 2011, the reserves had declined so that they would only be sufficient for a few months, and according to some reports were completely gone. The chaos of 2012 could only mean that the situation is worse. Once the reserves run out, the results could be devastating, as Iran's government and economy are highly dependent on oil revenues. Saudi Arabia has claimed that its excess production capacity is sufficient to cover Iran's exit from the international oil market, although this is not a truth universally acknowledged, especially after the Saudis have used at least some of their excess capacity to pressure OPEC rivals and make up for Iranian oil lost to sanctions.

Oil facilities can employ thousands of personnel, many of whom are drawn from pools of migrant labor with little oversight. This makes the infiltration of saboteurs relatively easy. This could allow a campaign of sabotage to be sustained for very long periods, resulting in a small de facto loss of production capacity that could last for months. Shiite populations in places like Saudi Arabia's Eastern Province could also be angered enough by a strike on Iran that they would carry out minor acts of sabotage on the facilities they work in, without any Iranian involvement.[61]

Some authors have speculated that non-Gulf oil producers might also be victims of Iranian retaliation. Iraqi Kurdistan and especially Azerbaijan are known to have good ties with Israel, so they would be natural targets. Some authors have even suggested that an Israeli attack could include the use of facilities in Kurdistan or Azerbaijan, which would make the risk of retaliatory attacks to Iran's northwest particularly acute. Such attacks would risk drawing in Turkey, though, and it would be insane for Iran to risk warfare with one more regional power in the wake of strikes.

Oil facilities have always been prone to long offline periods when attacked. If the major facilities in the Gulf experience a similar level of damage, the impact on the global economy would be serious. There are several factors to consider when using these cases as a guideline for possible attacks on Gulf oil:

- Delays could be aggravated by repeat attacks, a factor not present in many of the cases.
- Delays could be aggravated by the use of trained personnel and higher-quality weaponry. The Iranian military obviously has an abundance of domestic oil facilities to examine, allowing for improved attack planning. While Iran's military industry is not incredible, it can certainly provide Iranian operatives or proxies with fairly high-quality munitions for use against the facility. The net effect would be an attack that is significantly more effective than those by UNITA, Iraqi, or Nigerian insurgents.
- Delays could be mitigated by the urgency with which the world would attempt to restore production. Rapid rises in the price of oil would create very strong financial incentives for involvement by all capable parties.
- Delays would be mitigated by the massive size of some of the facilities involved—total devastation is impossible without nuclear weapons.

NOTES

1. Patrick Clawson and Michael Eisenstadt, "The Last Resort: Consequences of Preventive Military Action against Iran," WINEP, June 2008, www.washingtoninstitute.org/policy-analysis/view/the-last-resort-consequences-of-preventive-military-action-against-iran.

2. Ashton B. Carter, "Military Elements in a Strategy to Deal with Iran's Nuclear Program," CNAS, June 2008, http://belfercenter.ksg.harvard.edu/files/Military%20Elements%20in%20a%20Strategy%20to%20Deal%20with%20Irans%20Nuclear%20Program.pdf.

3. Vali Nasr, "The Implications of Military Confrontation with Iran," CNAS, September 2008, www.isn.ethz.ch/isn/Digital-Library/Publications/Detail/?ots591=0c54e3b3-1e9c-be1e-2c24-a6a8c7060233&lng=en&id=57089. Jeffrey White, "What Would War with Iran Look Like?," *American Interest*, July–August 2011, www.the-american-interest.com/article-bd.cfm?piece=982.

4. Carter, "Military Elements."

5. Ashton B. Carter and William J. Perry, "Plan B for Iran: What If Nuclear Diplomacy Fails?," The Preventive Defense Project, September 2006, www.carnegieendowment.org/static/npp/reports/carter_9-19-06.pdf.

6. Bruce Bueno de Mesquita has suggested that the crucial elite in Iran consists of roughly two thousand people. A campaign that killed some percentage of these and made communication difficult among the rest might have serious implications for the regime's politics. This would be a threat to the current leaders of the regime, but it is

hardly certain that a reshuffled elite would be any easier to deal with—and it might be significantly worse and significantly more resilient.

7. White, "What Would War with Iran Look Like?"

8. White, "What Would War with Iran Look Like?"

9. Anthony H. Cordesman and Abdullah Toukan, "Study on a Possible Israeli Strike on Iran's Nuclear Development Facilities," CSIS, March 2009; also referenced by Robert Gates in his confirmation hearing for the Defense Department, http://csis.org/publication/study-possible-israeli-strike-irans-nuclear-development-facilities.

10. Yaakov Katz, "Israel Worried Syria Weapons Going to Terrorists," *Jerusalem Post*, Jan. 3, 2012, www.jpost.com/Defense/Article.aspx?id=251944.

11. Reuel Marc Gerecht, "Should Israel Bomb Iran?," *Weekly Standard*, July 26, 2010, www.weeklystandard.com/articles/should-israel-bomb-iran.

12. Clawson and Eisenstadt, "The Last Resort." George Friedman, "Rethinking American Options on Iran," STRATFOR, August 2010, www.stratfor.com/weekly/20100830_rethinking_american_options_iran.

13. Sharon Udasin, "Israel Able to Fulfill Energy Needs—but with Costs," *Jerusalem Post*, Apr. 28, 2011, www.jpost.com/NationalNews/Article.aspx?id=218149.

14. There has been speculation that the other Lebanese forces, while claiming the gas fields, ultimately prefer a negotiated solution with Israel. These factions reportedly fear that Hezbollah's zero-sum stance stems from a desire to exploit the gas fields for its own enrichment.

15. "Israel Boosts Patrols around Naval Gas Fields, Fearing Guerrilla Attacks," *Haaretz*, Nov. 21, 2011, www.haaretz.com/news/diplomacy-defense/israel-boosts-patrols-around-naval-gas-fields-fearing-guerilla-attacks-1.396861.

16. The Israeli vessel was even designed to have a low visibility to radar. See Amos Harel, "Missile Attack on INS Spear: IDF Probe Faults Navy, Ship's Crew," *Haaretz*, Nov. 8, 2006, www.haaretz.com/print-edition/news/missile-attack-on-ins-spear-idf-probe-faults-navy-ship-s-crew-1.204672 and Amos Harel, "Soldier Killed, 3 Missing after Navy Vessel Hit off Beirut Coast," *Haaretz*, July 15, 2006, www.haaretz.com/news/soldier-killed-3-missing-after-navy-vessel-hit-off-beirut-coast-1.193112.

17. Associated expenses would include the obvious (repairs to the facility, insurance payments, cleanup, etc.) and the less obvious (a slight global natural gas price spike, changed gas transport patterns, purchasing alternative fuels, energy use restrictions, etc.).

18. See Al-Habib, Maria, "Iran Builds on Outreach to Taliban," *Wall Street Journal*, July 31, 2012, http://online.wsj.com/article/SB10000872396390444130304577560241242267700.html.

19. Reuel Marc Gerecht, "To Bomb, or Not to Bomb: That Is the Iran Question," *Weekly Standard*, Apr. 24, 2006, www.weeklystandard.com/Content/Public/Articles/000/000/012/100mmysk.asp.

20. Iranian actions to provoke Shia risings in Iraq would likely be seen as part of a broader Iranian campaign to spread the influence of pro-guardianship clerics throughout Shiadom. Al Sistani, who like most Shia does not agree with Khomeini's more intensive vision of guardianship, is threatened by the ascent of such forces.

21. Gerecht, "Should Israel Bomb Iran?"

22. Chuck Freilich, "Decision Time in Jerusalem," *Journal of International Security Affairs* 18 (Spring 2010): 55–64.

23. Nasr, "The Implications of Military Confrontation with Iran."

24. Ioana Emilia Matesan and John Gay, "El Arish and the Sinai Peninsula Underworld, Egypt," *National Strategy Forum Review* 20, no. 3 (Summer 2011), www.nationalstrategy.com/NSFReview/Summer2011Vol20No3BlackSpots.aspx

25. Ashton B. Carter, "Military Elements in a Strategy to Deal with Iran's Nuclear Program," CNAS, June 2008. The seizure of the embassy of the United Kingdom in late November 2011 highlights the real danger of grassroots—or Astroturf—Iranian violence against diplomatic missions. However, several nations took steps to protect their

diplomatic missions in Tehran after the incident, which may mitigate the impact of any future actions.

26. Seelke et al., "Latin America and the Caribbean: Illicit Drug Trafficking and U.S. Counterdrug Programs," Congressional Research Service, January 25, 2011.

27. This could be expensive, as smugglers are typically very careful to keep a low profile in destination countries with well-developed enforcement, and they will be especially wary of attracting the attention of counterterror forces.

28. In the Saudi case, the operative attempted to use a Mexican drug cartel to carry out the attack—a high-visibility operation that he should have known would have been unappealing to most criminal networks. In the second, there were two accidental explosions—one blew up the operatives' safehouse, and another seriously wounded one of them.

29. For discussion of the small boat threat, see the U.S. Office of Naval Intelligence's Fall 2009 report, *Iran's Naval Forces: From Guerrilla Warfare to a Modern Naval Strategy*.

30. See Eugene Gholz, "Threats to Oil Flows through the Strait of Hormuz: Implications for American Grand Strategy," LBJ School Hormuz Working Group, March 2007.

31. Caitlin Talmadge, "Closing Time: Assessing the Iranian Threat to the Strait of Hormuz," *International Security* 33, no. 1 (Summer 2008): 82–117.

32. Colin K. Boynton, LCDR, "Operations to Defeat Iranian Maritime Trade Interdiction," Apr. 5, 2009, www.dtic.mil/dtic/tr/fulltext/u2/a502907.pdf.

33. Ashton B. Carter, "Military Elements in a Strategy to Deal with Iran's Nuclear Program," CNAS, June 2008, http://belfercenter.ksg.harvard.edu/publication/18280/military_elements_in_a_strategy_to_deal_with_irans_nuclear_program.html. "Iran: US Concerns and Policy Responses," Congressional Research Service, Apr. 18, 2011.

34. This technique is known as minebreaking (as opposed to "sweeping" or "clearing") and has been used in history—it is even practiced today using unmanned ships. Gholz suggests that just six VLCCs would be lost in clearing the Strait of Hormuz this way. There is a flaw in the mathematics—the Gulf's intense currents would likely redistribute mines, undoing some of the earlier sacrifices. However, it is an excellent proof of concept, and the use of a mass flotilla of non-tankers might also allow the clearance of the strait by "breaking."

35. "Iran Oil Exports Top 844mn Barrels," PressTV, June 16, 2010, http://edition.presstv.ir/detail/130736.html.

36. According to some reports, the reserves have run dry.

37. Clawson and Eisenstadt, "The Last Resort."

38. Michael Connell, "The Artesh Navy: Iran's Strategic Force," Middle East Institute, Jan. 31, 2012, www.mei.edu/content/artesh-navy-irans-strategic-force.

39. Stephen Fidler and Roula Khalaf, "Iran Seizes 15 British Marines," *Financial Times*, Mar. 24, 2012. www.ft.com/intl/cms/s/0/5dde7972-d9ad-11db-9b4a-000b5df10621.html#axzz22ESHGNK0.

40. Anthony H. Cordesman, "Iran's Revolutionary Guards, the Al Quds Force, and Other Intelligence and Paramilitary Forces," CSIS, Aug. 16, 2007, www.csis.org/files/media/csis/pubs/070816_cordesman_report.pdf.

41. Dennis Blair and Kenneth Lieberthal, "Smooth Sailing: The World's Shipping Lanes Are Safe," *Foreign Affairs* 86, no. 3 (June 2007): 7–13; see also Talmadge, "Closing Time," 82–117.

42. Blair and Lieberthal, "Smooth Sailing," 7–13. Recall also that Saudi Arabia has a long history of interventions to stabilize global oil markets; the key question is not whether they would intervene, but whether they would have the capacity to do so.

43. Talmadge, "Closing Time," 82–117.

44. White, "What Would War with Iran Look Like?"

45. Frederic Wehrey et al., *Saudi-Iranian Relations Since the Fall of Saddam* (Santa Monica, CA: RAND, 2009), 33, www.rand.org/pubs/monographs/2009/RAND_MG840.pdf.

46. See, for example, "Bahrain Targets Shia Religious Sites," *Al Jazeera English*, May 14, 2011, http://english.aljazeera.net/video/middleeast/2011/05/2011513112016389348.html.
47. Joshua R. Itzkowitz Shifrinson and Miranda Priebe, "A Crude Threat: The Limits of an Iranian Missile Campaign against Saudi Arabian Oil," *International Security* 36, no. 1 (Summer 2011): 188.
48. Shifrinson and Priebe, "A Crude Threat," 193.
49. Note that Shifrinson and Priebe do not consider Iran's cruise missile arsenal. However, cruise missiles can be engaged by Saudi Arabia's formidable air defenses, making them less of a threat than ballistic missiles, which can only be effectively defended against using specialized equipment.
50. Shifrinson and Priebe, "A Crude Threat," 181.
51. Shifrinson and Priebe, "A Crude Threat," 178.
52. Given the 450–610 m CEP, the missile has a standard deviation of 497–674 m about its aimpoint. The figures are taken from a pair of 100,000-shot Monte Carlo simulations. Even factoring in high failure rates and unprecedented combat performance by missile defenses, the Iranians would have good odds of putting at least a few warheads into Abqaiq if they launch large numbers of missiles.
53. "Shahab-3/Zelzal-3," Federation of American Scientists Military Analysis Network, 2008, www.fas.org/programs/ssp/man/militarysumfolder/shahab-3.html.
54. Based on a series of 10,000-shot Monte Carlo simulations.
55. Samuel Glasstone and Philip J. Dolan, *The Effects of Nuclear Weapons*, 3rd ed. (Washington, DC: United States Department of Defense and United States Department of Energy, 1977), 130.
56. Glasstone and Dolan, *Effects of Nuclear Weapons*, 166.
57. Glasstone and Dolan, *Effects of Nuclear Weapons*, 204.
58. Glasstone and Dolan, *Effects of Nuclear Weapons*, 205.
59. Glasstone and Dolan, *Effects of Nuclear Weapons*, 227–28.
60. Glasstone and Dolan, *Effects of Nuclear Weapons*, 128–30.
61. Wehrey et al., *Saudi-Iranian Relations*, 33. Observation from interviews with Saudi Shia and Saudi security forces.

FIVE

Evolving Crisis, Challenging Exit

Let us presume that America chooses to attack Iran, and the strike is successful in destroying all major Iranian nuclear program sites (Natanz, Fordow, Arak, and Esfahan) and any significant sites not known to the general public. Iran's nuclear program will be seriously set back, with no imminent capability for breakout. Iran's military, meanwhile, will not be seriously degraded in its crucial sectors. Airstrikes would obviously deal heavy damage to Iran's air defenses and to certain elements of its military command and control; the navies and air forces (IRGC and regular) would be all but eliminated. The real movers and shakers—the senior officials of the IRGC and the regular army—would be largely untouched, though their ability to use ordinary means to communicate with their subordinates may be significantly damaged. The air campaign would presumably last about a week, as in the scenario we used to generate the cost estimates found in the appendixes.

Iran will be faced with an ongoing choice as the campaign continues and closes—how to respond? There are three basic paths Iran can take. The first is to respond as Iran has said in its propaganda, with an aggressive, all-out attack. This could include ballistic missile launches against its neighbors and regional U.S. bases, mining the Strait of Hormuz, missile and boat attacks on the U.S. Navy, and mass sabotage and terror. The second path is to initiate a campaign of "pinprick" attacks against this target set—an explosives-laden speedboat here, a missile launch or a massacre there. This campaign will be at a much lower tempo than the all-out option. The third path is to merely ignore the attacks.

Of course, Iran's capabilities allow it to choose from among many options between total aggression and total passivity. Iran can vary the pace and destructiveness of its response at will; Iran's leadership may be said to possess a dimmer switch. Iran also has good relations with numerous proxies, including Hamas and Hezbollah, and can be assumed to have contacts in Shia communities around the region; this, coupled with the general regional instability and discontent that will be provoked by an airstrike, will give Iran the ability to mask its actions. Iran thus really possesses three dimmer switches—it can retaliate at various rates and levels of destruction and it can vary the ease with which these attacks can be properly attributed. This will pose immense challenges to the United States. As it has seen in Iran's interference in Iraq, a war/peace binary is not applicable to the U.S.-Iran relationship; after a strike the situation could become even murkier. This will be to Iran's advantage. The international community will already be angry with the United States for carrying out the initial strike, and it will be all but impossible to craft a response to Iran's retaliation that satisfies both them and domestic American actors. The primary means of action for the United States have very little variability of attribution,[1] and the deeper American involvement in the international community heavily regulates tempo.[2] The U.S. dimmer switch thus operates in fewer dimensions and at a lower fidelity than Iran's.

MASS RETALIATION

Massive retaliation is a risky option for Iran. It might benefit in the long run from a greater perceived threat in Hormuz, even if it is unable to capitalize on the short-term price spike caused by its actions. A big effort would also show the Iranian people and Iran's neighbors that the regime is powerful and able to seriously destabilize the region at will. However, massive retaliation would invite—or even force[3]—a massive military response. This would include major attacks on Iran's leadership and military assets. The risks of attacks on leadership are obvious; the loss of key military assets would cost Iran regional clout and hinder domestic crackdowns. It is possible that general warfare would strengthen the regime—the early days of the Iran-Iraq War, for instance, saw massive crackdowns on opposition factions like the MEK and stabilized the Khomeini faction's rule. However, the world's inevitable and heavy-handed response[4] to a major Iranian retaliation would give the mullahs an opaque future. They would likely wish to avoid this outcome unless there are no better alternatives.

Massive response would also run counter to Iran's long-term vision for the region. Iran would prove itself to be a serious threat. In the past, states like Qatar have feigned neutralism towards Iran for leverage against Saudi Arabia. Iran's retaliation (which, according to back-channel threats, would include a missile strike on the emir's palace) would make it more difficult for states to ever pursue "third paths" between the Islamic Republic and the kingdom, and it would become less likely that they

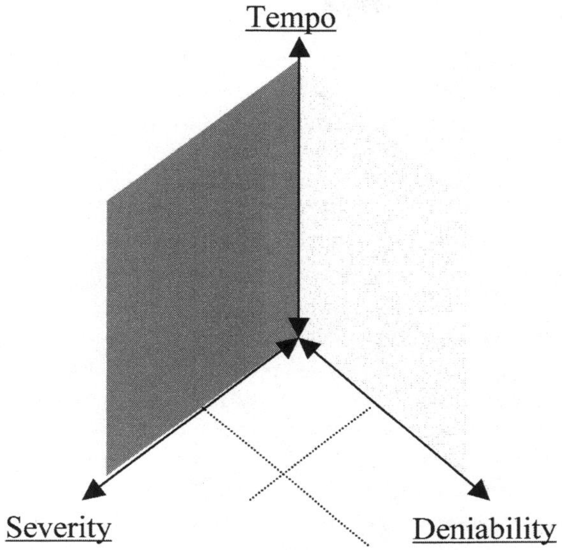

Figure 5.1. The three-dimensional space created by Iran's response options. Unlike Iran, America has little variation on the deniability axis—few of its options are highly deniable.

would align with anyone other than America and the Al Saud. In the years after the attacks, states would attempt to counterbalance Iran, building up their militaries even more (perhaps this time with more focus on competence and professionalism) and cementing their alliances. The United States presence in the region would become even more certain. Domestic Shia groups would see renewed repression, and states could even attempt to reopen the Iraqi and Lebanese civil wars to challenge the current Shiite-friendly order and undermine Iran's influence. A severe enough retaliation, especially if it includes targets in Israeli ally Azerbaijan, could even prompt Turkey to restrict trade. The net result of all this would be an isolated, impoverished Iran with greatly diminished regional influence.

NONRETALIATION

Nonresponse to an attack is also risky. The revolutionary regime derives much of its legitimacy from its ability to keep Iran secure from Western interference. An open intervention by the West would show Iranians that the regime is inadequate to that task. Failure to respond forcefully could make the regime look weak, surely the impression it would not wish to convey in a post–Green Revolution, post–Arab Spring world.

MIDDLE PATHS

Iran's ideal and most likely reply is thus a less serious response, one which punishes Washington for its actions and which demonstrates the regime's resilience without critically undermining its interests in the region or exposing it to serious retaliation. The solution is a campaign of pinprick attacks that, as discussed above, will seriously challenge the United States' ability to respond in a way that will satisfy both domestic and international actors. The challenge for Iran will be identifying the amount of retaliation that the United States will tolerate or only weakly challenge, and then conducting operations as close as possible to that limit. This will require a careful balance. Attacking prominent symbols of American might like U.S. Navy ships in regional ports or American embassies would show the Iranian people that the regime is still capable, but a proportional—that is, large—response would be inevitable. Smaller attacks, like attacks on establishments frequented by American expatriates, might be ignored by an America eager to avoid a new foreign entanglement, but would also show a lack of resolve. Iran thus seems likely to launch significant attacks on prominent American targets. The assassination attempts against Israeli diplomats will likely be visited on Americans, as well—indeed, this may be the primary manifestation.

AMERICAN RESPONSE AND CYCLICAL VIOLENCE

The American response to Iran's retaliation could be substantial. Similar attacks on America in the past, like the 1998 bombings of American embassies in Kenya and Tanzania and the 1993 Iraqi assassination plot against former president George H. W. Bush, provoked rapid, brief responses that were roughly at the midpoint of America's retaliatory capabilities—attacks with large numbers of cruise missiles, but not much more. Given the large number of American military assets that will be present in the region and the heavy usage of cruise missiles in the initial attack on Iran's nuclear program, American policymakers will likely be inclined to a slightly heftier response led by aircraft. IRGC facilities will likely be targeted, as they will almost certainly be responsible for Iran's retaliation. However, the United States should take caution before attacking the IRGC too forcefully, because it is vital for repressing dissent and controlling the regular army. Severely weakening the IRGC could cause the regime to fear for its existence—or even fear that the United States is attempting regime change. This could provoke a highly aggressive response, as the regime may feel it has nothing to lose. Other facilities, like the IRGC's extensive economic interests or nonrepressive assets like its navy, make better targets.

The U.S. retaliation, even if it is carefully calibrated, will pose another challenge to the revolutionary regime's legitimacy. This challenge will demand a response just as the initial attack did. However, the challenge will not be as serious as the first. If the United States destroys Iran's nuclear program, it will have destroyed one of the regime's premier sources of prestige. There will be no equivalent target available for the second strike, and the U.S. response will not seek one out. Thus, Iran will have an opportunity to de-escalate the conflict slightly by responding with smaller pinprick attacks rather than continued large attacks. Either response will provoke a proportional U.S. retaliation, so *ceteris paribus* the Iranians would prefer to be subjected to a smaller retaliation and therefore choose a smaller response. The regime may feel that its initial response, if it was bloody, brutal, and bold enough, answered any who questioned the regime's legitimacy. If it indeed feels this way, its response will be directed more towards American decision makers and public than towards the Iranian public. Given high American casualty sensitivity, a response calibrated to these audiences would require less force.

However, regardless of the magnitude of the Iranian response, it will likely provoke an American reply, which will provoke an Iranian reply, ad infinitum. The need to respond to an individual attack will weigh on the minds of policymakers against the increasingly apparent cycle of violence. The unpleasantness of sustained conflict will thus be accompanied by a severe risk of miscalculation, miscommunication, and escalation. Neither country's interests would be served by a war. The United States has a strategic interest in avoiding new Middle Eastern entanglements as it seeks to restore its own economy, its military, and its international reputation. We cannot say with certainty that the Iranian leadership considers war the worst possible outcome. Iran's current leadership was forged in the fires of the Iran-Iraq War, which saw serious dissent activity but also allowed the revolutionary regime to consolidate its position with crackdowns on political rivals. Growing economic strains and losses of legitimacy following the 2009 election have put the regime in a difficult position. A war would be immensely destructive for Iran and for its already fading foreign influence, and it could be the regime's death sentence, but if it is desperate enough it could start a war and hope to ride through it on a wave of nationalism. An opaque future is better than no future at all.

In any violent confrontation, determinations of advantage and disadvantage, victory and defeat, success and failure, and even war and peace will be extremely difficult. The United States possesses an immense conventional advantage against Iran, but Iran's ability to choose from a range of responses at varying levels of attribution, tempo, and destructiveness could keep it in the fight indefinitely. Iran's military forces are no doubt trained to rapidly disperse in the event of hostilities. The United

States would then be forced to rely on its intelligence apparatus to identify targets; military dispersion in urban areas would necessitate a rapid and effective intelligence cycle to find targets and kill them with minimal harm to civilians.[5] In a lower-level conflict, Iran could periodically take pressure off of itself by using its proxies against America or its allies. This would make things especially difficult for Washington. Iran's goading would be obvious, but evidence might not be incriminating enough for American policymakers to feel comfortable facing the international scrutiny they'd provoke by retaliating. In a brief, intense conflict, America's advantage against Iran is obvious; in a long, low-intensity conflict, the outcome becomes less certain. Iran would be devastated, but America may find itself forced into an expensive second phase of its efforts to secure itself against terrorist acts.

NOTES

1. Iran might not perceive it this way, as perceptions that the Islamic Republic is beset by "enemy agents" and the like, if generally held, might make the mullahs think that they are the apprentices of dimmer switch warfare, and the Americans are the masters. In reality, the only plausible low-attribution actors for the United States are the various extremist groups in Iran. However, a low-attribution response will not be appealing if there is a public thirst for revenge.
2. For instance, the United States would be condemned for responding to an Iranian terrorist attack with three small air raids: one two days later, one two months later, and one two years later, because international norms dictate that aggressive actions have a close temporal connection with the events that justify them.
3. If Iran seals the Strait of Hormuz with mines and missile strikes, a mass military operation would be required to restore safe navigation.
4. The United States would obviously be in the lead of this response, but affected regional powers would also have strong reasons to join; the growing military capabilities of the region's minor powers would add to the strain on Iran.
5. This intelligence will be quite difficult to gather; the humanitarian criticisms of Israel's intervention in Gaza (Operation Cast Lead), which saw thousands of buildings destroyed, might be repeated against the United States.

SIX

Regional Oil

What will be the impact of a strike on oil markets and the U.S. and global economy? Despite a considerable amount of writing on other issues related to a strike on Iran, including some extremely detailed studies of American and Israeli military options that have been outlined in the previous chapters, there has been less discussion of the economic consequences of a strike. This section outlines a range of economic consequences based on different sets of assumptions about the global economy, the nature of the strike, and possible Iranian responses. Given the precarious state of the global economic recovery since the 2008 financial crisis, it is important to make good judgments about the impact of a military campaign in Iran. Military action has direct costs—munitions, wear and tear, fuel, and so on—but the impact on oil markets is potentially much greater than the cost of a campaign. The Gulf region is the world's most important producer and exporter of petroleum and it depends heavily on one narrow access route—the Strait of Hormuz. Regardless of what happens in the first hours of a military strike, the oil market will almost certainly see a sharp rise in price. What happens after that is dependent on how the war progresses.

The United States faces unique vulnerabilities to changes in oil prices due to its economic structure. Transportation accounts for nearly 10 percent of American GDP, and depends heavily on oil, with over 90 percent of its energy needs sourced from petroleum products. As the mover of people and goods, price increases in transportation impact all other sectors of the economy.[1] A spike in oil prices increases the cost of shipping products and thus the cost of living, resulting in less disposable income. Because there are no immediate alternatives to road transportation, oil is an inelastic commodity: major price increases will not cause major demand decreases. Only in the long run will high oil prices shrink the market enough to produce a significant fall in demand.

But oil spikes are not the same. Sudden spikes in the price of oil occurred in the early 1970s, the late 1970s, and the late 2000s. The impact of these spikes depended on the overall health of the global economy and the flexibility of the oil market. When global demand for oil is relatively high because the major economies of the world are growing, there will be little slack on the supply side and price spikes can be very large. Supply reductions, like that which would be caused by a closure of Hormuz, can quickly turn a tight market into a serious shortage. There are a few ways to reduce the impact of abrupt spikes; the simplest remedy is an increase in production.

The problem is that in the short run worldwide production is near capacity. Only Saudi Arabia has significant extra capacity that could come online quickly. The kingdom has invested heavily in security and redundancy at its oil facilities, including alternative pipeline routes for getting oil to the market. However, if a closure of Hormuz, perhaps amplified by sabotage of alternative routes, keeps Saudi Arabia from playing its role as the world's "supplier in the last resort," consumers would be dealt a heavy blow. This could force the release of oil stockpiles which have been accumulated to meet this contingency, such as the Strategic Petroleum Reserve (SPR), or it could mean allowing the market to raise prices sufficiently to reduce demand—a very painful alternative. If circumstances become truly dire, rationing and other restrictions could be put in place. These are politically unappealing actions for the leaders of consumer countries and would have a direct, negative impact on economic growth and employment.

GULF OIL: IRAN'S ROLE

About 17 million barrels flow through the Strait of Hormuz every day.[2] Should Iran ever block access to the strait, there are some alternate export routes from the Gulf. The East-West Pipeline, which crosses from Abqaiq in eastern Saudi Arabia to the Red Sea port of Yanbu, is the best alternative for transporting Saudi oil without going through the Strait of Hormuz. It has a theoretical capacity of about 5 million barrels per day (bpd).[3] In 2005, the Gulf exported roughly 37 percent of the world's oil.[4]

Before the sanctions began to bite, Iran produced 4.1 million barrels per day, but consumed 36 percent of that at home.[5] It produced 5.5 million bpd immediately prior to the Islamic Revolution, and had plans to expand to nearly 8 million bpd. The oil industry has experienced war damage and decades of neglect; facilities have not been adequately maintained and control of the oil ministry has become a political bargaining chip.[6] Production under the Islamic Republic has been much lower than

Table 6.1. Oil Exports of Gulf Area, 2011

State	Barrels per day	Notes
Bahrain	3,400	Larger refinery sector; limited extraction.[1]
Iran	2,500,000	Prior to sanctions.[2]
Iraq	1,800,000	Some believe there is potential for major expansion.[3]
Kuwait	2,100,000	[4]
Qatar	1,100,000	Also has a massive natural gas industry.[5]
Saudi Arabia	7,300,000	[6]
United Arab Emirates	2,300,000	[7]

[1] Energy Information Agency: Bahrain.
[2] Energy Information Agency: Iran. February 2011.
[3] Energy Information Agency: Iraq.
[4] Energy Information Agency: Kuwait.
[5] Energy Information Agency: Qatar.
[6] Energy Information Agency: Saudi Arabia. See appendix G for a more thorough breakdown of Gulf oil and gas.
[7] Energy Information Agency: United Arab Emirates.

its potential; with the sanctions hitting, it has fallen still further, by about one million barrels per day, and Iran has struggled to find buyers for what it does produce. Consumption at home has continued apace, eating away at Iranian exports—and thus at Iran's hard currency flows.

Oil production is concentrated in the southeast of the country, with many fields near the border with Iraq and in the eastern Gulf. The vast majority of Iranian oil flows through just one shipping terminal—Kharg Island on the southeastern coast.[7]

Oil Prices and Iran's Economy

Like many oil-exporting Middle Eastern states, Iran's annual budget is drawn up based on anticipated oil prices. When prices surpass expectations, this is a windfall—Saudi Arabia, for instance, did not budget for the price increases of the Arab Spring, and thus received a massive surplus.[8] Iran's government is highly dependent on oil revenues for stability, as it has long used those revenues to support subsidies for its population. The recent major reform of the subsidy system did not significantly reduce this dependence, as an estimated 35 percent of the budget goes into the monthly payments that replaced the subsidies.[9] This explains Iran's longstanding hawkishnessness in OPEC negotiations and regular remarks by Iranian leaders that oil prices of $100 or more are natural. With high oil revenues, Iran's solvency becomes much more certain. With low oil revenues, Iran could be forced to choose between keeping the government fully funded and functional and the stability brought by paying the people.

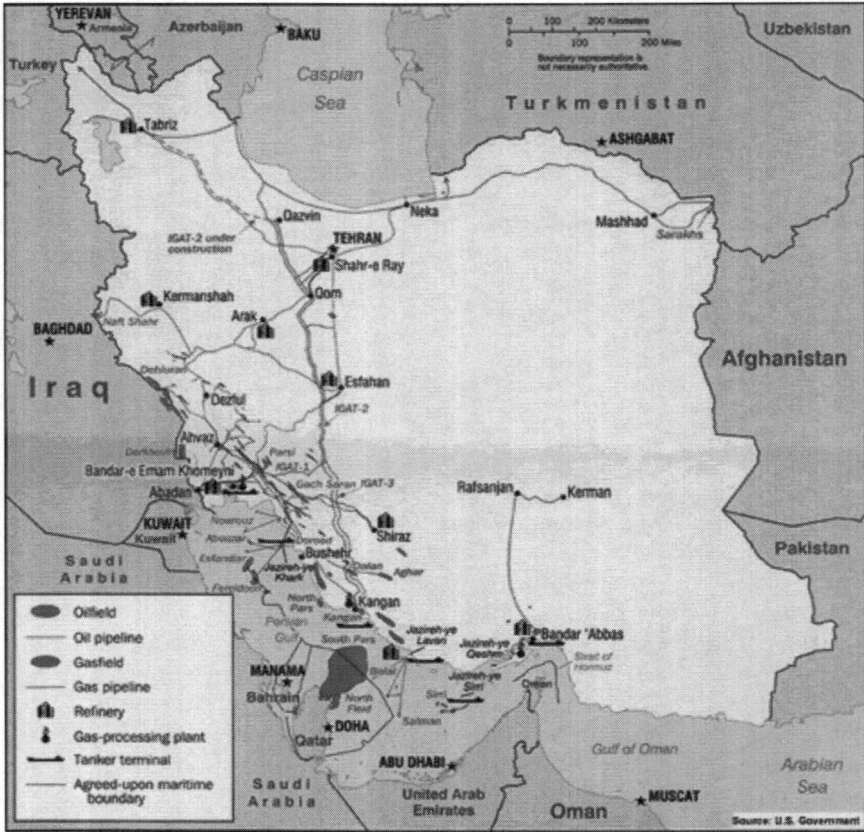

Figure 6.1. Iran's oil and gas fields and pipelines. ***(U.S. Energy Information Administration.)***

Unanticipated drops in oil prices could thus provoke a crisis in Iran. If oil prices returned to mid-2009's low $60s, Iran would be spending 60 percent of its budget on the monthly payments, excluding payments to its industries,[10] and even prices in the low $70s can "expose economic vulnerabilities."[11] Iran can use its hard currency reserves to make up for shortfalls for a time, but the reserves have thinned due to the sanctions of the regime. The implications are obvious—at lower oil prices, Iran becomes less capable in all domains of government action; at critically low prices political upheavals may occur. While oil prices have remained well above the critical levels above, Iran's ability to capitalize on higher prices is not clear, and on top of the problems due to the sanctions, there may be other unsustainability—the Iranian oil sector has been making noise for

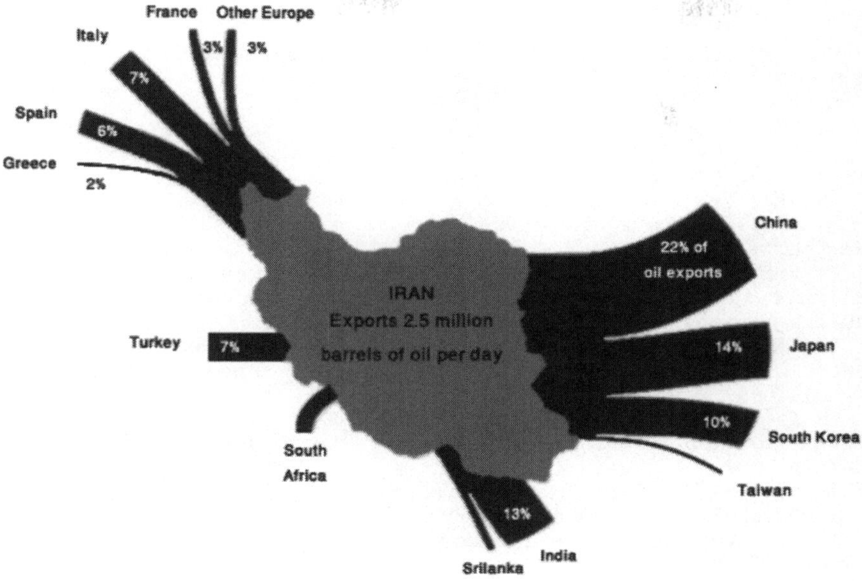

Figure 6.2. Iran's oil exports. ***(Wikimedia.)***

major increases in the share of its revenues that are reinvested in it, and has been partially thwarted.[12]

The United States and the European Union have tightened sanctions on Iran, including major moves against the Iranian oil sector. The European Union agreed to cut off imports of Iranian oil by July 2012, which forced Tehran to find a new outlet for hundreds of thousands of barrels of oil. Washington has been less successful at convincing Asian nations to end imports from Iran, but has seen many cut their imports or demand special accommodations. China previously cut hundreds of thousands of barrels per day, and India has begun paying for its purchases with nonstandard currencies or with other commodities (some of which the Iranians might not really need), and Iran has reportedly begun to sell oil at a $20 per barrel discount.[13] However, the four Asian nations of China, India, South Korea, and Japan are purchasing increasing amounts of oil from Iran, accounting for over half of Iranian oil exports. This backtracking follows a previous reduction in imports by those countries in response to new threatened penalties from the United States and the European Union.[14] There has been serious trouble insuring ships and finalizing transactions, and Iranian shippers have been heavily targeted. The sanctions may have a net impact of cutting Iran's revenue in half.[15]

NOTES

1. More than 70 percent of the value moved by transportation travels by fuel-intensive trucks and aircraft.

2. Energy Information Agency, "Iran Country Analysis Brief," 2010.

3. "Persian Gulf Oil and Gas Exports Fact Sheet," Marcon International.

4. Energy Information Agency, "International Energy Annual 2006," June 2008.

5. Energy Information Agency, "Iran," Feb. 2011.

6. The growing role of the IRGC in Iranian oil, culminating with the recent assignment of an IRGC commander as oil minister, has paralleled the its increasing role in Iran's economy.

7. Energy Information Agency, "Iran," Feb. 2011. There are similar choke points in the oil streams of Iran's neighbors—see appendix G for a few examples identified by the U.S. government.

8. They spent the surplus quickly—experts estimated that if they were to sustain the same level of spending every year, their 2030 breakeven price would be more than $300/barrel.

9. Patrick Clawson, "Iran Makes Itself More Vulnerable to Outside Pressure," Washington Institute Policy Watch #1838, www.washingtoninstitute.org/templateC05.php?CID=3391.

10. Clawson, "Iran Makes Itself More Vulnerable."

11. Simon Henderson, "OPEC Deliberates: A Saudi Opportunity."

12. Calls were made for near 100 percent increases in some state company budgets, and for $50 billion in investment in upstream processing facilities; the budget appears to have covered about 20 percent of the latter figure, and instead focused on providing substantial funding to assure the settlement of oil contracts. See reports on Shana.ir, a.k.a. the Petroenergy Information Network.

13. Peg Mackey, "Insight: Catch Me If You Can—Oil Sanctions against Iran," Reuters, March 6, 2012, www.reuters.com/article/2012/03/06/us-iran-oil-sanctions-idUSTRE8250UG20120306.

14. Ilan Berman, "Iran's Asian Lifeline," *Wall Street Journal*, Aug. 16, 2012, http://online.wsj.com/article/SB10000872396390443324404577592851646756614.html.

15. Gary Sick, interviewed by Bernard Gwertzman, "Crisis-Managing U.S.-Iran Relations," Council on Foreign Relations, March 6, 2012, www.cfr.org/iran/crisis-managing-us-iran-relations/p27558.

SEVEN

Oil and War

MILITARY CONFLICT AND GLOBAL OIL PRICES

Estimates of the impact of the various military options against Iran on the oil market will depend on two sets of assumptions: first, about the nature of the attack and the extent to which the perpetrators are backed by an international consensus in favor of an attack, or whether they are acting unilaterally; second, about the prevailing conditions in the oil market. Any disruption of Gulf supplies would drive prices higher, with obvious negative consequences for the U.S. and the global economy.

Recent History

However, the history of oil disruption in the Gulf suggests a more mixed picture. A number of significant oil supply and demand shocks have occurred since 1970 that reveal patterns in their economic impact. Following the outbreak of the Yom Kippur War in October 1973, the Arab oil producers announced an embargo for the United States and the Netherlands for their support of Israel. The embargo reduced oil production by 30 percent and increased prices by 30 percent.[1] These measures lasted until Israeli troops withdrew back across the Suez Canal in March 1974. As oil prices rose, fuel prices increased by over 40 percent.[2] The American economy experienced a recession during this period, with GDP growth decreasing by 8 percent the next year.[3] Inflation increased by over 11 percent from 1974 to 1975[4] and remained persistently high until the mid-1980s. The shock led to the expansion of new sources of oil and alternative energy technologies, and was the impetus for the creation of the Strategic Petroleum Reserve.[5]

A second disruption in Gulf oil supplies occurred in the late 1970s around the overthrow of the shah of Iran. The Islamic Revolution and

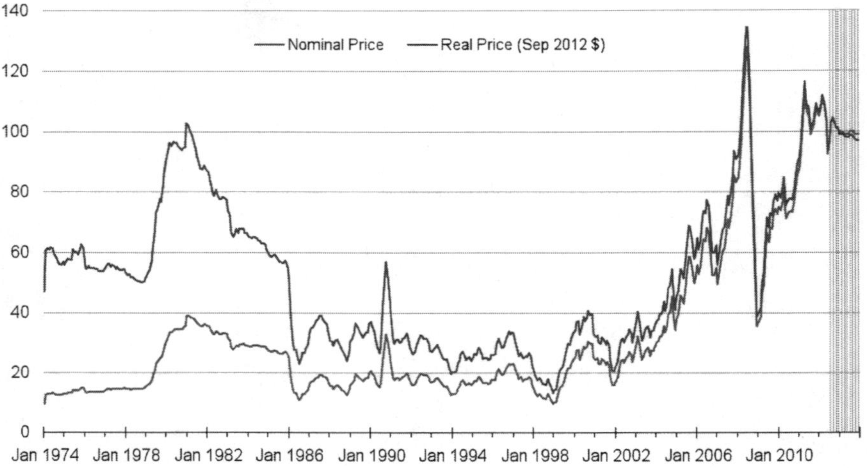

Figure 7.1. Monthly imported crude oil price. ***(U.S. Energy Information Administration.)***

associated labor strikes severely reduced Iran's production for several months, and afterwards exports remained lower due to the Revolution's negative effects on industry.[6] The price of oil increased by 80 percent. In an attempt to mitigate these increases, Saudi Arabia and other OPEC producers increased production,[7] but higher oil prices lasted until early 1983. U.S. core inflation increased,[8] and real GDP declined 2 percent in 1979 and another 3 percent in 1980.[9] This shock further encouraged the development of alternative sources of oil, including the Alaskan oil fields, and saw the elimination of price controls.[10] Japanese automakers began to have more success in the American market, as they were able to produce cheaper, more fuel-efficient cars than their American competitors.

The 1980–1988 Iran-Iraq War had a very different impact. The conflict between two major oil producers, with many facilities near the front lines, saw a significant decline in oil production. Despite this, oil prices decreased, and American GDP increased by an average of 3.4 percent each year during the decade.[11] This was possible because new supplies of oil were coming online in Canada, the North Sea, Mexico, and Nigeria,[12] while Saudi Arabia kept production high to starve Iran's war machine of oil revenues. Meanwhile, demand for oil decreased due to greater fuel economy for passenger cars and increased electricity production from non-petroleum sources.[13] The decrease in demand outweighed the decrease in supply, creating a glut and driving down prices.

Similarly, the oil shocks of the 1990–1991 Gulf Crisis and War had little lasting effect. Though rumors of war saw prices double, this only lasted for several months. Price hikes were mitigated by significant Saudi production increases and the release of 17 million barrels from the Strategic Petroleum Reserve. This replaced some of the lost Iraqi production and drove down prices. The long-term effect on the cost of oil was minimal.[14]

The Asian financial crisis of 1997 was a demand shock. Past high levels of growth in the region and attendant increases in demand made producers put new sources of oil online to meet future needs. However, growth slowed and demand fell. As a result, there was too much oil on the market, depressing prices. The glut reduced growth in exporting countries like Russia and helped growth in importing countries like the United States.

The 2000s saw an extended price increase, its collapse, and then a second rise. By July 2008, the cost of a barrel of crude had risen from $25 to over $147. The increase was driven by demand from emerging market countries, a shrinking supply of oil, speculation, and inflation. The world financial crisis made high prices unsustainable, and oil had fallen to $32/barrel by December 2008.[15] Oil prices have since increased due to decreased production and new shocks, including the uprisings in the Arab world.

The history of oil shocks thus indicates that there is a strong relationship between increases in oil prices and decreases in GDP growth, and that the main factor keeping oil prices down is excess capacity. As a result, their impact is blunted during an oil glut. Furthermore, radical changes in oil prices tend to change the composition of industries and drive the development of new technologies and new sources of energy.

The irony of this history would suggest that an optimal time to engage in military activity against the Iranians would be when oil prices are low, perhaps $20–$40 a barrel. This is only likely to happen in the event of a global depression. Prices have fluctuated dramatically over the past twenty years and could do so again. Low oil prices would likely make Iran more vulnerable since demand for their product would already be low and other producers would likely fill any gap in Iran's production given that they would probably not be producing at capacity.

Compounding the irony, low oil prices are likely to reduce the urgency of attacking. Because of the serious strains that Iran has experienced during periods of low prices, it becomes very pliant when its oil revenues cannot cover the government's needs. Iran would likely offer, or pretend to offer, concessions in exchange for sanction relief. This would create a political climate extremely unfavorable to military action; as discussed elsewhere, the climate at the time of action is key to ensuring that tactical successes create genuine strategic changes.[16]

Impact of a Military Strike on Iran

Nevertheless, it is clear that any military strike against Iran's nuclear facilities will cause panic in the world's financial and oil markets. It is important to distinguish between the direct effects that military strikes might have on the production and supply of oil from the Gulf as distinct from the indirect or more psychological effects on financial markets (the so-called oil risk premium).

Much of the direct impact will depend upon the nature of the attack. If it is limited to major nuclear facilities, it is unlikely that there would be any physical impact upon Iran's production or export capacity, given that Iran's major oil fields and distribution systems, including the Kharg Island shipping terminal, are not immediately adjacent to nuclear facilities. The exception would be the new Bushehr light water reactor, which is just 42 miles away from Kharg Island.[17] An attack on Bushehr that ruptured the core and spread radiation could affect Kharg Island and therefore export capacity. Radioactivity could also spread across the Gulf to other major exporters like Kuwait, Iraq, Saudi Arabia, the UAE, and Qatar.[18] However, it is assumed that if this is likely, Bushehr's core will not be targeted by either Israel or the United States.

Of course, an effective strike on Iran would have to include attacks on Iran's air defense and maritime assets. Military actions around Iranian ports and coastal defense sites could reduce shippers' willingness to operate in the Gulf. Insurance rates will rise and tankers will be reluctant to move as long as combat continues.

IMPACT OF AN ATTACK ON IRANIAN OIL FACILITIES

In theory any strike against Iran could target its extensive oil facilities. Given the capabilities of United States, and to a lesser extent Israeli, airpower, serious damage could be inflicted very quickly on the production and distribution system of the Iranian oil network. This option is not likely to be chosen under any ordinary circumstances—it would be extraordinarily provocative and would likely create a backlash among other oil-consuming countries—particularly in India, China, and Japan. Nevertheless, it cannot be ruled out that under some extreme circumstances, such as an aggressive Iranian attack on its neighbors' oil facilities, there would be an attack.

In any attack on Iran's nuclear program, hitting Iran's oil facilities would not be a high priority. The attacker would have several key tasks to accomplish in a short time frame with limited (very limited in the case of Israel) resources; hitting oil stations would divert those resources. The nuclear program is a large and dispersed target set, while Iran's retaliatory apparatus is larger and more dispersed. These two target sets and the air defenses that protect them would be getting virtually all of the attacker's attention, as destroying the former would be the purpose of the attack and destroying the latter would limit threats in the Strait of Hormuz.

Nevertheless, attacking Iran's oil facilities could be a part of a longer campaign. Because Iran's oil production is so central to its economy, taking it offline for an extended period would have severe economic, political, and societal consequences. Thus, the attackers might consider using anti-oil strikes as a punishment for extreme Iranian actions such as major terrorist attacks on the United States and Israel.

Tehran could also stop oil exports of its own accord in an effort to punish its opponents. It has three production options in case of a limited strike. It can continue exporting oil at the same rate, reduce exportation, or stop it entirely. Continuing current levels of production and export would be intended to keep the Iranian economy on an even keel, since about half of Iranian state revenue comes from the oil industry.[19] Most importantly, currency reserve loss rates would be unchanged, providing insurance against future disruptions in trade.[20] The drawback of keeping production steady is that it would fail to punish the United States or Israel for the attack.

Cutting off exports would be extremely risky. The increase in global prices would hurt "enemy" economies, pressuring them to end their campaign, especially if there should be significant opposition to the campaign in Israel or the United States. There are two major drawbacks for Iran under these circumstances. First, if Saudi Arabia has enough excess capacity, it may be able to increase its production so that global production remains essentially the same. Market tightening would be the primary cause of a price increase that would follow. The second drawback is that cutting off oil would cause severe damage to the Iranian economy. Most of Iran's $64 billion in annual oil export revenues goes toward central government expenses for jobs for bureaucrats and payments to the poor. Without oil money, a significant portion of the population would be out of work and wages would collapse. Tehran would be forced to use its currency reserves to import goods that it previously paid for with oil revenues. The political consequences for the regime would be dangerous.

Iran's middle path is to merely reduce exports rather than cutting them off entirely. This allows Iran to inflict some punishment while maintaining some economic activity. There are two risks. First, the Saudis could negate the reduction with their excess capacity, and it would be easier to do if Iran does not totally cut off production. Second, anything less than a full shutdown may fail to inflict sufficient pain and signal that Iran is not fully committed to the tool of economic coercion. This will reduce the credibility of Iranian threats.

Due to the potential domestic impact and the uncertain efficacy of manipulating production, Iran will likely have no choice but to continue production at previous levels. However, if Iran successfully blocked or negated Saudi Arabia's excess capacity, reducing production may become more effective.

IRAN'S OPTIONS AGAINST REGIONAL OIL

Attacks on the Gulf region's oil production are one of Iran's most aggressive retaliatory options. The world's oil markets are very tight, with IEA-estimated demand above production and Saudi excess production capacity partly soaked up by production losses in Libya, Sudan, and Syria. Further reductions in global daily oil production could have serious consequences for the global economy.

The region's concentrated oil resources give Iran a wealth of potential targets. Massive facilities like the petroleum stabilization plant at Abqaiq, Saudi Arabia, are especially likely to be targeted, as they are more vital, but their large area requires a large force to effectively disable. Smaller resources like refineries and wells are highly redundant—the destruction of one would have little impact.[21] However, Iran has several ways of attacking. The IRGC can infiltrate teams into neighboring states, and its Quds Force can train and equip local "resistance" groups. Individual agents or sympathizers can commit small acts of sabotage. Oman and the United Arab Emirates may become targets or see infiltration through their lands, as the UAE has hundreds of thousands of Iranian residents and hundreds of boats travel from Iran to Oman every day.

Iran's missile forces can bombard the larger targets in the region—cities and the largest oil centers—and Iran's naval forces can mine the Strait of Hormuz and attack oil tankers. Vulnerabilities extend beyond the Gulf. Azerbaijan and Iraqi Kurdistan both have good relations with Israel, and could plausibly offer some accommodation to Israeli attackers. Even if they don't, Iran might elect to target them as Israeli proxies.

Because Iran has so many possible avenues of attack, it would be unrealistic to predict the impact of an Iranian attack on its neighbors' oil. It would be much more useful to show the possible impacts of the discrete elements that could be part of the Iranian response.[22]

Action in the Strait of Hormuz

At least some Iranian military action in Hormuz is all but inevitable. As with news of the attack on Iran, incidents in Hormuz will cause rapid and potentially disproportional hikes in oil and drops in other markets, as investors will be unsure whether the events are isolated or the beginning of a long campaign.

Iran might begin sustained, small-scale harassment, firing a few missiles every few days or laying small numbers of naval mines—in other words, it might reuse the tactics of the Tanker War. This kind of action drives up shipping insurance rates, but the increases will likely have a minimal impact on price when distributed across a million-barrel cargo. The loss of individual tankers is not a serious risk—the strait is much too big to be physically blocked by a sunken ship, and the global tanker fleet is enormous. The real impact (independent of speculation's impact) would be no more than a few dollars more per barrel, or a few cents more for a gallon of gasoline.

Larger-scale harassment would be difficult to maintain, as it would deplete Iran's arsenal of antiship missiles (a depletion that might be accelerated by U.S. retaliatory strikes on missile launchers). Tankers can physically survive the damage from as many as ten antiship missiles,[23] requiring a rate of launches that would plow through Iran's arsenal quite quickly, but damage to critical areas by even one missile can make a ship useless.[24] Iran probably wouldn't need ten missiles to put a tanker out of service, but it would be unable to sustain a missile campaign indefinitely. Each missile launch would risk the launcher's detection and destruction; assuming regional militaries have learned the lessons of the failed Scud-hunting campaigns of the Gulf War, attrition might grow. Depending on Iran's selection of launch rate and launch areas, its missile campaign could last anywhere from nine to seventy-two days.[25] A missile campaign wouldn't be devastating, but Tehran would be squarely in the driver's seat.

Iran's most aggressive option against Hormuz is an attempt to make it so unsafe that ships cannot pass. This could only be sustained with naval mines. Iran has an arsenal of thousands of mines, possibly including

Figure 7.2. Satellite image of Iranian submarines in Bandar Abbas port. On the left are four midget submarines (anchored in pairs). On the right is a *Kilo*-class submarine, a Russian import. *(Produced with Google Earth.)*

advanced models received from Russia as part of the deal for Iran's *Kilo*-class submarines. These submarines are Iran's most effective minelaying tool, as its large dedicated minelayers are very easy targets. The submarines could be assisted in their task by Iran's many naval small boats and by vessels disguised as civilian craft. Most experts do not believe Iran is capable of an extended closure, but Iranian minelaying would provoke a severe panic in world markets. Real impact would begin to occur within days of any Iranian blockade. The most worrisome outcomes follow prolonged closure. One estimate suggested that the strait could be rendered unsafe for as long as 112 days,[26] which would have extreme consequences. However, this estimate was a worst-case scenario, and bringing it into being would make Iran a leper to the international community while guaranteeing severe retaliation.

Attacking Arab Oil Facilities

Iran could use its commandos, proxies, sympathizers, and missiles to attack the refineries, terminals, wellheads, and plants of regional oil companies. Price spikes would result when news of this tactic broke.[27] The impact would not be as serious for small attacks, as heavy redundancy would prevent significant losses.[28] The only added expenses would be for repairs.

A major campaign against the oil facilities might do more damage, but it would need a large amount of resources—or luck—to actually cause a serious loss in production. If this loss occurs, it could reduce global supply by millions of barrels per day for weeks or months, as relatively nonredundant facilities like the stabilization plant at Abqaiq use unique parts that cannot be readily cannibalized from other plants.[29]

Oil production is very vulnerable—pipelines are too long to effectively secure, and other facilities require large numbers of laborers, allowing for easy infiltration of saboteurs. However, in major production states like those around the Gulf, oil facilities are built in large numbers. The destruction of a few refineries or pipeline segments would have little or no impact on the successful exportation of oil. The Saudis have prepositioned pipeline repair equipment around the country, and claim that they can restore any section of pipeline within thirty-six hours of trouble. Each refinery has internal redundancies—if a key element like a distillation tower is destroyed, operators can redirect flows within the facility to continue operations—and refineries are quite numerous, with seven in Saudi Arabia and many more around the world. (Because oil can be easily shipped in crude form and refined closer to the consumer, Middle Eastern countries have refining capacities that are very limited in comparison to their production. For example, oil-poor Japan and South Korea have a refining capacity greater than the entire Middle East.)

Iran's ability to use conventional means against oil is thus uncertain at best. Iran's air force is small and outdated; it would quickly fall against its neighbors' relatively advanced air defenses. Iran's missiles are too inaccurate to reliably hit the region's handful of key chokepoints.[30] Iran's special forces and proxies could probably mount a surprisingly effective campaign, but they would have difficulty using their limited firepower to destroy large industrial targets.

Mobilizing the Saudi Shia Population

Iran may be able to disrupt Saudi excess capacity. Saudi Arabia's Eastern Province, home to the lion's share of its oil resources, has a very large Shiite population. Because of their religious ties to Shiite Iran and their second-class status in Sunni Saudi Arabia, there are longstanding concerns that the kingdom's Shia might resist the Al Saud in response to an attack on Iran. Research suggests that they do not currently favor violent resistance on Iran's behalf, even in the event of conflict, and that only minor sabotage is likely.[31] Indeed, the Saudi Shia see themselves as likely to be the victims, rather than the perpetrators, of extremist violence.[32] There were attempts to instigate an Arab Spring movement among the Saudi Shia, but these were tamped down so quickly by the authorities that one must doubt it had widespread and enthusiastic support. The violence experienced by Shia in Iraq during the civil war after the U.S. invasion, in Iran after the 2009 election, and in Bahrain during the Arab Spring protests received a similarly quiet response. Either the Saudi Shia realize that public action will only invite a crackdown, or the Saudi security apparatus is very effective at deterring and breaking up dissent networks; both may be the case. This may be gradually changing—the arrest and injury of the fiery cleric Nimr al Nimr led to unrest—and one must wonder whether Iran might be able to stir up similar unrest through false flag outrages. However, despite substantive dissatisfaction with their treatment by the Al Saud, the Saudi Shia will be difficult to rouse.

Other avenues of resistance in the wake of an attack might still be open to the Saudi Shia. A sympathy strike by oil workers is certainly possible. Strikes require organization and communication, both of which the royal authorities can target, but they do not intrinsically require mass protests. Simply by staying home, the Saudi Shia might be able to undermine the oil industry. Again, though, their willingness to engage in such actions, especially on behalf of Iran, is doubtful. There are Iran-aligned opposition groups in their ranks, but they are not the largest or most influential Shia faction, as few Shia choose to abandon respected ayatollahs like Ali al-Sistani for Ali Khamenei and his second-class religious credentials, and more local Shia leaders like Hassan al-Saffar offer a clearer and more viable form of opposition to anti-Shia excesses in Saudi

Arabia than the Supreme Leader. Shia-Iranian collusion is thus not presently a serious risk.

Use of Weapons of Mass Destruction

Iran's leadership might also consider using weapons of mass destruction against neighbors' oil. Iran is not known to possess chemical weapons, and was a victim of chemical warfare during the Iran-Iraq War, creating much popular revulsion with them. Declassified intelligence estimates suggest Iran does pursue "dual-use" chemical warfare technologies that give it a weaponization capability.[33] However, reports do not specify whether these were common industrial technologies that Iran would have reason to acquire or less common technologies whose development would be suspicious.[34] Nevertheless, in theory, Iran could attempt to use chemical weapons against oil facilities. Effective deployment of chemical weapons in a highly populated oil town or a facility with many employees could cause mass casualties and strain local infrastructure. However, most chemical weapons disperse or decompose so rapidly in open air that they do not remain deadly for more than a few hours or days, meaning they would be ineffective for denying use of oil-producing areas for more than a brief period.[35] The use of chemical weapons would also be extremely inflammatory and could invite a strong American response, possibly with weapons of mass destruction.

While nobody currently suspects that Iran has nuclear weapons, it openly admits to the possession of a range of radioactive materials. Iran could use some of these materials to produce a dirty bomb and then use this against a key oil facility, again with the aim of area denial rather than physical destruction. However, dirty bombs may not be very effective weapons—the level of contamination they produce is typically fairly small and dangerous only in the long term. Even the mass radiation releases of the Chernobyl disaster resulted in only thirty-one immediate deaths, and many of the thousands more that will be killed by it are still alive two and a half decades later.[36]

A dirty bomb has never been detonated, so there is no solid data on the sort of panic that they would cause—the "fear factor" is its most dangerous feature. As the dirty bomb worries in the United States several years ago showed, the hype has become so thorough that many experts on radiological bombs begin their discussions by carefully explaining that the detonation of a dirty bomb does not result in a massive Hiroshima-like explosion. Public misunderstanding of the device's danger coupled with general fears of the effects of radiation and cultural peculiarities could lead to massive, unpredictable panics in affected states.

Iraq and Azerbaijan

It is not only Gulf oil that would be directly affected in the event of U.S.-Iranian hostilities. Perceived Israeli allies to the north and west might also see attacks. Iraqi Kurdistan produces limited quantities of oil that it exports via Turkey. Kirkuk (not in Kurdistan) is more important to production, with a 1.6 million bpd pipeline. More important are the considerable energy assets of Iran's Caspian neighbor, Azerbaijan. Many of its oil and natural gas facilities are offshore in the Caspian Sea, an area where the two states have unresolved claims. There are several major pipelines and oil terminals in Azerbaijan that could be attacked, most notably the Baku-Tbilisi-Ceyhan Pipeline, carrying up to 1 million bpd, and the Sangachal Terminal, with a 1.2 million bpd capacity. (Each of these facilities was listed as a "critical foreign dependency" in American internal documents betrayed to Wikileaks, as were many hydrocarbon facilities in the greater Gulf.) A demonstration of local vulnerabilities could challenge other pipeline projects in the area, with geopolitical consequences that would reverberate through Eurasia.

NOTES

1. See appendix C.
2. CBC News, "In Depth: Oil."
3. See appendix E.
4. See appendix F.
5. Energy Information Agency, "25th Anniversary of the 1973 Oil Embargo," 2000.
6. "Business: Oil Squeeze—TIME."
7. "Business: Oil Squeeze—TIME."
8. See appendix F.
9. See appendix E.
10. Energy Information Agency, "25th Anniversary of the 1973 Oil Embargo," 2000.
11. See appendix E.
12. Energy Information Agency, "25th Anniversary of the 1973 Oil Embargo," 2000.
13. Energy Information Agency, "25th Anniversary of the 1973 Oil Embargo," 2000.
14. See appendix C.
15. See appendix C.
16. In brief, an attack that successfully destroys Iran's nuclear program would still be a failure if the international community is so outraged that Iran feels it can safely resume or even accelerate development. If the international community quietly supports the attack, Iran might decide that its program has only earned it isolation and war, and refrain from resumption.
17. It is, however, upwind in typical conditions.
18. See discussion in Toukan and Cordesman, "Iran, Israel, and the Effects of a Nuclear Conflict in the Middle East," CSIS Burke Chair in Strategy, 2009, and Toukan and Cordesman, "Study on a Possible Israeli Strike on Iran's Nuclear Development Facilities," CSIS Burke Chair in Strategy, 2009. Appendix H lists key facilities in the area that may be affected by a leak.
19. Energy Information Agency, "Iran," Feb. 2011.
20. Energy Information Agency, "Iran," Feb. 2011.

21. Joshua R. Itzkowitz Shifrinson and Miranda Priebe, "A Crude Threat: The Limits of an Iranian Missile Campaign Against Saudi Arabian Oil," *International Security* 36, no. 1 (Summer 2011): 167–201.

22. See appendix I for a scenario-set which informed the discussion in this section.

23. Lieberthal and Blair, "Smooth Sailing: The World's Shipping Lanes Are Safe," *Foreign Affairs*, May/June 2007, www.foreignaffairs.com/articles/62604/dennis-blair-and-kenneth-lieberthal/smooth-sailingthe-worlds-shipping-lanes-are-safe.

24. Charles Dragonette, Glenn Davis, and Randy Young, letter to the editor, *Foreign Affairs* 86, no. 5 (September–October 2007), www.foreignaffairs.com/articles/62840/glenn-davis-charles-dragonette-and-randy-young/dangers-at-sea.

25. Caitlin Talmadge, "Closing Time: Assessing the Iranian Threat to the Strait of Hormuz," *International Security* 33, no. 1 (Summer 2008): 82–117, http://belfercenter.ksg.harvard.edu/publication/18409/closing_time.html.

26. Talmadge, "Closing Time."

27. See appendix H for a list of crucial facilities. If any of these names appears in the headlines in connection with an attack, the market will react especially negatively. However, as we discuss, many of these facilities are not as "critical" as the government analysts identifying them suggest.

28. Joshua R. Shifrinson and Miranda Priebe, "A Crude Threat: The Limits of an Iranian Missle Campaign against Saudi Arabian Oil," *International Security* 36, no. 1 (Summer 2011): 167–201, http://web.mit.edu/polisci/people/gradstudents/papers/shifrinson.priebe.isec_a_00048.pdf.

29. Shifrinson and Priebe, "Crude Threat," 167–201.

30. Shifrinson and Priebe, "Crude Threat," 167–201.

31. Wehrey et al., *Saudi-Iranian Relations Since the Fall of Saddam* (Santa Monica, CA: RAND, 2009), 33.

32. "The Shiite Question in Saudi Arabia," Crisis Group Middle East Report No. 45, Sept. 2005.

33. Deputy Director of National Intelligence, "Unclassified Report to Congress on the Acquisition of Technology Relating to Weapons of Mass Destruction and Advanced Conventional Munitions."

34. The Chemical Weapons Convention makes a distinction between schedule I, II, and III chemicals. Schedule I chemicals are only useful as weapons and have no legitimate use. Schedule III chemicals are quite commonly produced in large quantities for commercial purposes. Schedule II chemicals are somewhere in between—they have some purposes other than warfare but are not needed in large quantities. Thus, schedule II and III chemicals could both be classified as dual-use, but the acquisition of large quantities of schedule II chemicals would be worrisome. The unclassified DNI report cited above does not discuss this distinction and thus is not useful for determining Iran's intentions.

35. The exception is the nerve agent VX, which can persist for weeks. VX is not known to be possessed by Iran. The psychoactive incapacitating agent BZ is also persistent, but is much less effective at entering the body and is not very lethal. Blister agents, like the easily manufactured and used mustard gas family, can persist for up to three days. The dispersal of an agent like this in a key area like Abqaiq or one of the oil terminals would have negative economic implications, but it would not permanently disable the facility. The high heat found in the region, especially when not in winter, would accelerate the natural decontamination process. Information on persistence via "Chemical Warfare Agents," GlobalSecurity.org, 2011, www.globalsecurity.org/wmd/intro/chem-table.htm.

36. Scott Stewart, "Dirty Bombs Revisited: Combating the Hype," *Stratfor*, Apr. 22, 2010, www.stratfor.com/weekly/20100421_dirty_bombs_revisited_combating_hype.

EIGHT

Preparing for Oil Disruptions

MITIGATING THE IMPACT OF OIL DISRUPTIONS

In the event that oil flows through the Strait of Hormuz are disrupted, policymakers will have several means available to reduce economic impact, including rerouting oil flows, boosting production, reassuring investors, and reducing demand. Mitigation actions like these can have a major impact on market outcomes. For example, the 1990–1991 Iraqi invasion of Kuwait provoked a major increase in the price of oil as investors feared export disruptions. A range of actions were taken under the auspices of the International Energy Agency, including release of reserves, demand suppression measures, production increases, and fuel substitutions, putting 2.5 million barrels per day on the market;[1] Saudi Arabia boosted production by 2.7 million barrels per day.[2] Meanwhile, the coalition of forces aligned against Iraq quickly racked up impressive victories against Saddam Hussein's forces, and the apocalyptic retaliation he had promised did not materialize. The cumulative effect was dramatic: on January 16, 1991, crude oil at Cushing closed at $32.00 per barrel; on January 17, crude closed at $21.44 per barrel, an incredible 33 percent one-day decline that dwarfed other major daily price shifts and left many bullish speculators with huge losses.

Rerouting Oil Flows

In theory, the simplest way to deal with trouble in the Strait of Hormuz is to bypass the strait altogether. The deserts of Arabia and Mesopotamia are crisscrossed by a huge array of oil pipelines, allowing the redirection of flow to ports far from Iran's reach. These pipelines can even use special chemical additives—drag reduction agents (DRAs)—to boost their flow by 50 percent or more during emergencies. However, some of the best-positioned pipelines for addressing the crisis have been out of commission for decades due to political struggles between host states, and others remain on the drawing board.

Perhaps the best route for addressing the Iranian threat is the Abu Dhabi Crude Oil Pipeline (ADCOP) from Abu Dhabi to the emirate of Fujairah on the Gulf of Oman. Opened in July 2012, ADCOP can accommodate 1.5 million bpd in normal conditions. Also important is the Petroline in Saudi Arabia, connecting the oil facilities at al Jubail on the Gulf to the Red Sea port of Yanbu and carrying up to 5 million bpd. The 1.6 million bpd Iraq-Turkey pipeline could also help relieve pressure on Hormuz.

Given enough warning and political will, inactive pipelines might also be resurrected. The most important of these is the Iraqi Pipeline in Saudi Arabia (IPSA), a 1.65 million bpd route to Yanbu that was shut down during the first Gulf War, seized by the Saudis as reparation, and remains divided; the Saudis have reportedly maintained their portion of the pipeline.[3] Secondary routes include the Trans-Arabian Pipeline (Tapline), a

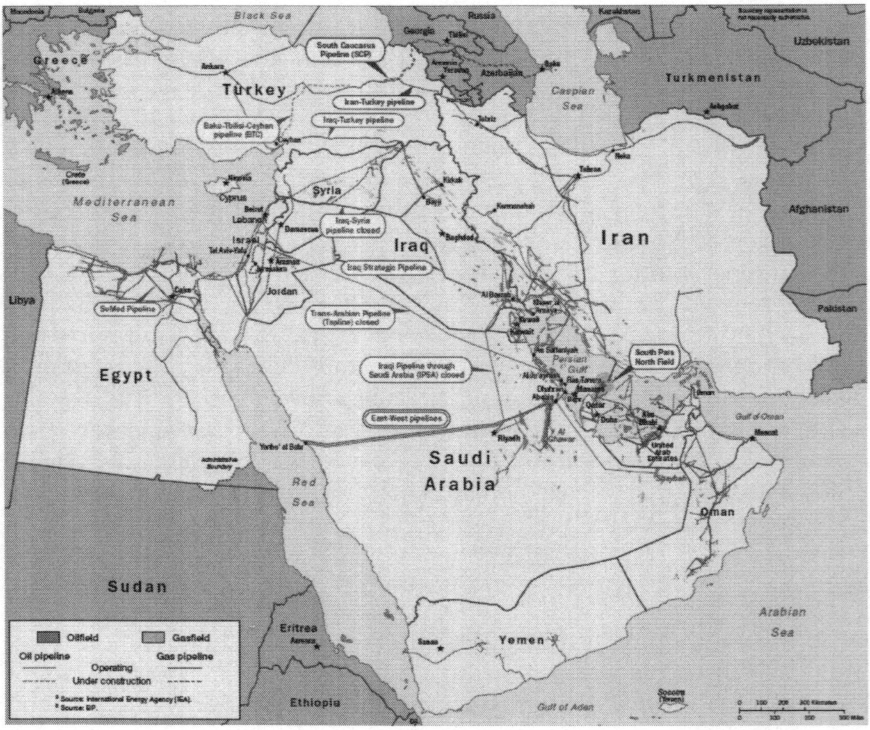

Figure 8.1. Selected Oil and Gas Pipeline Infrastructure in the Middle East. ***(U.S. Energy Information Administration.)***

500,000 bpd line from Saudi Arabia to Lebanon that has long been sealed due to disagreements with Syria, and the Iraq-Syria-Lebanon pipeline, which nominally carried up to 700,000 bpd but tended to actually carry 300,000.[4] There have been talks on reactivating this line while building new line capable of handling 2.7 million bpd, but the unstable situation in Syria will likely keep this from being realized for some time.

There are thus presently 8.1 million bpd of ready-to-use pipeline capacity, plus 2.85 million bpd if pipelines currently closed for physical and political reasons are repaired and reopened. Recall that chemicals can boost the capacity of pipelines—with their use, the line networks perform as follows:

Table 8.1.

	Nominal (thousands of barrels per day)	***With DRAs, conservative estimate (+50%) (thousands of barrels per day)***	***With DRAs, optimistic estimate (+65%) (thousands of barrels per day)***
Active lines (including ADCOP)	8,100	12,150	13,365
Inactive lines	2,850	4,275	4,702
Total	10,950	16,425	18,067

The existing pipeline network thus cannot fully cover the sealing of the Strait of Hormuz, even if drag reduction agents are especially effective and demand is exceptionally low. (During the 2008–2009 recession, daily flow through Hormuz fell to 15.5 million barrels a day, meaning even in the optimistic estimate the world export loss would be equivalent to the world's fourth-largest exporter, the United Arab Emirates, sealing its ports.)

There are some added costs to rerouting. The use of drag reduction agents (DRAs) is not free—they must be stockpiled, added to the oil, and then removed from it at the destination. The value of the changes that must be made to use DRAs is likely in the area of $600 million.[5] The Saudi port of Yanbu to which much of the rerouted oil will be traveling is also further from Asia than ports on the Gulf, adding several days of transit time. This adds a little expense, but it also puts more tankers in transit, resulting in a 10 percent loss of delivery capacity.[6] Since this is functionally a decrease in supply and an increase in demand for tankers, leasing costs will presumably increase and be passed on to consumers.[7]

There is a more fundamental problem with the notion that the world can pipeline its way out of an Iran crisis. While pipelines like ADCOP were obviously built to reduce reliance on the strait, they also have a commercial role and are used to transport oil even when the region is at peace. It is thus deceptive to represent their total flow capacity as the volume of oil they can reroute around Hormuz, because a large portion of that total capacity is already in use. The actual re-routable capacity is at least the volume added by use of DRAs, and is probably a few hundred thousand barrels greater because some of the pipelines (both active and inactive) typically function(ed) below their maximum. Re-routable volume is thus closer to:

Table 8.2.

	With DRAs, conservative estimate (+50%) (thousands of barrels per day)	*With DRAs, optimistic estimate (+65%) (thousands of barrels per day)*
Active lines (including ADCOP)	4,050	5,265
Inactive lines	1,425	1,852
Total	5,475	7,117

Even if we assume that there is a lot of unused capacity in addition to the DRA boosts, it is hardly enough to keep oil flowing uninterrupted indefinitely.

Excess Capacity

Spare oil production capacity can be key for relief of a crisis. Saudi Arabia has long been known for its attempts to keep oil prices relatively low via production boosts during shortages, and in some market conditions other states also have some excess capacity. Though some suggest that the Saudi excess capacity might not be as great or as accessible as is commonly believed,[8] the U.S. government officially estimates that OPEC has 2.3 million barrels per day in spare capacity.[9] Price shifts, new discoveries, and improved extraction methods make global excess highly variable as producers bring new resources online to take advantage of high prices or wait for higher prices to resume pumping. As oil prices peaked just before the 2008–2009 recession, excess capacity fell to about 1 million barrels per day; as the recession hit and Saudi Arabia simultaneously developed new fields, excess capacity grew to 4.65 million barrels per day.[10]

Part of this variance likely stems from the economics of oil extraction. Removing crude oil from the ground, transporting it to processing facilities, processing it, and then transporting it to consumers costs money. Some crudes cost more than others—for instance, it is more expensive to extract oil from tar sands or from fields that are running dry, and crudes that are high in sulfur require processing before they can be transported. Some oil is thus only economical at high market prices, so assertions that spare capacity *drops* when prices go up likely stem from a measure of production capacity that assumes a fixed and relatively high price. Spare capacity thus might not really be higher at lower price levels. However, if a crisis drives up prices enough that producers begin extracting from more expensive fields, the figures for capacity based on a fixed high price are likely reasonable.

Of course, excess capacity is only relevant if it can be brought to market. If travel through Hormuz is unsafe, Gulf excess capacity will become irrelevant. For much of 2012 and 2011 the only excess capacity available was in Gulf states; in 2010 the same was the case, with the exception of 150,000 barrels per day in Libya. The blockage of Hormuz would bottle up almost all the world's extra oil; the United States has begun to seek to lock in purchases from a diverse set of small suppliers outside the confines of the Gulf.[11]

Assurance

Market psychology will play a key role in the crisis. The amount of oil traded on paper exceeds the amount physically traded, creating potential for volatility and panic. In the event of a crisis with Iran, investors must be quickly and convincingly informed that the global oil trade is not in jeopardy. A two-pronged approach of information sharing and physical demonstration will be most effective.

Dissemination of information that is accurate and critical of Iran's capabilities in the strait will be the first prong. There is a widely held belief among laymen that Iran can seal off Hormuz for a long period, a belief that is not shared by the majority of experts. Lay exposure to mainstream expert opinion could mitigate panicked flows of wealth around the market by balancing the influence of investors. In oil markets, investors will be anticipating sustained increases in price due to physical disruption of flows in Hormuz. They will thus buy up futures contracts, fueling price spikes. Smart investors will know that the physical disruption will not be so serious, and will short the market to profit off of its imminent downturn. They will thus flood the market with borrowed futures, tamping down prices. An opposite effect will occur in non-oil sectors. Investors will anticipate a collapse in prices and will thus short the market, flooding it with borrowed shares; smart investors will go long and purchase these shares, reducing the downward pressure on prices.[12] In both cases, the ability of wise investors to mitigate panic depends on their resources. If the vast majority of trades are by fearful investors, the panic could be significant; if smart investors predominate, shifts would more closely approximate the small increase in economic vulnerability that a war entails. It is thus wise to inform investors of the true level of danger on the strait—knowledge is a defensive asset for the attacker and for neutral states.

The second prong of reassurance will be visible actions that show the United States and regional powers are prepared to deal with a crisis. Positioning additional minesweepers (and reminding the world of those already in place) is one such action; increased security in locations vulnerable to Iranian attack (both in the Middle East and elsewhere) is another.

These paths have been tested before. As oil prices fell during the 1980s oil glut and Iran became desperate for revenues to fund its war with Iraq, Tehran began threatening to cut off flow through Hormuz in an apparent bid to induce a panic and drive up oil prices. The Reagan administration launched a global diplomatic initiative to counter this narrative, and price levels remained relatively steady. The key to deadening the blow to the markets is thus an effective communications strategy that is deeply integrated into planned responses.

PREPARATION

While mitigation measures will play a crucial role in the event of a crisis, careful preparation can make them more effective and less urgent. Expanded oil storage and transport will delay the flow's decline, and a range of legal and infrastructural changes in importer countries can make them more able to accommodate disruption.

Expanding Reserves

Petroleum reserves allow consumer states to cope with a disruption in oil markets. The largest single oil reserve is the United States Strategic Petroleum Reserve (SPR). The entire system holds over 727 million barrels of oil, with a maximum output of 4.5 million barrels per day, exceeding daily Iranian oil production and giving the United States the ability to fully replace Iranian oil production for 180 days.[13] Similar reserves, public and private, exist around the world; the member states of the International Energy Agency hold a combined 4.1 billion barrels in reserve. Given the limited capacity of global oil reserves, their release could only temporarily mitigate the impact of the closure of the Gulf—they are a holding measure, not a permanent defense.

The world's strategic reserves currently hold more than four billion barrels, which at IEA-planned withdrawal rates are enough to stave off the impact of a Hormuz closure for thirty days, and mitigate it for months.[14] Expanding them will extend this period, and the mere threat of their release in a crisis will deter all-out speculation. Laws are already in place in the United States to expand the Strategic Petroleum Reserve from its current capacity to one billion barrels, and parallel expansions can presumably occur in other IEA reserve nations.

Part of the process of filling expanded reserves, or a parallel track, could be the prepositioning of oil from producer states via leasing. This will reduce prices for filling the reserves while reassuring producers that they will not be undercut by massive reserve holdings. Negotiations on

Figure 8.2. Shibushi oil stockpile site (Kagoshima Prefecture, Japan). ***(Wikimedia.)***

U.S. oil leasing have occurred in the past, so dusting off these processes could be a positive step.

Pipeline Preparation

As we suggested earlier, the region's pipeline networks are currently unable to fully redirect the flow of oil from the Gulf. There are several steps that should be taken to ensure the effectiveness of the networks that do exist and the availability of enough capacity to make a difference in a crisis.

If Iran attempts to shut the Strait of Hormuz, it may use proxies and agents in the region to attack pipelines and thus magnify the effects of a shutdown. As discussed above, pipeline security is already an extremely high priority for states like Saudi Arabia, and the Saudis accordingly claim that, thanks to prepositioned stocks of spare parts, they can restore flows anywhere in the massive kingdom within thirty-six hours.[15] However, Iran will likely attempt to attack weakest link locations along pipelines, perhaps in less-prepared countries. In 2011, multiple weeks-long interruptions of natural gas flows into Israel and Jordan caused by attacks on pipelines in the Sinai showed the impact that prepared attackers can have on an unprepared target; regional and world powers would be wise to underwrite pipeline security and rapid repair capabilities throughout the region, sharing techniques devised by nations that are at a higher level of readiness.

Preparation can be made for massive DRA use to pipe extra oil out of the Gulf area. Beyond the stockpiling of DRAs in multiple places within multiple facilities (to prevent their becoming a target of sabotage), governments can expand facilities needed to introduce and remove the chemicals before and after piping. The cost of these improvements has been estimated at $600 million,[16] a hefty sum, but one whose expenditure would weaken the Iranian threat to the strait.

Resolution of the tension between Saudi Arabia and Iraq could restore flow through the Iraqi Pipeline in Saudi Arabia, adding 2.72 million barrels per day of potential flow redirection with DRAs, an amount nearly as great as the total daily production of the United Arab Emirates. Improving Saudi-Iraqi relations has been a priority of the U.S. government since the 2003 war, though there has been little success, symbolized by the sustained refusal of the Saudi government to open an embassy in Baghdad. As Iraq plans to expand its oil production, restoration of the IPSA might become more appealing, even if costly repairs on the Iraqi side are necessary.

Saudi Arabia is not the only route out of the Gulf. The several pipelines that flow to the Mediterranean have been shut for decades due to disagreements with Syria. The Iraqi government currently has plans for a several million barrel per day pipeline corridor through Syria. However, if the House of Assad falls and successor regimes are stable and moderate, the Saudis and other Gulf states may also be able to pipe oil directly to the Mediterranean. Tireless optimists might also point out that an Arab-Israeli peace, even if Syria is excluded, would allow a similar arrangement.

Removal of Bottlenecks

Most damage to pipelines can be quickly and easily repaired, so the limited number of pipelines running all the way to ports far from Gulf oil fields is not a serious issue. An Iranian-backed attack would likely only cause a few hours' interruption. Similarly, most facilities in the oil production stream, like wellheads and refineries, exist in great numbers around the region, making destruction of a handful insufficient to shut off production. Even oil terminals can be restored relatively quickly if buoyed terminal systems are kept close by. However, there is a bottleneck in the Saudi system: the stabilization facility at Abqaiq, which removes sulfur from oil to make it safe to ship. Millions of barrels must pass through Abqaiq before being exported. The facility is still very unlikely to be wiped out—with an area three square kilometers, only a nuclear-armed Iran could seriously threaten it. However, reducing dependency on one facility will make Iran's anti-oil deterrent weaker, and will reduce the threat that a nuclear Iran, should one eventually emerge, will pose.

Abqaiq currently operates well below capacity in spite of its central role, and can accommodate Saudi Arabia's near-term production expansion plans. Thus, it may be more fruitful to seek security improvements at Abqaiq than to seek the immediate development of new stabilization facilities. Many of the parts used at Abqaiq are unique, which would slow repair in the event of an attack. These unique parts should thus be stockpiled in great numbers.

Preparing to Reduce Demand

Supply assurance only addresses one aspect of a crisis; demand reduction completes the picture. The IEA's plans for addressing shortages include contributions by all countries; since many cannot boost oil production, substitute fuels, or release reserves, they are obliged to reduce their consumption. The United States' primary contribution to the IEA system is through the Strategic Petroleum Reserve, but it can certainly develop a significant demand reduction capability. The legal framework for tomorrow's contingencies can be put in place by today's legislatures.

The IEA's demand reduction system is likely worthy of emulation, as it is structured to allow policymakers to carefully tailor responses so they are proportional to the crisis. Voluntary measures and public service announcements are sufficient to resolve minor problems. As problems become more severe, less light-handed measures, like dramatic reduction of public transportation fares, come into play. The worst crises need heavy-handed responses.

Example measures include:[17]

A comprehensive use of demand reduction measures could reduce IEA members' consumption by about 3.8 million barrels per day, at a cost of $10 billion.[18] This reduction would be enough to cover loss of supply from any exporter other than Russia or Saudi Arabia.

Middle-term preparations allow more flexibility. Increased fuel economy standards, oil product taxes, and use of electric cars could reduce

Table 8.3. Measures to Reduce Oil Demand

Light-handed				*Heavy-handed*
Voluntary measures	Increased service by public transportation	Public transportation free	Telecommuting encouraged	No driving on every tenth day
PSAs		Designated carpool lanes	Lowered speed Limits	Four-day, ten-hour per day work week
				Fuel rationing

demand, as could more utilization of natural gas, coal, and other non-petroleum energy sources. Increased telecommuting and better insulation in oil-heated homes are other options. In the long term, deeper structural shifts can significantly reduce dependence on foreign oil: increased use of rail transport for both products and people, less air travel, use of unconventional oil, and abandonment of heating oil would all have significant effects.[19]

Readying the Refinery Network

Refineries are becoming increasingly specialized for processing the crude they typically receive, reducing their ability to process new inputs if a crisis shakes up the market.[20] They are also becoming rarer due to restrictions on their construction, though refining capacity has still increased. Most troublingly, they have very little excess refining capacity that would allow them to process more oil after an interruption—in 2010 and the first six months of 2011, 85.6 percent of U.S. refining capacity was in use, leaving an excess that averaged 686,000 barrels per day. This is a significant improvement over 2004 and 2005, which saw spare capacity drop to just 35,000 barrels per day, but it is still a tiny fraction of daily U.S. demand for refined petroleum products. A refining sector with a minimal ability to play catch-up is a liability. In 2012, the situation remained nonideal—two refineries on the U.S. East Coast, and one in the Caribbean, have been shut down, and there are prospects for several more to join them. Washington will face some logistical strains to keep its domestic markets in order, exacerbated by legal restrictions on internal oil shipping (the Jones Act).[21]

Several measures can remedy these problems. Allowing the construction of new refineries is the most straightforward way to boost refining capacity. In addition, tax incentives, subsidies, or regulatory fiat can support the development of a refining sector that carries significant excess capacity and is able to accept a broader range of oils as inputs. Streamlin-

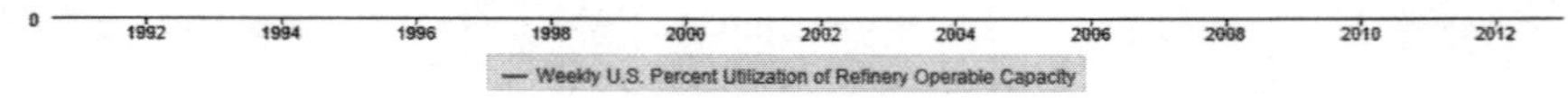

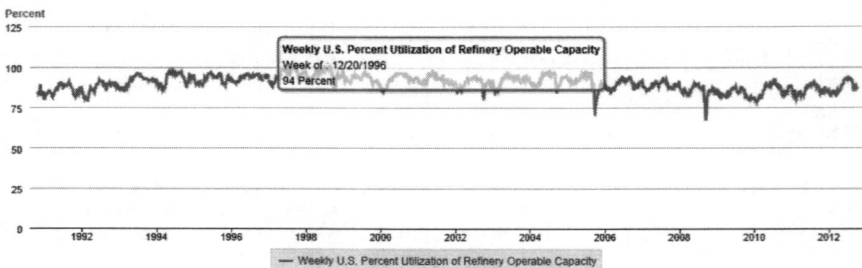

Figure 8.3. Weekly U.S. Percent Utilization of Refinery Operable Capacity. ***(U.S. Energy Information Administration.)***

ing the regulatory process is also important—in the past, the refinery sector has been presented with contradictory instructions by different elements within the federal government, imposing unanticipated compliance costs. In addition, measures can be put in place to temporarily scale back environmental restrictions on refineries and other key elements of the oil sector in the event of a severe shortage—as has been the case in the past with the Jones Act restrictions on oil shipping. Analysts propose that such measures can receive consensus support if the temporary regulatory breaks are balanced by tighter regulation on their termination to ensure that the net environmental impact of the regulatory reform is positive.[22]

"Pre-assuring" Investors

As has already been argued, a crucial element of mitigating a crisis in the Strait of Hormuz is offering investors reassurance—and proof—that traffic through the strait will not be interrupted. The best and most credible way to do this is to build confidence before the crisis even begins. The same information campaigns described earlier of course apply. However, middle-term measures can make future responses more credible and more effective. The U.S. minesweeping force is currently at a low, though the resale of some elements of the force to allied nations means the decline is not as serious as it seems. In past conflicts in the region, nations that pride themselves on "peaceful" foreign policies, such as Japan, have been willing to contribute minesweeper support to even highly contentious conflicts. However, the U.S. military's reputation for relative effectiveness means that American minesweepers will have a greater impact on market stabilization than those from other nations. Thus, expansion of the minesweeper force and basing of additional minesweepers (there are already several at Manama, Bahrain) in the Gulf and Indian Ocean is prudent.

Regional naval powers, like the United States, regularly practice clearing Hormuz and thus have an understanding of their capabilities. However, it is apparent from several of the academic works[23] that have attempted to estimate Iran's ability to interfere in the Gulf that this information has not been effectively distributed to the public, even in a basic form that still protects sensitive information. Even the most careful analysts are forced to rely on estimates of minesweeper effectiveness based on either highly outdated or highly disanalogous cases—common sources of clearance rates are the Second World War (in which both minesweeping technology and mines were not nearly as advanced) or operations off Kuwait (which did not take place during wartime, and in which maps of mine placement were provided to the minesweepers by the Iraqi military). Other estimates[24] ignore both modern mine technology and the ability of the Gulf's currents to redistribute mines after their deployment, yielding misleading figures. The net result is the unavailability of esti-

Figure 8.4. USS *Dextrous* (MCM-13) steams through the waters of the Persian Gulf. *(U.S. Navy, photo by Photograph's Mate 2nd Class Michael Sandberg.)*

mates based on accurate assumptions, which debases both the academic and public discourses on the Iran threat and keeps them from vetting whatever information emerges from the military. It would thus be beneficial for the military to release—or better advertise, if it has released—figures on the effectiveness of its mineclearing forces against modern mines, unless these forces are so ineffective that the information's release would make investors less confident. Demonstrations of the ability of U.S. minesweeping forces to work seamlessly with local forces are also appropriate.

NOTES

1. For a detailed breakdown, see the IEA report by Richard Scott, *The History of the International Energy Agency*, Vol. 2, *Major Policies and Actions of the IEA* (OECD/IEA, 1994), www.iea.org/Textbase/nppdf/free/2-ieahistory.pdf.
2. "Saudi Arabia: Oil and Gas," Asia Trade Hub, www.asiatradehub.com/saudiarabia/oil.asp.
3. Dagobert Brito and Amy Myers Jaffe, "Reducing Vulnerability of the Strait of Hormuz," in *Getting Ready for a Nuclear-Ready Iran*, ed. Sokolski and Clawson (Strategic Studies Institute of the U.S. Army War College, 2005), 219.
4. Zhdannikov, "Russian Firm Signs Deal to Fix Iraq-Syria Pipeline," Reuters, March 26, 2008, http://in.reuters.com/article/2008/03/26/russia-iraq-contract-idINL2673766420080326, and EIA Country Analysis, "Iraq," www.eia.gov/countries/cab.cfm?fips=IZ.
5. Brito and Jaffe, "Reducing Vulnerability," 209–24.
6. Eugene Gholz, "Threats to Oil Flows through the Strait of Hormuz: Implications for American Grand Strategy," LBJ School Hormuz Working Group, March 2007.
7. Since there may be tankers sunk or in jeopardy in the Gulf area during a crisis that necessitates rerouting through Yanbu, decreases in tanker supply will be even greater, and insurance rates might also go up; the cumulative effect might be note-

worthy. However, past tanker shortages have added only about $0.70/bbl, or $0.06/gal (c.f. Gholz).

8. Clifford Krauss, "Saudi Cut in Oil Production Stirs Speculation," is the most credible such source.

9. "The Availability and Price of Petroleum and Petroleum Products Produced in Countries Other Than Iran," Energy Information Agency, Aug. 24, 2012, www.eia.gov/analysis/requests/ndaa/.

10. James L. Williams, "OPEC Excess Capacity," 2011, www.energyeconomist.com/a6257783p/opec/capacity/excesscapacity.html.

11. Timothy Gardner, "U.S. Seeks Oil Supply Cushion as Iran Sanctions Loom," Reuters, Dec. 14, 2011, www.reuters.com/article/2011/12/14/us-usa-oil-diplomacy-idUSTRE7BD22620111214.

12. Note that in all areas, the fearful investors will lose money, and that the deeper their fears are (i.e., the more committed they are to the notions that there will be a reduction in the availability of oil and this reduction will be sustained) the more they will lose.

13. U.S. Department of Energy, "Strategic Petroleum Reserve Inventory 2005." Of course, the 4.5 million barrel drawdown rate is a mere fraction of what passes through Hormuz, so straightforward replacement of the entire Hormuz flow is not possible.

Strauss Center, "About the Strait," August 2008.

14. Brito and Jaffe, "Reducing Vulnerability." Of course, once drawn down, reserves must be refilled, which would create an artificial boost in oil demand and thus, presumably, a parallel increase in price in the months or years required to refill the reserves would result. If the reserves are seriously depleted in the crisis, their ability to balance future disruptions would be reduced, potentially creating a price premium.

15. Shifrinson and Priebe, "A Crude Threat: The Limits of an Iranian Missile Campaign Against Saudi Arabian Oil," *International Security* 36, no. 1 (Summer 2011).

16. Brito and Jaffe, "Reducing Vulnerability," 209–24.

17. See Clawson and Henderson, "Reducing Vulnerability to Middle East Energy Shocks," Washington Institute Policy Focus #49, Nov. 2005, and International Energy Agency, "IEA Response System for Oil Supply Emergencies," 2011.

18. Clawson and Henderson, "Reducing Vulnerability to Middle East Energy Shocks."

19. See Toni Johnson, "Expert Roundup: Reducing U.S. Oil Consumption," Council on Foreign Relations, June 11, 2010, www.cfr.org/energyenvironment/reducing-us-oil-consumption/p22413.

20. Clawson and Henderson, "Reducing Vulnerability to Middle East Energy Shocks."

21. "Potential Impacts of Reductions in Refinery Activity on Northeast Petroleum Product Markets," Energy Information Agency, Feb. 2012, www.eia.gov/analysis/petroleum/nerefining/update/pdf/neprodmkts.pdf.

22. Clawson and Henderson, "Reducing Vulnerability to Middle East Energy Shocks."

23. See, for example, Talmadge or Shifrinson and Priebe.

24. See esp. Gholz, "Threats to Oil Flows through the Strait of Hormuz."

NINE

Economic Consequences

WIDER ECONOMIC FACTORS

Growth Patterns and Oil Markets

Increased demand for energy in Asia has driven a long-term tightening of the global oil market. The era of globalization has seen the influence of emerging markets economies (EME) increase significantly. These economies are growing and industrializing quickly, shifting dynamics of global output and increasing global linkages. These countries, especially China, have dramatically increased their imports of oil and other sources of energy over the last decade in order to power their respective economies.[1] In the long term, rapid EME growth could devour the world's limited excess capacity.

These patterns of growth may be disturbed by the current economic turmoil. The American economy grew at a rate of 1.3 pecent in real terms in the first quarter of 2011 and 0.4 percent in the second quarter, though it has since picked up the pace; the European financial crisis has held back the economies of the EU.[2] Furthermore, slow growth may continue for an extended period, and broaden to the EMEs.[3] Emerging economies are not immune to their own problems; in addition to the danger of decreasing growth due to slowdowns in developed economies, there is a risk of inflation, which could hurt consumer spending in countries like China and reduce the competitiveness of their products overseas, further reducing demand.[4] As a result, growth may be down worldwide for an extended period of time, putting downward pressure on global oil prices.

Nevertheless, there is a long-term trend of increased oil demand from emerging market countries, especially China and India. Near-term weaknesses may mitigate their role, but they will continue to take more and more oil from the global market. If unconventional oil sources cannot be extracted efficiently and in great volume, the effect will be a tightening of the global oil market, an increase in prices, and heightened importance of the security of Gulf oil.[5]

Oil Price Increases and Supply Interruption

Estimates of price increases following a fall in supply suggest that a decrease in production of 1 million barrels per day leads to an 8 percent increase in price, or approximately $8.46 per barrel at current prices.[6] Assuming this relationship is linear (at least for the physical, not psychological, market impact), we can estimate changes based upon different scenarios for production disruptions. Given that Iran produces approximately 4 million barrels per day and oil prices are around $105 per barrel, a decrease in production of 50 percent would lead to a 16 percent increase in price to $121.80 per barrel; a total loss of production would lead to a 32 percent price increase, to approximately $138.60 per barrel. Saudi Arabia's likely maximum production loss is about 5 million barrels per day given the redundancy of its facilities and relative invulnerability of non-redundant facilities like Abqaiq.[7] This loss would cause a price increase of 40%, to $147 per barrel.[8] In combination with a reduction in production from Iran, the total increase in price could be up to 72 percent, which would translate to $180 oil. The nightmare scenario, a stoppage of Hormuz, would take 17 million barrels per day off of the market, leading to $248 oil. This would translate to a nationwide average gas price of roughly $8.30 per gallon. Market psychology could drive prices even higher.

Oil Price Increases and Economic Recovery

The cost of oil spikes to the U.S. economy is very high due to America's large daily oil consumption. Given that recent consumption has averaged around 18.1 million barrels per day, the cutoff of oil from Iran or a similar medium disruption would cost the American economy about $300 million per day. Assuming very optimistically that a conflict with Iran results in two weeks of such supply problems, the back-of-the-envelope cost to the American consumer would be $4.2 billion. A sustained confrontation, with interruptions coming in fits and starts over the next several months, would cost much more.[9]

Several econometric studies have attempted to quantify more precisely the impact that oil prices have on the economy. These studies have concluded that a 10 percent increase in oil prices will result in a 0.4 percent to 0.6 percent decline in U.S. GDP growth.[10] The impact of oil price changes has decreased over time as the role of oil in the economy has decreased.[11] It would therefore be reasonable to assume that the future growth cost of an increase in oil prices would tend more towards 0.4 percent than 0.6 percent. The effect is not linear, however. Decreases in oil prices do not result in significant increases in growth, indicating that the impact occurs in a single direction.[12] After a damaging price hike, a matching decrease in prices will not restore lost growth.

Oil price increases also have an impact on employment. While they create jobs in the energy sector, they also destroy jobs in manufacturing and other energy-intensive industries. An example of that relationship can be seen during the 1979 oil crisis: the Gulf Coast experienced a boom as oil exploration and extraction increased while the rest of the economy faced a recession. Estimates suggest that for every 10 percent increase in the price of oil, 290,000 manufacturing jobs will be lost, while 30,000 oil industry jobs will be created.[13]

Spikes in oil prices can have destabilizing financial effects in seemingly unrelated sectors. Many oil-producing states have "shallow" economies with little ability to absorb new wealth in vast amounts. Oil spikes thus force sovereign wealth fund managers to invest their windfalls abroad, flooding markets, driving up prices, and potentially creating bubbles—as was the case, it has been suggested, with the 2008–2009 housing bubble. Thus, oil disruptions can have a serious negative impact on every sector.

Threats to the Dollar

If key economic powers like China were strongly opposed to a U.S. intervention in Iran, could they retaliate by ending the dollar's role as the global reserve currency? Some have suggested an analogy to the 1956 Suez Crisis, when the United States, furious with Britain and France for not informing the Eisenhower administration of their plans, pulled the

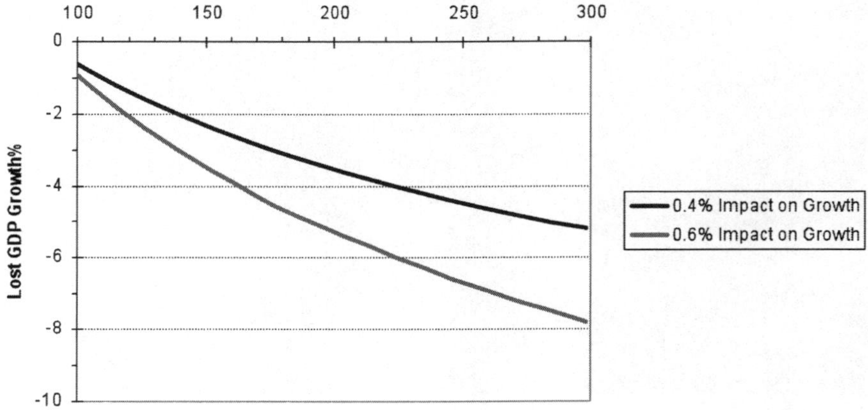

Figure 9.1. Increases in oil prices vs. GDP growth. ***(Courtesy of the authors.)***

rug from under the British pound and forced British prime minister Anthony Eden to stop military operations.[14] History aside, an increase in the price of oil, such as one due to an oil shock, would increase the American trade deficit due to the greater value of imported oil. This would cause the dollar to depreciate, since dollars must be exported to cover the cost of oil. There would in theory be both political and economic reasons to abandon the dollar in favor of another currency.

The modern world is not totally happy with the dollar's status as a de facto global currency, and with the significant influence that the increasingly dysfunctional American government has on global finance. The Chinese government has expressed concern about the depreciation of the dollar and the impact upon its dollar-denominated holdings. The Gulf Arab countries are also worried, as the dollar's central role in oil transactions gives them extraordinary exposure to American exchange rate fluctuations. If China, the Gulf States, and other countries reached the limits of their tolerance, could they move away from the dollar? If they do, the consequences could be dire. Reduced demand for the dollar would cause further depreciation. Reduced demand for American debt would increase the interest rate at which the United States must pay to borrow money.

Figure 9.2. Smoke rises from oil tanks beside the Suez Canal hit during the initial Anglo-French assault on Port Said, 5 November 1956. ***(Imperial War Museums, London.)***

Though the United States may appear vulnerable to Suez-like measures following a unilateral attack on Iran, the situation of the United States, the role of the dollar, and the state of the global economy are not similar. One key difference is the nature of the exchange rate regimes. The dollar, like most currencies in the post–Bretton Woods era, floats freely, with its value set by the foreign exchange market. Even in periods of volatility, the Federal Reserve has intervened very little in its price. The United States is thus less vulnerable to a speculative attack on the dollar, as the Federal Reserve has not staked a position that it would be willing to defend. In contrast, the British pound of 1956 had been given a hard peg of $2.80 per £1. The British Treasury maintained a reserve of $5 billion to defend the peg against speculative attacks. To be effective, this reserve had to be maintained and replenished by the IMF. The United States could thus twist Britain's arm by threatening its IMF funding.

The pound was also not the global reserve currency at that time. The stability of the international financial system did not depend then on the pound as it does today on the dollar. Many international transactions are conducted in dollars, many debts are denominated in dollars, and many countries hold securities denominated in dollars. The Chinese hold approximately $1.3 trillion, or 20 percent of their GDP, in dollar-denominated U.S. government debt. The Chinese government, among many others, has a vested interest in ensuring the stability of the dollar and the fiscal health of the United States.

Alternatives to the Dollar?

Despite its recent depreciation, there is no clear challenger to the dollar. The euro is currently in crisis because some of its members, notably Spain, Italy, Greece, and Ireland, are facing default, and in the longer term it will be strained by Europe's rapid graying; an oil price spike due to events in the Strait of Hormuz could be too much for it to bear even if the other threats are manageable. The euro's short- and long-term instability would make it difficult for (as one example) oil markets to be priced in euros, as oil producers would face serious currency instability. These issues make the euro an unstable store of value and therefore a bad reserve currency. The Chinese yuan, though it is the currency of one of the world's largest economies, is even more unsuitable. It does not freely float—indeed, its artificial valuation is subject to extensive criticism—and the Chinese financial system is not transparent. This is a very unappealing investment climate.

Presently there are few realistic alternative global reserve currencies. No matter how angry world states are in the aftermath of an American attack, they would still have to act against their own core interests to effectively wield the monetary weapon. As long as world leaders are relatively rational, the risk to the dollar is diminished.

However . . .

In the long run, this situation could change. China, America's major international creditor, has a complex and changing economy whose future is difficult to predict. However, one school argues that China's economy will continue its relentless growth. By 2030, it could have a per capita GDP of $33,000 and a significantly different economic structure with more consumption and less production. No longer urgently needing to create a favorable climate for exportation, the PRC may be willing to stop buying up huge volumes of American debt. The United States, meanwhile, shows no signs of seriously reforming its deficit-funded public sector, so it will in all likelihood continue to need foreign credit. Thus, China could threaten the United States just as the United States threatened Britain in 1956, refraining from bond purchases and using its influence to prevent an IMF bailout.[15] If the oil states of the Middle East are no longer friendly with the United States, they too will refuse credit, creating a crisis and possibly forcing American obedience.

This projection, however, is for 2030 and not 2012. Presently, the Gulf oil states are all extremely vulnerable to outside intervention and thus must seek patronage. These vulnerabilities stem from severe geopolitical weaknesses—small populations in open terrain—that have shaded their politics for centuries and will not change in the next three decades.[16] For similar reasons, even as China's naval capability and oil consumption grow, it will still have difficulty projecting power into the Gulf for many years, because its ships must pass through the Straits of Malacca and around India. China is thus unlikely to replace the United States as the guardian of the Gulf anytime soon.

One also wonders whether an attack on Iran would be sufficient to provoke China to take dramatic action. China sees its interests threatened by the United States' commitment to Taiwan and role in its neighborhood, so it would be more reasonable to expect the use of the currency weapon in this theater. Free traffic through the Strait of Hormuz is a key Chinese economic interest, given its growing demand for oil. However, if China is to be a flexible power in 2030, it will have to stabilize its domestic situation enough that low growth will not produce unrest. A China that can threaten to destroy the dollar is thus a China that can weather an economic storm—a China that will have less incentive to destabilize the world economy in an act of vengeance.

IMPACTS IN THE MIDDLE EAST

Regional Conflicts

Iran's ability to inflame conflicts on its borders allows it to impose new costs. U.S. operations in Afghanistan cost $110.3 billion in FY 2011, while operations in Iraq cost $43.4 billion in the same period. Current U.S. budgetary plans revolve around massive savings from the reduction of expenditures in these two countries. Iran thus does not need, for instance, to return Iraq to the bloody days of 2004 or 2006 to cause the United States great pain. Merely causing the United States to return to Iraq or delay withdrawal in Afghanistan could force the expenditure of hundreds of billions of dollars.[17] This new expenditure would stress the American economy, and could fuel recurring impasses over the federal budget deficit.

Continued instability in Iraq would also impose costs on the global economy. The Iraqi oil industry plans to expand its production capacity to 12 million barrels per day by 2017, an increase of more than 9 million barrels.[18] There are many who doubt that Iraq can adequately develop its production stream resources in just a few years, but it is certainly true that increased supply would have a favorable impact on the price and volatility of oil, and thus on the economy as a whole. The loss of that extra capacity and the increasing instability could be the opportunity cost of a war with Iran; the Iraqi government's comparatively lower revenue might also keep it from returning to its role as a regional balancer against the Islamic Republic and thus sustain Tehran's post-2003 freedom of action.

If Iran's Lebanese proxy Hezbollah can be persuaded to unleash its missiles against Israel after an attack, there is a risk of an Israel-Hezbollah or general Levantine war. It would be foolish to predict the nature of the latter, for Syrian, Egyptian, Palestinian, and Turkish stances are continually and rapidly evolving, and a conflict with Israel could force symbolic participation by any number of regional powers.

The 2006 war between Israel and Hezbollah had a limited impact on the global economy. However, Israel and Lebanon each saw losses, with Israel's economic growth forecast being revised downward from 5.4 percent to 4.5 percent,[19] and Lebanon going from 6 percent growth to -5 percent;[20] damage to Lebanon was valued at $7 billion.[21] Calculated against their 2005 GDPs, the nations lost a combined $3.6 billion in growth; a conflict of identical economic impact now would cost $6.2 billion. A renewed war would likely be worse—Hezbollah's more advanced armament and closer ties to the Lebanese government would likely provoke a deeper and bloodier Israeli intervention, leading to significantly higher expenses that could easily reach the tens of billions.

A broader war with Israel is also possible, though the United States would likely be able to compel states like Saudi Arabia and Iraq to give no more than cursory assistance, and it is difficult to imagine Syria putting up much of a fight in its present state. However, renewed hostilities would impose billions of dollars in direct costs, tens of billions in repairs, and hundreds of billions in forgone growth, trade, and investment in regional states, while heightened oil prices and risks to trade in Suez and the eastern Mediterranean would rattle the global economy.

American Trade

It is quite possible that an American or Israeli strike on Iran would provoke a wave of anti-American sentiment in the Middle East, and that regional governments would seek to punish the United States for its risky actions by cutting trade with American companies. Studies suggest that the quality of relations between states can affect their trade. Statistical tests of the impacts of crises on U.S.-Arab trade found the following significant relationships:[22]

Table 9.1.

	1991 Gulf War	*2003 Iraq War*
Increased U.S. market share	Kuwait, Oman, Saudi Arabia, GCC, Arab world	
Decreased U.S. market share		Oman, GCC, Arab world

It thus appears that many of the Arab states boosted trade with the United States as a reward for its actions in 1991, and reduced trade with the United States as a punishment for its actions in 2003. The measurable impact on trade was substantive—for instance, the United States lost 1.3 percent of its market share in 2003 in anti-war Saudi Arabia, at an immediate cost of about $200 million in today's dollars.[23] A comparable loss of trade today in the Arab world as a whole would reduce U.S. exports to the region by almost $11 billion, or 0.8 percent of total U.S. exports. The qualitative impact of such a trade loss on U.S.-Arab relations is more worrisome than the quantitative impact, as it could create openings for China, which recently acquired a greater market share in the Arab world than the United States and which may, in the wake of a strike on Iran, be viewed as a more reliable, less intrusive partner.

However, that is a very gloomy account. While the United States lost market share in almost every Arab state in 2003, this cannot be conclusively attributed to the Iraq War, and exports to the Arab world more than tripled by 2008.[24] The U.S. is losing to China in many key areas, but it is noteworthy that even when exports to the kingdom fell in 2003, losses were concentrated in low and medium technology manufacturing; almost every type of high technology export expanded. The Arab states showed indiscipline in their effort to discipline the United States for Iraq; moreover, there is a range of goods for which the United States remains a competitive manufacturer.

It is also unlikely that many of the Gulf states would realign their trade to punish the United States for a strike that they've been secretly calling for (as was unveiled in the documents betrayed to Wikileaks) for years. Any U.S. trade losses in the region are more likely to stem from a general economic slowdown that would follow a successful Iranian mass retaliation.

THE IMPACT OF THE SANCTIONS

Sanctioning Iran has a major impact on the Iranian economy. Part of the impact has been the weakening of the national currency, with the rial losing more than 60 percent of its value between October 2011 and October 2012. In response, Iran has set up a set of multiple exchange rates for different goods, with goods the state feels are needed more receiving better exchange rates. This system is intended to ration out what limited hard currency supplies it still holds.[25] Venezuela made a similar attempt to maintain a tiered peg, and the consequences were severe—it led to misallocation of resources, damaged sectors producing goods that could be imported at the state's fixed rates,[26] and rewarded a range of corrupt activities while encouraging off-the-books transactions.[27] The Revolutionary Guards, with their major involvement in the economy and in smuggling, may be able to derive significant benefits from the tiered rate; if they are able to challenge other importers or force them to collude, they may even be able to artificially boost prices by creating shortages. This would increase the guards' power while increasing political tension.

The official rate of inflation has also continued to rise, from 21.8 percent at the end of March 2012 to 22.9 percent at the end of July 2012.[28] The IMF estimates total 2012 inflation will be over 25 percent, and will remain at high levels in 2013. The rial's rapid loss of value in late 2012, however, suggested unofficial inflation may be higher; hyperinflation expert Steve Hanke estimated it at nearly 70 percent *per month*.[29] As a comparison, the United States Federal Reserve estimates U.S. inflation in 2013 will fall between 1.6 and 2.0 percent per year,[30] while the European Union in recent years has seen a median inflation below 4 percent.[31] Since the sanctions started, buyers have disappeared and Iranian storage tankers became full. As a result, Iran's oil exports have declined by 20–30 percent—a daily drop in shipments of 52 percent. In late summer 2012, analysts estimated the sanctions and embargos against Iran are costing the state $133 million per day.[32] Additionally, sanctions have made international transactions much more difficult, and have scared foreign investors away from Iran's key industries. India, for example, faced difficulties in trying to pay for its oil purchases from Iran due to the sanctions on banking. Iran's oil customers often make payments for their purchases into accounts in their own country denominated in their own currency; Iran then buys their goods with the money and imports them.[33] Iran's earnings from its oil are thus decreased in value—while they may be paid in currency, the value of the currency can only return to Iran in the form of goods, that is, a barter-like system, with potential for inefficiencies that will work against Iran.

However, the most significant consequence of these economic hardships caused by the sanctions may be the pressure they have created on the Iranian government. Ahmadinejad's government is extremely concerned about the public discontent and political instability that these sanctions have created and will create. The most noteworthy public expression of discontent were protests in Neyshabour, near Mashhad, over the high food prices and the "Chicken Crisis," where people shouted "Death to the looter of public treasure." The increasing high prices and the short supplies of chicken—at around 65,000 rials, or over $5 at the official exchange rate, a kilo (2.2 lb) of chicken is now nearly three times the price it was a year ago—have become an issue in national politics. Some Ahmadinejad opponents found the opportunity to publicly denounce the current administration for not being prepared for the crisis. However, the government has tried to lessen the crisis by offering reduced priced chicken at government sponsored centers, and it has also stepped up imports of frozen chicken and meat from abroad. But getting the reduced price chicken can be a very daunting process, as the lines are very long and those chickens are offered for a limited time during the

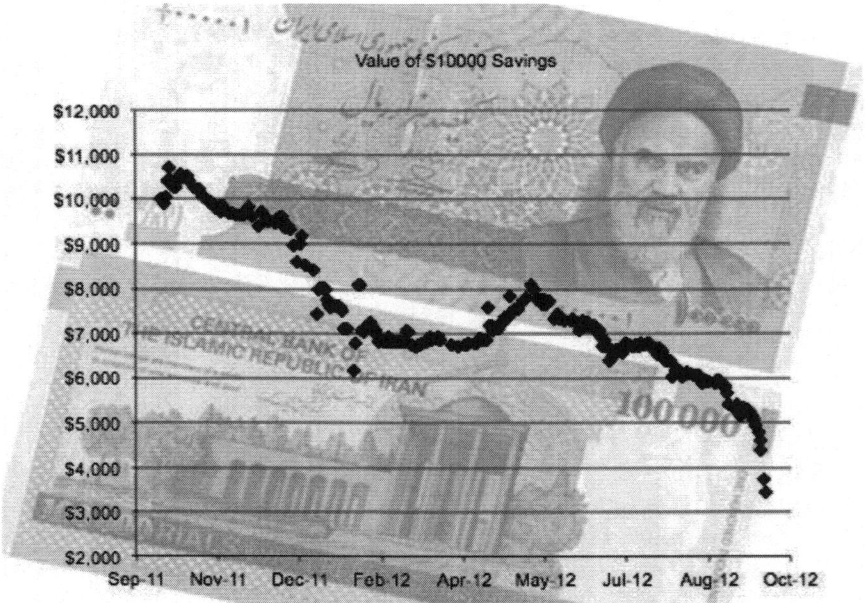

Figure 9.3. Value of rial-denominated savings with initial value of 10,000 USD. *(Courtesy of the* National Interest.*)*

week. Police Chief Esmail Ahmadi Moghaddam urged television channels to avoid broadcasting images of people eating chicken saying: "Certain people witnessing this class gap between the rich and the poor might grab a knife and think they will get their share from the wealthy."

The public is becoming more frustrated and less content with their country's deteriorating economy. Preschool teachers who lost their jobs due to budget cuts and men complaining that they were owed back pay protested in front of Iran's parliament building during the end of July 2012. In order to ease the discontent and encourage people to remain loyal, religious leaders, such as Ayatollah Ahmad Alamolhoda and Grand Ayatollah Naser Makarem Shirazi, reminded worshipers of the importance of standing up against the western sanctions and being determined to wage up the economic war on the Islamic republic. "If there is a shortage in chicken meat then change your diet and look for other sources of protein. Do not expect to continue the lifestyle you currently have," advised Ayatollah Ahmad Alamolhoda during Friday prayer. However, the Ayatollah failed to address the fact that sanctions have affected most basic staple available to poor Iranians—bread. Before 2010, the Iranian government subsidized the price of bread for the public. However, as a result of the sanctions against the state, subsidies were removed, and the price of bread has increased between the December

Figure 9.4. Iranians wait in line for government-subsidized chicken, 2012. ***(Iranian Students' News Agency)***

2010 and July 2012 by an astronomical 1500 percent.[34] In early June 2012 alone, bread prices increased by 33 percent.

Sociologist Kevan Harris argues that the government is allowing inflation on "luxury" goods like chicken while ensuring continued supply of rice via barter and special exchange rates. Still, the inflation is rapidly eating away at middle-class savings. Harris notes that this inflationary pattern hit Russia in 1999 and Argentina in 2001, and that the result was the rise of nationalistic leaders—Putin and the Kirchners.[35] It is not clear how this pattern could repeat in Iran. Though new nationalist hardliners in power would certainly be problematic, the public is fed up with the nationalist Ahmadinejad government, suggesting some new variety of nationalism would be needed. Forces close to Khamenei may attempt to provide this in the form of a more clerical form of nationalism than the lay and secular nationalism identified with Ahmadinejad.

The September–October 2012 collapse in the rial's value led to further serious consequences. Unable to price their goods effectively under rapid currency fluctuations, Tehran's Grand Bazaar shut down; large protests followed. The state attempted to suppress the black market for foreign currency. Ahmadinejad then gave a rambling press conference in which he argued that the troubles were caused by foreign sanctions and "psychological warfare," in addition to a small network of currency manipulators operating in Iran; his rivals countered that the collapse was in large part his fault. Tensions within the Iranian elite had been simmering for years, but the currency crisis brought them to a boil.

Other countries also suffer losses due to sanctions. Persuading them to participate in the U.S. sanctions regime thus comes at a cost, and this cost might be diplomatic or financial. If the Iranian bomb begins to appear inevitable, local states may require larger incentives to participate in sanctions, as they will otherwise be inclined to rebalance their relations with Tehran to reflect its new power, but states further afield may do the opposite as they seek to avoid Iranian nuclearization with greater urgency.

CONCLUSIONS

Any attack on Iran by the United States or Israel will lead to an immediate spike in world oil prices. How long the spike lasts, and by how much prices will rise, will depend upon what happens in the days following the outbreak of hostilities. If the attacks are restricted to one-time targeting of nuclear facilities, collateral damage to Iran's oil facilities will be minimal, and the markets might quickly adjust. But if the strikes involve major military operations against Iranian air and maritime assets, damage to Iranian oil facilities is quite possible and prices will almost certainly remain high.

Equally important will be the Iranian response. Iran could stop exports. Such action would hurt their economy and undermine their internal political stability. In extremis, Iran could interfere with traffic in the Strait of Hormuz and attack Arab oil facilities. While this is no easy task, the psychological impact on the oil markets could propel prices to unforeseen highs. However, oil price rises will be tied to prevailing market conditions. If confrontation occurs at a time of low global oil prices—for instance, at the height of a recession—the impact would be less serious than if they occur when the global market is tight and oil prices are already high.

In these circumstances, the role of Saudi Arabia would be key to reducing the long-term impact of supply disruptions and price increases. Similarly policies taken with respect to the release of the Strategic Petroleum Reserve in collaboration with actions of other major importers will be an essential part of the operation. The degree to which the United States could expect cooperation will depend on the circumstances under which the conflict started and the degree to which there is support, at least in the Arab world, to some form of military operation against the Iranian weapons program.

The worst time to launch an attack on Iran would thus be when the global economy is on the cusp of recovery, but where a precipitous rise in oil prices could tip it back into recession. Similarly the most dangerous political circumstances to undertake such an attack would be when the United States and Israel have no support from the international community and key Arab oil producers. While both states have the capability to unilaterally inflict significant damage to Iran's nuclear program, mitigating the impact of the resulting economic shocks will require deep multilateral cooperation.

The economic sanctions on Iran appear too biting, and may provoke Iran's return to the negotiating table with the P5+1. However, they have also contributed to a tightening of the global oil market, as spare capacity has dropped, demand has increased, and producers have gone offline in a number of countries experiencing instability. When combined with the temporary strains on U.S. refinery capacity, the situation is worrisome indeed. If an attack on Iran cuts supplies now, America may find itself seized by a perfect storm in the oil markets.

NOTES

1. Energy Information Agency, "China."
2. "BEA National Economic Accounts," U.S. Bureau of Economic Analysis (BEA).
3. Binyamin Applebaum, "Its Forecast Dim, Fed Vows to Keep Rates Near Zero."
4. Keith Bradsher, "As Inflation Climbs, Chinese Policy Makers Face a Problem."
5. If unconventional oil and natural gas can be extracted efficiently and in great volume, the opposite could be true. Prices might not see dramatic drops, as unconven-

tional oil is expensive to produce and thus is only viable at high price levels, but the dependence of oil markets, or at least the American oil market, on the Strait of Hormuz would be lessened.

6. Charles Robertson and Mark Cliffe, "Attacking Iran: The Market Impact of a Surprise Israeli Strike on Its Nuclear Facilities," ING, January 2007, http://media.ft.com/cms/8c72c46c-afac-11db-94ab-0000779e2340.pdf. "2011 West Texas Intermediate Crude Oil (WTI) Prices," Union Pacific, www.uprr.com/customers/surcharge/wti_2011.shtml.

7. Shifrinson and Priebe, "A Crude Threat: The Limits of an Iranian Missile Campaign Against Saudi Arabian Oil," *International Security* 36, no. 1 (Summer 2011).

8. Robertson and Cliffe, "Attacking Iran."

9. Note that these calculations assume perfect inelasticity of demand, and thus are very rough estimates.

10. Rebecca Jimenez-Rodriguez and Marcelo Sanchez, "Oil Price Shocks and Real GDP Growth: Empirical Evidence for Some OECD Countries," European Central Bank Working Paper 362 (May 2004).

11. Hillard Huntington, "Shares, Gaps, and the Economy's Response to Oil Disruptions," *Energy Economics* 26 (2004): 415.

12. James Hamilton, "What Is an Oil Shock?" National Bureau of Economic Research, Working Paper #7755 (June 2000).

13. Stephen Davis and John Haltiwanger, "Sectoral Job Creation and Destruction Responses to Oil Price Changes," National Bureau of Economic Research, Working Paper 7095 (April 1999).

14. After Egyptian leader Gamal Abdul Nasser nationalized the Suez Canal in July 1956, Britain and France met secretly with the Israelis to plan an attack that would restore the Canal to their control. The Israelis would invade the Sinai and approach the Canal; as fighting intensified, the British and French would occupy the Canal area, saying that international economic interests must be protected. This justification would allow them to occupy the Canal indefinitely, as the Egyptians would have been shown incapable of keeping it secure.

The military operations were initially successful. Israel made rapid gains and Anglo-French airborne forces moved in. However, the United States and the rest of the world initiated strong diplomatic pressure. Britain's currency reserves plummeted as Saudi Arabia initiated an oil embargo. The United States blocked IMF aid and refused to offer oil assistance. Faced with a crushing economic blow, a ceasefire was quickly announced, and British prime minister Anthony Eden soon fell from power.

15. Arvind Subramanian, "The Inevitable Superpower?," *Foreign Affairs*, September/October 2011.

16. See, e.g., John M. Collins, *Military Geography for Professionals and the Public* (Washington, DC: National Defense University Press, 1998), which notes that desert terrain favors offensive operations. In the local historical record, we see the incredible speed of the Islamic conquests, pre-Abdulaziz Saudi raiders, the 1956 and 1967 Arab-Israeli Wars, and the 1991 and 2003 American interventions in Iraq.

17. The failure of the United States to renew its Status of Forces Agreement with Iraq and the subsequent withdrawal of almost all U.S. troops by the end of 2011 mitigates, but does not eliminate, added military costs to the United States. In a post-strike context of open Iran-U.S. confrontation, answering a cry for help from the Iraqi government might be seen as an urgent national priority.

18. Energy Information Agency, "Iraq," 2011.

19. Sharon Wrobel, "2006 GDP Growth Tops Forecasts," *Jerusalem Post*, Jan. 1, 2007.

20. United Nations Development Program, "About Lebanon." www.undp.org.lb/about/AboutLebanon.cfm.

21. Paul Salem, "The Future of Lebanon," *Foreign Affairs*, Nov.–Dec. 2006.

22. Nader Habibi, "GCC States' Import Demand: The Effect of Geopolitics," Crown Paper #6 (2011), 28. Note that the author's regression analysis also included variables

for exchange rates, total volumes of trade, the Asian Financial Crisis, and the Second Intifada/ September 11. Most regressions did not yield significant results.

23. Statistics can be found in the STAN Bilateral Trade Database at http://stats.oecd.org.

24. Data from the U.S.-Arab Chamber of Commerce, www.usarab.org/arab-world/trade.html.

25. "Iran Introduces Tiered Exchange Rates for Imports," Reuters, July 21, 2012, www.reuters.com/article/2012/07/21/iran-currency-imports-idUSL6E8IL1FI20120721.

26. Imported "essential goods" that are eligible for an artificially strong exchange rate are essentially being subsidized, while domestic goods are not.

27. "Venezuel'a Unsustainable Economic Paradigm," Stratfor, Aug. 4, 2010, www.porvenezuela.org/KeyIssues/VENEZUELA_ECONOMIC_PARADIGM.pdf.

28. "Inflation Rate in Iran Rises to 22.9%," *Ya Libnan*, Aug. 6, 2012, www.yalibnan.com/2012/08/06/inflation-rate-in-iran-rises-to-22-9/.

29. Steve H. Hanke, "Hyperinflation Has Arrived in Iran," *Cato@Liberty*, Oct. 3, 2012, www.cato-at-liberty.org/hyperinflation-has-arrived-in-iran/.

30. Michael S. Derby and Kristina Peterson, "Fed Lowers 2012 Growth Forecast; See Higher Jobless Rate, Lower Inflation," *Wall Street Journal*, June 20, 2012, http://online.wsj.com/article/BT-CO-20120620-710990.html.

31. "Inflation Rate," About Inflation, www.aboutinflation.com/glossary/inflation-rate.

32. Anthony DiPaola and Isaac Arnsdorf, "Iran Loses $133 Million a Day from Sanctions as Oil Buoys Obama," *Bloomberg News*, Aug. 1, 2012, www.businessweek.com/news/2012-08-01/iran-loses-133-million-a-day-from-sanctions-as-oil-buoys-obama.

33. Benoit Faucon, "Iran Barters and Bargains to Help Oil Sales," *Wall Street Journal*, Aug. 7, 2012.

34. "Killing Them Softly: The Stark Impact of Sanctions on the Lives of Ordinary Iranians," ICAN, July 2012, www.icanpeacework.org/wp-content/uploads/2010/01/Iran9.pdf.

35. Kevan Harris, "The Drama of Iran's Erratic Rial," USIP Iran Primer, Aug. 16, 2012, http://iranprimer.usip.org/blog/2012/aug/16/drama-iran%E2%80%99s-erratic-rial.

TEN

Conclusions—the Challenge of Getting Out, the Costs of Staying Home

EXIT STRATEGY FOR WAR WITH IRAN

Any sustained conflict with Iran would drain America by requiring a significant security commitment to ensure regional peace and by imposing a "security premium" on oil prices. America would want to find a way out. What options would be available?

Regime change would be one option, but it carries obvious risks and would be extremely expensive, so it would only be pursued as a last resort. If Iran's retaliatory actions are unbearable or carried out in a morally reprehensible fashion (for example, terrorism affecting hospitals, children, etc.), or if Iran openly commits major resources to the development of a bomb, policymakers may wish to simply change the regime and be done with the political ayatollahs regardless of short-term costs—like peeling a Band-Aid. However, another regime change operation in the Middle East might cause key world powers to see a threatening revisionist streak in post–Cold War American foreign policy. The impact of this could be global and grave. Russia and China, great powers able to counter or undermine American action if they choose, were deeply angered when they backed resolutions intended to prevent atrocities by the Gaddafi regime in Libya, but saw NATO then carry out a regime change operation. They were also displeased when American diplomats criticized their ties to the Assad regime in Syria, despite America's apparent unwillingness to intervene. These actions strengthened historically shaky ties between the two powers, creating a strategic challenge to the United States. War with Iran would continue this trend, and may force the two to begin to balance American influence more actively—a recipe for increasing global tension.

Insurgency and entanglement could occur if factions like the IRGC are ideologically committed enough that they will keep fighting even if the regime falls.[1] The collapse of the central government, if the U.S. attempts regime change from afar[2] or its attempts to form a government are not fully successful, could provoke dangerous separatism among the Kurdish, Arab, Azeri, and Baluchi populations. Regional actors like Iraq, Turkey, and Pakistan would see the formation of ethnic enclave states in Iran as seriously dangerous to their interests. Additionally, collapsing the government will not be sufficient to change Iranian society in such a way that radicals do not remain a key power center—deep reform would be needed.[3] We should not be too pessimistic, though. Iran is not another Iraq. Its diversity does not threaten the integrity of its Persian core, and it has been more supportive of its ethnic minorities over the years than neighboring states like Iraq;[4] accordingly, there is less discord. Still, an American regime change operation would require extraordinary luck and extraordinary skill to avoid a number of pitfalls that could turn the conflict into a multigenerational catastrophe with significant geopolitical impact. The potential consequences are so severe that if the United States finds itself sucked into a land campaign in Iran, it might consider more traditional war goals, using its forces not to remove the Iranian government but to force it to make concessions.

An American or Israeli attack on Iran can likely destroy Iran's key nuclear infrastructure. However, it cannot in itself destroy Iran's will to possess risky nuclear technologies; in fact there is a strong chance war will merely convince Iran's leadership that a weapons program is the only path to security from foreign intervention. Recognizing this, some Israeli thinkers have argued that Jerusalem should be prepared to mount new antinuclear raids every few years, a process referred to as "mowing the lawn." This would be a deeply destabilizing pattern, as Tehran would not sit back and wait for the Israelis to attack them again and again. The Levant could erupt with new conflicts, and Israel's cafes and buses may again be unsafe. Similar troubles may befall America if it carries out the attacks. Simply put, attacking will only temporarily and imperfectly resolve the strategic challenge of a risen Tehran, leading to sustained crisis.

There is a parallel problem. While the limited strategic consequences of an antinuclear strike might lead Iran to refrain from the most aggressive retaliation, this will not be Iranian leaders' only consideration. They must also factor in the costs before domestic and international audiences of going back on years of threats. Additionally, they will have some ideological considerations—the Iranian foreign policy community includes many nationalist and Islamist neoconservatives, and conceives of Iran as a key seat of non-Western power. De-escalation will hardly be the only option presented to the Supreme Leader, and Iran has a wide selection of asymmetric levers it can pull.

These two problems indicate the substantive risk that America may find itself involved in a longer confrontation with Iran than it planned, that a strike may be followed by more than a few desultory rounds of Iranian retaliation and American response. American policymakers will begin to consider new ways of breaking the cycle. They will certainly consider deepening the conflict. Regime change will be discussed. The fall of the mullahs has been in the back of American policymakers' minds for decades, and the potential destabilization of the regime has long been one of the supporting arguments for sanctions. Policymakers may perceive targeting the regime itself with both air and ground capabilities as the logical next step if air power fails to resolve the crisis.[5] This is a mistake. The costs of regime change are well known after Iraq, and would be far greater in Iran. A larger population, longer supply lines, tougher terrain, and well-prepared resistance forces would await.

If policymakers feel that circumstances are forcing them to put troops on the ground in Iran to end a conflict, goals short of regime change would be necessary. What would such a war look like? After all, Iran is unlikely to risk conventional battle with the United States, as defeat would be all but certain, but allowing Iran to simply wait for the United States to overextend itself and create vulnerability to guerrilla attacks (say, by attempting regime change) would play into Tehran's hands.

There are three paths for expanding a conflict short of regime change in a way that allows the United States to use its military effectively. They will be discussed in order of cost to the United States. All of these actions would have the goal of increasing the cost to Tehran of continued resistance, forcing a political settlement.

First, the United States could expand its air campaign to include a range of strategic targets. The first choice would be the IRGC's economic arm, as it makes up a substantive portion of Iran's economy and there can be no doubt that it is a legitimate target of war. However, some of its most valuable activities (smuggling, for instance) would be all but impossible to target. The oil industry is a secondary tier of targets, as it relies on fixed assets and is of great importance to the state's ability to sustain warfare; tertiary targets would include infrastructure and non-IRGC economic targets. This campaign would allow American policymakers to calibrate their response relatively finely and would impose significant and long-term costs to the Iranian government without expanding the size or duration of the American mission.

Second, the United States could take actions of its own in the Persian Gulf. If Iran's naval forces are spent and American control of the Gulf is uncontested, the United Arab Emirates would have the opportunity to regain control of Abu Musa and the Tunbs, a set of small islands off its coast that were seized by the shah on the departure of British forces in

1971. Emirati actions would likely require mere acquiescence from the United States, followed by some modest commitment to the preservation of the status quo. If this were not enough, there are a large number of other Iranian islands that America or its allies could seize. At minimum, these could serve as bargaining chips for peace negotiations. Their occupation by friendly military forces would weaken Iran's natural advantages in the Gulf, albeit at the cost of some stability, so longer-term occupation of islands other than Abu Musa and the Tunbs would require judgment and careful weighing of strategic balances. Occupation like this may be the only permanent solution to the geopolitical challenge posed by Iran as long as the Iraqis remain weak and the GCC states remain disorganized, but the forces required would impose a significant opportunity cost on the United States. Policymakers would have to consider which other areas they'd need to take troops from, and which contingencies they'd no longer have the flexibility to address. They would also have to recognize that Iran may turn the islands into targets—a threat that will be amplified if it gains nuclear weapons—and that this could allow Iran to control the narrative of future crises.

Third, the United States could launch limited land warfare within Iran. Even without the goal of regime change, this would be extraordinarily costly, so it would only be worthy of consideration if Iran's retaliation is especially loathsome in method or enormous in magnitude. There are three reasonable areas of operation: Bushehr and Bandar Abbas, for their strategic importance (both to the economy and the oil state, the latter to Iran's naval activity), and the greater Khuzestan area in Iran's southwest. None of these objectives would require the United States to operate in or beyond the Zagros Mountains, where America's advantages would begin to fade. The Khuzestan area could be particularly amenable to campaigning, given its flat, open terrain and significant number of Arabs (far more familiar to the American military than Persians, and less likely to resist on behalf of Iran[6]). Depending on circumstances and forces available, holding ground may not be desirable; in either case the prevention of steady flows of oil, imports, and exports would be the goal. Air power could do more or less the same thing with fewer risks and lower costs (though land warfare would allow more reversibility—bombing an oil terminal does more damage than seizing it). Thus, any land action would have to be taken in only the most serious of circumstances, and only with a clear and robust conception of the *political* objectives that the action would achieve.

A more realistic way out of conflict is for either the United States or Iran to simply ignore the latest blow and allow the cycle to end. However, there is a risk that the other side would not stop attacking. We must remember that Iran has been sponsoring deadly attacks on American forces in Iraq for years. If the United States does not reply to Iranian actions, Iran may continue probing to bleed America and see what it can get away with in the post-strike era. Tehran's hardliners will attempt to move the goalposts and attain a de facto norm of higher day-to-day resistance to American regional presence. This would of course magnify the American domestic discontent that leaving an attack unanswered would have created, and it will hinder American influence and access to the broader region. The opposite is also possible—in Tehran's view, America has always been trying to overthrow the Islamic Republic, and because of this the regime has been forced to take a difficult road in order to defend itself. Some analysts have suggested that the details of America's sanctions measures indeed constitute a de facto policy of regime change,[7] and it is difficult to argue that there would be many tears shed in Washington if the Islamic Republic collapsed. In the aftermath of a strike and retaliation, Iran will not be the only party driving the conflict.

One potential way out of a cycle of small-scale violence would be legal measures. The United States could capture the Iranian proxies or illegal agents that were responsible for the latest attack and try them. This would satisfy the domestic desire for justice in a fashion that would not perpetuate the cycle and would hopefully thus allow it to end. However, if the captured personnel are Iranian citizens or government employees, Iran may see them as prisoners of war and see their detention as a sign that the conflict with the United States continues; the integration of their cases into the legal system would make it more costly domestically to return them as part of a peace settlement. The outcry in the United States and the United Kingdom over the release of Libyan agent Abdelbaset al Megrahi (the Lockerbie bomber) might be repeated.

Trial is a two-edged sword. If an attacking aircraft is downed, the airframe will likely be put on display in an attempt to embarrass its owners (as happened in late 2011 with an American drone). If an aircrew is captured, they could be paraded on TV or subjected to show trials in an effort to influence public opinion in the attacking country. It would be unclear when they would be released, as the conflict itself would be ambiguous and asymmetric. The prisoners could, in fact, be a long-term source of conflict as the attackers attempt to free them. If they are Israeli, matters could be even worse—the state could deal with them in a much harsher manner, and elements in the IRGC that have been acting out of late may attempt to carry out punishment independently, which would be a major international incident.

The most obvious way out of a cycle of violence would be a ceasefire deal between the two states. There is some history of this—there are rumors that a secret U.S.-Iranian agreement during part of the Iraqi insurgency created a drop in Iran-backed attacks, and even in the chaos after the Islamic Revolution, the United States and Iran were able to agree to the Algiers Accords to free American hostages and resolve financial claims. However, in the aftermath of a U.S. strike on Iran and an Iranian retaliation, both sides would find peace to be, as Khomeini famously remarked about the peace with Iraq, like drinking hemlock.

INTERNAL POLITICAL IMPACTS

One unpredictable element present throughout the crisis is the threat of a coup. Like most countries in the Middle East, Iran follows the ancient tradition of keeping parallel militaries—one regular army and one special army kept near the seat of power to prevent the regular army from intervening in politics. This anti-coup army is given special privileges to ensure it has a vested interest in the survival of its patron in the regime. However, leaders from Caligula to Saleh have learned that these guards are not always loyal—their self-interest and proximity to the levers of power can cause them to desert or even turn on the leader they protect. The IRGC, Iran's parallel army, has several currents in it that could pose challenges to the regime. Some have strong ties to the economic sector—the appointment of the head of the guards' main economic arm as oil minister over an Ahmadinejad ally in late 2011 shows both the influence that the guards command in the economy and their political clout. These elements have a strong interest in supporting the regime, but that interest could decline significantly if their assets are being targeted or the regime falls. The most dangerous element of the IRGC is thus not these men, but those who are most loyal to the regime's ideology, people like those in the Qods Force that are charged with assisting proxies. In the aftermath of an American attack, they will be eager to retaliate with all their might; further American strikes will likely target them, which will add to their eagerness. However, the regime will only allow a partial response, provoking discontent in the ranks.

There is a possibility that this will lead to some form of silent coup. It would be dramatic to see the guards directly challenge Supreme Leader Khamenei, even with his weak religious credentials, but it would be quite unsurprising to see them arrest parliamentarians, senior officials, or perhaps even the president before installing themselves in positions of power.[8] They could also "offer" Khamenei strong "advice" on the regime's direction. This would be dangerous. In order to ensure loyalty, the guards are indoctrinated into the regime's ideology but not necessarily its pragmatism. Their policy choices could diverge significantly from rationality due to different valuations of outcomes—for instance, mass martyrdom in battle might not be considered the worst possible outcome. From a conventional perspective, aggressive actions like sealing Hormuz and attacking neighboring regimes have little to offer Tehran; we cannot have a comfortable level of certainty that regime's more ideological elements would make the same assessment. Even if the Guards do not choose immediate aggression, their dominance of the political sphere would put

Iran on a pushier path—analysts have even compared an IRGC-led Iran to the military-dominated and aggressive Japan of the late 1930s.

THE COST OF INACTION

One obvious conclusion from the preceding analysis is that that there are significant costs to an attack on Iran. However, it would be erroneous to think the choice is between expensive action and free inaction. Resisting Iranian nuclearization has costs, costs that will grow significantly as Iran's nuclear program becomes more advanced and grow further still if the program succeeds. The Iranian oil industry is also much less productive than it could be due to unavailability of parts and expertise, investor worries, and heavy regulation. With regulatory reform and global market access, Iran's heightened oil production could yield a 10 percent decrease in oil prices, saving the United States roughly $70 billion; total economic benefit to the United States could approach 0.4 percent of GDP, plus the less quantifiable impact of deeper long-term business ties.[9]

If Iran chooses to pursue the bomb, it will be in gross violation of the international nonproliferation regime. Policymakers will demand harsher measures. Tougher sanctions will have their own costs, and could prompt defections from the sanctioning alliance. New costs may come into play, such as a heightened military presence in the Gulf area, new covert operations, and Cold War–style intimidation patrols. Aerial operations to intimidate Iran would likely cost at least $2 billion per year, if not significantly more.[10] The United States would also need to boost its troop presence in the region. Estimates for keeping one U.S. soldier in Iraq for one year have famously approached one million dollars;[11] costs per soldier of quieter operations in South Korea are above $500,000.[12] Expanding regional military presence by 25,000 soldiers (for example) could thus cost between $12.5 and $25 billion per year.[13] If these troops are deployed in Saudi Arabia, it is quite reasonable to expect some increase in terrorism; the rule of the al Saud might even be challenged, which would have unfathomable effects on oil markets.

Missile defense against Iran would also become more of a priority. This could have very significant diplomatic costs, as missile defense assets must be placed in countries that may require convincing to serve as hosts. Russia has long regarded U.S. missile defense as a threat to its own security, so defending against Iran could antagonize Russia and create a risk of confrontations or arms races. Missile defense also has high development costs—the FY 2012 budget includes $8.6 billion for this, and inflation-adjusted total costs rival the Apollo program at $150 billion[14]—and the Iranian threat has come to play a key role in justifying continued investment. The elimination or dramatic reduction of the perceived Iranian missile threat, if it produces a concurrent reduction in missile defense funding, could save enormous amounts of money—for instance, a 50 percent reduction in costs would take less than six years to save the equivalent of the cost of the Three Gorges Dam project.

If Iran obtains the bomb, the price is steeper. Intimidation and sanctions costs would remain high. Markets would certainly suffer an immediate and visible blow, but subtle long-term costs would also appear. Iran would now be able to threaten Hormuz more effectively, as it could back up closure attempts with nuclear threats; it would also be a greater threat to its neighbors and might feel more freedom to back terrorist groups.[15] All of these would depress markets and encourage sharper price spikes whenever relations become tense; the insecurity premiums on oil would also climb. Iran could use its status as a nuclear power to attempt to expand its regional role, which would create crises with attendant economic shocks. The economic impact of a strike would be large, but brief; the impact of an Iranian bomb would be smaller, but continue indefinitely. The only hope for resolution in the latter case would be a gradual stabilization and normalization of Iran's international role resulting from its new responsibilities as a nuclear power.

CONCLUSIONS

Iran's nuclear progress continues, but bold claims of new centrifuge technologies and massive centrifuge halls have not been substantiated by IAEA reports, and plans to test improved centrifuges in large numbers have not materialized. Analysts have called Iran's nuclear program a "saunter," not a "race," to the bomb—while states like North Korea need the bomb to survive, Iran wants the bomb to expand its influence and thus is not in a rush. Iran is working from "aspiration," the DPRK from "desperation."[16] A strike may be superfluous as long as oil prices are low and Iran's economy is in crisis, and as long as sanctions regimes hinder payment on what oil Iran does sell. Nuclear components and expertise are expensive.

The risks of a military strike are substantial. However, there remains a possibility that Iran will begin to pursue the bomb more openly. The United States and the world will need policy options that will show Iran that it will not be allowed to go nuclear. Though the United States and Israel have long emphasized that military options are on the table, it is difficult to attribute the pause in Iran's development to fear of military strikes, especially with the United States already entangled in three conflicts in the greater Middle East and struggling economically. The political will for an attack is absent, reducing the credibility of claims that military actions are a possibility.

As many commentators have pointed out, the United States has used words like "unacceptable" to describe the nuclear quests of both Iran and

Figure 10.1. Standard Missile-3 (SM-3) is launched from the Pearl Harbor–based Aegis cruiser USS *Lake Erie*, during a joint Missile Defense Agency, U.S. Navy ballistic missle flight test. *(U.S. Navy.)*

North Korea, yet it has so far tolerated both programs. Acquiescence to North Korea's program may have been forced due to the extreme circumstances found on the Korean peninsula,[17] but it did not advance the value of America's word; accepting a nuclear Iran after similar rhetoric would further decrease that value. There is thus reason to develop options that increase pressure on Iran but that will reduce the risk of warfare.

This risk of warfare is present in all policy choices, given the regular confrontations at organic levels that have the potential to spiral out of control.[18] Policymakers must thus evaluate choices regarding Iran by the changes in war risk they entail (including risks from anti-Iranian anger they may have to stir up in order to justify certain choices to the public), the nature of the conflict they could provoke (open warfare, asymmetric responses, etc.), and the exit strategies and de-escalation options that would be available. The importance of exit strategy is likely not lost on the post-Iraq War policymaker, but it must be emphasized even more in examining conflict with Iran. Iran's ability to retaliate with open military force is somewhat overstated. However, it has a range of other ways of making things unpleasant for America, including difficult-to-attribute attacks by proxies, which would make sustained conflict an unpalatable option even if the United States were not already involved in a global war. It is thus imperative that policymakers maintain several specific and realistic plans for disengagement.

Options for increasing pressure on Iran without direct military engagement include economic measures—such as redoubled efforts to deprive the Islamic Republic of trading partners—or covert actions like assassinations, sabotage, and cyber warfare. Military escalation that does not provide pretext for war is also possible. A recent analysis recommended patrols by nuclear-capable aircraft near Iranian airspace to "undermine the narrative of hard-liners . . . that Iran's nuclear program increases its security."[19] Showing Tehran that it would be subject to Cold War–style confrontation and pushiness if it gets the bomb could be dissuasive, and could sate Iran hawks in the United States and Israel who feel that the current sanctions paradigm is not doing enough to force Iran to pursue an unambiguously peaceful nuclear program.

Small-scale military confrontation can also be considered. Iran will not find understanding in the international community if it responds to minor U.S. attacks with overwhelming force. Iran has given the United States multiple pretexts for attack in recent years that would have justified retaliatory action. However, Iran's ability to respond in asymmetrical fashions may give it the luxury of replying in a time and manner of its own choosing, meaning there are risks not only of spiraling confrontation but also of sustained pinpricks or unanswerable attacks. Direct tit-for-tat response might not be realistic from either party. Thus, policymakers should be careful in their selection of actions against Iran.

The United States will also have to consider the impact that its actions will have on international support for the sanctions regime—an attack that is a solid tactical success but that leads to significant abandonment of sanctions would be a strategic failure. However, this does not mean that small-scale force should be ruled out. Iran's backing of terrorism and support of Iraqi militias against U.S. forces have gone largely unanswered. This has been of necessity. With two wars in the region already in progress, Washington could scarcely afford to launch another. As withdrawals from Iraq and Afghanistan continue, American flexibility will increase, and with it the credibility of American threats. Actions that could demonstrate a renewed Middle East leadership to Iran and cause it to reduce its misbehavior certainly merit consideration.

The United States must consider the risk that both action and inaction pose to the global nonproliferation regime. If Iran withdraws from the NPT and acquires the bomb without significant consequences, other states may become less cooperative with its demands, which would result in less-secure radioactive material and greater proliferation risk. If Iran is attacked and withdraws from the NPT, the same result may occur. It's not clear that these are adequate foundations for a global arms race with a host of new players—global geopolitics have shifted dramatically since the atomic age. However, even without an arms race America could be forced to expand its nuclear coverage to balance Iran, imposing new costs and new risks while setting back its officially stated quest to reduce reliance on nuclear weapons.

As we discussed in the preceding chapter, an attack poses serious risks to the global economy. Oil price spikes have a direct negative impact on growth, and they can promote bubbles in other sectors. Iranian terrorism and use of proxies could cost the region billions. However, inaction has its own costs, including the tens of billions that can be saved in the United States if Iran's oil sector opens to global development, the tens of billions that could be spent to support troops and patrols needed to balance a nuclear Iran, tens of billions for extra missile defense, and the costs of oil spikes and confrontations resulting from an Iranian resurgence. If policymakers suspect that a strike on Iran will have highly decisive effects, cost-benefit analysis could favor action. Less decisive attacks would almost certainly yield higher economic costs than benefits, meaning policymakers would have to weigh noneconomic factors like security or credibility to justify an attack.

If American intelligence has a high ability to find clandestine Iranian nuclear sites, the military option is a viable short term counterproliferation strategy. Strikes can create an enormous material setback that will likely require a multiyear recovery period. This period can be extended by returning to attack again, though successive attacks will be more difficult (politically and militarily) and will require better information. However, strikes will make it quite likely that the U.S.-Iranian confrontation (which has long been, for all intents and purposes, a low-grade war) will become more open, more controversial, and more expensive in both blood and treasure. Still, a nuclear Iran, even one that is a completely "rational"[20] actor and highly stable (neither of which is by any means guaranteed), is costly. Several years remain between the present and Iran's development of a bomb or a strategically meaningful breakout capability. The international context will evolve in that period. The sanctions regime is currently imposing serious pains on the Iranian economy, so an attack now would be ill timed. This may not always hold, and it is certainly possible that future policymakers will find that even a crippling sanctions regime or extreme concessions are unable to rein in Tehran's nuclear ambitions. If this is the case, the policy options will have decayed into a stark dilemma: take military action and accept significant short-term risks or acquiesce to the long-term danger of an Iran that can take a more muscular role. Choice of paths in this case may be a consequence of a select set of policymakers' psychological and group dispositions towards risk.

Across the long history of human conflict, many grand ideas of military might have come up short when tested on the battlefield. Proposals for an attack on Iran tend to rest on the assumption that air power, aided by guided weaponry and advanced intelligence gathering, can have a dramatic impact on the enemy. The historical record of air power in the Middle East does not fully support this theory. The 1991 Gulf War saw air attacks do critical damage to Iraq's military, yet Saddam Hussein continued to behave in a manner that he should have known would make Washington see him as a threat. The 2003 war opened with a failed assassination strike on Saddam, and, as would happen in Afghanistan and Pakistan, saw pervasive and precise airpower unable to deal insurgencies a crushing blow. Similarly, the 2006 Israeli attack on Hezbollah, despite impressive levels of coordination and high sortie rates, failed to defeat the Shiite militia and gave it a propaganda coup. Estimates of the efficacy of air power against Iran, even when they take into account possible rates of aircraft loss or weapon failure, should thus be taken with a grain of salt. Iran is not invincible, but it has had the opportunity to learn from a string of Western wars in its neighborhood. A conflict is likely to take unexpected turns, and a "complete victory" in which Iran gives up its nuclear ambitions is not likely. However, Tehran is aware that it would suffer greatly in the event of a foreign attack on its nuclear infrastructure, and this has certainly had an impact on the decisions it has made about its program. Continuing to proclaim the existence of the military option keeps this cost in their minds. Still, the only way to reach any agreement with Iran on this matter is to assure the regime that it can have a place in the regional framework, and that nuclear weapons will do more harm than good to its regional standing. Presently, that is simply not the case. Without a solution to this more fundamental problem, Iran will continue its slow march toward the ultimate weapon.

NOTES

1. This has become less likely, as the IRGC has partially transformed into a paramilitary economic cabal aligned with the regime rather than a pure fighting force. If its investments are destroyed or signed over to "post-revolutionary" owners, many commanders may not feel resistance leads to any positive outcomes. Of course, we should not doubt that some elements in its ranks are deeply committed and will resist.

2. For instance, by destroying Iran's oil exports and thus starving the government of funds while harassing its ability to communicate orders via strikes and electronic warfare.

3. Removing the influence of the clerics would be both impossible and undesirable for an occupying power. The most viable path would be an effort to wrest the economy from the grasp of IRGC affiliates, and transfer it to a mix of state, bazaari, bonyad, and modern corporate control. This would likely require expropriation, arrests, careful monitoring, and the restoration of producer-oriented subsidies, and would still be very difficult. A foreign power implementing these measures would face an expensive and potentially lengthy path, and may face accusations of "disaster capitalism" or profiteering when foreign corporations inevitably enter the Iranian economy.

4. This is not a high bar.

5. Despite its tendency toward realism, an error of this kind was exhibited by the George H. W. Bush administration in the closing days of Operation Desert Storm: policymakers wanted to extract concessions that would ensure Iraq would not again threaten the peace, yet seemed to view regime change as the only further option, and one they did not wish to exercise given the risks of occupation. The wish for regime change led the administration to encourage rebellions in Iraq, yet it did not support them because of the costs, resulting in massacres and serious embarrassment, and further trouble with Iraq until the 2003 war. Other options for getting key concessions, such as further land attacks with goals short of regime change, do not seem to have been seriously considered.

6. The path chosen toward the Arab population, though, would be a matter fraught with danger—offering any sovereignty or seeking collaboration would ensure either entanglement or a repeat of the massacres that happened across the Shatt al Arab after Desert Storm.

7. Yousaf Butt, "Are Sanctions a Fatwa on Iran?," *National Interest*, Jan. 12, 2012, http://nationalinterest.org/commentary/are-sanctions-fatwa-iran-6363.

8. Recall that reformist president Khatami was presented with a letter from top IRGC leaders threatening a coup.

9. DeRosa and Hufbauer, "Normalization of Economic Relations: Consequences for Iran's Economy and the United States," National Foreign Trade Council, Nov. 2008.

10. This is a back-of-the-envelope style estimate, using $10,000 per square mile per year for no fly zone costs (taken from Harrison and Cooper, "Selected Options and Costs for a No-Fly Zone Over Libya," Center for Strategic and Budgetary Assessments, March 2011, which derived their figure from studies of no-fly zones over Iraq; we will assume that our case is analogous). The zones of operation we assume are one of 1,000 miles by 120 miles along Iran's southern coast, and one of 785 miles by 120 miles along Iran's border with Kuwait, Iraq, and Turkey.

11. Drew, "High Costs Weigh on Troop Debate for Afghan War," *New York Times*, Nov. 14, 2009.

12. Bandow, "Free Rider: South Korea's Dual Dependence on America," CATO Policy Analysis No. 308, May 1998.

13. This figure likely includes the costs of defense assistance in addition to raw troop deployments, an analogy that would likely hold with deployments in the Gulf.

14. Smith and Ratnam, "$35B Missile Defense Misses Bullet with Bullet," *Bloomberg*, Aug. 3, 2011.

15. Dagobert Brito and Amy Myers Jaffe, "Reducing Vulnerability of the Strait of Hormuz," in *Getting Ready for a Nuclear-Ready Iran*, ed. Sokolski and Clawson (Strategic Studies Institute of the U.S. Army War College, 2005), 209–24.

16. Patrick Clawson and Michael Eisenstadt, "The Last Resort: Consequences of Preventive Military Action against Iran," WINEP, June 2008, www.washingtoninstitute.org/policy-analysis/view/the-last-resort-consequences-of-preventive-military-action-against-iran.

17. Namely, the extraordinarily close proximity of the South Korean capital, Seoul, to the border. The city of more than ten million is within artillery range of North Korea, and war plans are at best ambiguous on whether the city would be held for the duration of a conflict. The human and economic cost of provoking a war between the Koreas is thus unfathomable; it is not at all clear that the same is the case with Iran.

18. For examples, see Simon Henderson, "Energy in Danger: Iran, Oil, and the West," WINEP, June 2008, 2–3, www.washingtoninstitute.org/policy-analysis/view/energy-in-danger-iran-oil-and-the-west.

19. Davis et al., "Iran's Nuclear Future: Critical U.S. Policy Choices," RAND Project Air Force, 2011, 26–27. If this option does not sate hawks, nuclear-armed patrols coupled with increasingly strident rhetoric—a lesser Operation Giant Lance—might force even Tehran's hardliners to take pause.

20. The use of this term has been a subject of intense debate among Iran watchers—by some measures, any leadership is rational if it engages in a careful, logically sound, deliberative decision-making process instead of caprice. Iran's leaders appear to meet this standard easily. However, they have also taken multiple actions at once which interfere with one another (in the Rafsanjani period, for instance, attempts at rapprochement with Europe were under way at the same time as plots on Kurdish dissidents in Germany), taken actions that grossly violate international norms (like the attacks on Israeli diplomatic personnel in third countries), and taken other steps which may have been arrived at by a rational process but which, to outsiders, appeared highly irresponsible.

Appendix A: International Policies and Actions toward Iran

BRITAIN

Along with the rest of the P5+1, Britain has demanded that Iran suspend its enrichment activities. Britain has participated in sanctions through the UN Security Council and the European Union as well as additional unilateral sanctions.[1] In July 2011, British foreign secretary William Hague stated: "The message to the Iranian government from the U.K. and its partners is clear . . . it needs to change its behavior before it will be treated as a normal member of the international community."[2] In November 2011, photographs showed troops from the Basij forces and members of the al-Quds Brigade assisting or standing by while citizens attacked the British embassy in Tehran, implicating the Iranian government and leading to the closure and evacuation of British officials from the embassy.[3] Hague called for tougher sanctions against Iran, including oil sanctions, but stated that the call for "intensification of sanctions" was not a response to the storming of the embassy in Tehran.[4] Several European countries also closed their embassies.

Speaking at the Conservative Party's 2011 conference, former defense minister Liam Fox said that a military option cannot be taken off the table, citing a potential arms race in a dangerous region if Iran became nuclear.[5] Leader of the Opposition Ed Miliband stated in an interview that the international community was taking the right course by pursuing a dual strategy of engagement and sanctions,[6] and Deputy Prime Minister Nick Clegg of the Liberal Democratic Party also voiced his support for the government's strategy of engagement coupled with sanctions.[7]

Overall, Britain wants to avoid a military strike if possible, and advocates for economic sanctions beyond the UN Security Council's measures. However, in November 2011, British defense ministry officials said that if the United States planned to attack Iran, America could "seek, and receive, U.K. military help."[8]

Britain's recent national defense strategy documents have repeatedly identified Iran, its proxies, and its nuclear program as a threat. There is particular concern at the "strong possibility" that Iranian nuclear ambitions will be copied by its neighbors, and that this general proliferation "would lead to high instability, precarious energy security, and . . . a severely damaging effect on the Middle East Peace Process." They propose no specific course of action. The documents imply that Britain is more urgently threatened by terrorism and natural disasters, and that budgetary problems cast a pall over the entire political sphere, including the military. Britain indeed faces a major threat from homegrown terrorism, with poorly integrated immigrant communities hosting large numbers—some estimates are in the thousands—of individuals with connections to terror. Policymakers can reasonably worry that an attack on Iran—whether supported by the UK or not—will lead to domestic terror. Coping with this and a potential energy crisis might be too much for the Cameron-Clegg government.

UK policy is thus likely to continue to focus on isolating Iran internationally and slowing its march toward weapon capability, though participation in a use of force should not be ruled out. Many of the tools Whitehall prefers—such as development aid—simply will not work at this time and in this context.

Official statements argue that a "rules-based international system" is most friendly to British interests abroad; much of the current international approach is taking place in a thoroughly legalistic and institutionalized context. Russia and China are quite likely to stand in the way of an internationally legitimized war, so any military effort would be in spite of international law. As is so often the case, an Iran conflict would find the UK torn between the more legalistic European Union and the freewheeling United States. This would be a very unpleasant situation, one in which British choices are all but impossible to predict, though traditional Euro-
skepticism in the Conservative Party may tilt the balance toward Washington. However, if Iran is foolish enough to retaliate massively, the UK is much more likely to join the effort.

FRANCE

France has endorsed sanctions by the UN Security Council and others on nuclear sectors of Iran's economy, and even called for stricter measures.[9] France has repeatedly called on Iran to "suspend its sensitive activities."[10] Current president Francois Hollande has maintained this line in the early months of his administration, though his rise provoked worries abroad that he would take a softer stance on Iran than his predecessor—not a tall order. Former president Nicolas Sarkozy suggested that Iran's persistence with their nuclear agenda could cause a preventive attack on Iran because "Iran refuses to negotiate seriously."[11] He argued that France should work "at all costs" to avoid a military confrontation, but did not explicitly state what path France would take should confrontation happen anyway. Similarly, in September 2011 French UN ambassador Gerard Araud said "there is a strong risk of military action" if Iran refuses to negotiate.[12] Across the aisle, Socialist Segolene Royal (a former presidential candidate and Hollande's partner-turned-rival) maintained that a diplomatic route was preferable, but also refrained from ruling out action.[13] France was among those who withdrew diplomats after the recent attacks on the British embassy in Tehran from the country.

French military doctrine allows for French participation in major conflicts far afield if they are multilateral *and* France can commit enough forces to ensure that it will be given key leadership roles within the coalition. Though France has hinted of force, these criteria will likely interfere with French participation in a war with Iran. Such an operation is most likely to be initiated unilaterally by Israel or the United States, and Hollande will be under pressure to condemn it. Once underway, it will likely not require substantial assistance within the immediate zone of combat—and furious France will be loath to provide it. Paris is thus unlikely to find either of its criteria for intervention fulfilled. However, in the event of Iranian retaliation it might need to become involved in cooperative security efforts, especially outside the Gulf theater.

GERMANY

In January 2011, Germany stated that it does not support military action against the Iranian nuclear program and would not participate in any such action. Germany does, however, support sanctions and international pressure.[14] Germany has been critical of the ways sanctions were implemented in the past. In 2007, when Iranian sanctions began to be more heavily considered, German officials criticized France and the United States for pursuing a third round of sanctions when many French and American businesses bypassed the sanctions already in existence.[15] Germany has long had a fruitful economic and political relationship with Iran and for that reason has been hesitant to support sanctions. "Germany has a traditionally good relationship with Iran. . . . The Iranians never fail to point out Germany's deep closeness with Iran." This close relationship makes Germany a valuable addition to the P5+1.[16]

In April 2011, Germany closed an Iranian bank based in Hamburg, which was widely believed to contribute to Iran's nuclear program.[17] Furthermore, powerful German companies such as Siemens, formerly strong partners with Iran, have begun withdrawing their business from Iran. They are implementing sanctions; however, the process will take several months and Germany recognizes that sanctions are not working fast enough.[18] In a 2010 meeting with Brazilian officials, German foreign minister Guido Westerwelle said, "We remain ready to negotiate. But since we have had the impression that our outstretched hand has nothing to grasp . . . we will have to talk about other measures."[19] In response to the International Atomic Energy Association's November 2011 report evaluating Iran's progress towards producing a nuclear bomb, Westerwelle said, "If Iran further refuses serious negotiations about its nuclear program, new and strict sanctions will be unavoidable. . . . The way of definitive and broadly applied sanctions is the right way. We reject any discussion of military options."[20] Germany has remained stalwart in its support for further nuclear sanctions and the opening of Iran's peaceful civilian nuclear power plant.

Despite Germany's vocal stance on Iranian sanctions, leaked documents revealed more about their policies. A German government-funded think-tank, the Institute for Security and International Affairs, reportedly advised the United States that "covert sabotage (unexplained explosions, accidents, computer hacking, etc.) would be more effective than a military strike, whose effects in the region could be devastating."[21]

In 2011, Germany, France, and the UK spearheaded a new round of European Union sanctions on Iranian business.[22] In the weeks after the release of the IAEA report, the United Kingdom's embassy in Tehran was attacked,[23] and Germany launched an investigation into an alleged Iranian plot to strike U.S. bases on German soil if the United States were to attack Iran.[24]

Germany's most recent defense white paper (released in 2006, only the second since the Cold War) explicitly identifies proliferation as "one of the greatest threats and challenges to the security of the international community."[25] However, it couches proliferation as purely a problem of non-state actors and terror groups, rather than one that can be a deliberate product of state policy, and the proposed mechanism for preventing proliferation is stronger international law and deeper disarmament. While it identifies "convincing Iran to find a constructive solution in the nuclear dispute" as a crucial priority for the international community in the Middle East,[26] it does not propose a means of convincing. In the event of a military conflict over Iran's nuclear program, Germany would likely pursue an ambiguous policy, condemning the attacks but doing little that would impact the course of the conflict. Its quietist approach may continue even in the event of substantial Iranian retaliation (including within Germany), though a major minelaying in the Strait of Hormuz would lead to strong international calls for the employment of Germany's large fleet of counter-mine vessels.

RUSSIA

Historically, Iran has been on the contested fringe of Russian influence and Russia has been among Iran's top trading partners. In 2010 Russia's trade with Iran was over one billion euros.[27] Russia has coordinated energy sales and sold arms to Iran in an attempt to become an influential power in the region. Together, Iran and Russia control 20 percent of the world's oil reserves and almost half the world's natural gas reserves. This energy partnership provides Russia with the opportunity to invest in the Iranian energy sector in a way that benefits its own economy and energy sector. Russia has also sold many weapons, submarines, and weapons systems to Iran.[28] A 2006 report describing these arms sales said:

> Since 1992, Russia has sold Iran hundreds of major weapons systems, including twenty T-72 tanks, ninety-four air-to-air missiles, and a handful of combat aircraft like the MiG-29. Late [2005], Russia agreed to sell Iran a $700 million surface-to-air missile defense system (SA-15 Gauntlet) along with thirty TOR M-1 air-defense missile systems, ostensibly to defend its soon-to-be-complete, Russian-built nuclear reactor at Bushehr. Moscow also plans to upgrade Tehran's Su-24, MiG-29 aircraft, and T-72 battle tanks.[29]

Experts disagree over whether or not these sales make Iran's military arsenal a threat. The sales have primarily focused on air defense.[30] In 2007 Russia agreed to sell Iran the S-300 air defense system, but cancelled the sale in 2010 in response to UN sanctions on Iran.[31] The S-300 could have significantly increased the vulnerability of aircraft attacking Iran's nuclear facilities.

Russia's defense sector amounts to more than 4 percent of its gross domestic product,[32] equal with agriculture. Defense manufacturing has long been a high national priority, so we must wonder if Russia feels it is giving a lot by participating in the embargos on Iran.

In 2011 Russia helped complete the Bushehr nuclear power plant despite pressure on Russia from the international community.[33] Russia continued to work on the reactor while expressing support for sanctions that directly target the nuclear program.[34]

Russia's Step-by-Step Plan

In August 2011, Russia proposed a "step-by-step" plan, which provides a phased framework to ease sanctions in exchange for Iran meeting certain benchmarks. The United States has resisted this approach, arguing that it will allow Iran to make minor concessions to break off parts of the coalition without genuine moves for settlement. Given Iran's years of relative success at duping and dividing the international community, this is a realistic worry. However, if no other path to settlement is possible, the step-by-step plan offers at least a small delay of Iranian nuclearization, and increases the diplomatic cost Iran must pay to renege. Little prevents Iran from getting the bomb eventually. If it must stab one of its few friends in the back on the way, it is a net gain for Western interests.

Both Iran and Russia have been quiet about the contents of the step-by-step plan, making it difficult to evaluate. However, a March 2012

Boston Globe op-ed by Hossein Mousavian,[35] a top Iranian nuclear negotiator during the Khatami administration, might be similar to the proposal. Mousavian proposes a path for negotiation:

- Identify each side's bottom lines. For Iran, this will likely be the right to a nuclear program with enrichment; for the P5+1, this is the prohibition of an Iranian bomb and the resolution of Iran's disputes with the IAEA.
- The West must cease pushing for regime change in Iran.
- The West must understand that sanctions offer delay, not resolution.

Negotiations launched with this shared understanding, argues Mousavian, will have a chance at success. An ultimate agreement might feature the following phases:

1. Iran limits enrichment and stops enrichment to 20 percent. The P5+1 provides fuel rods for the Tehran Research Reactor, and the United States and European Union suspend sanctions on Iranian oil and its central bank.
2. Iran implements several IAEA measures that will yield greater transparency. The P5+1 recognizes Iran's right to enrich, and suspends UN nuclear sanctions.
3. Iran permits complete IAEA surveillance of its centrifuges and ceases putting centrifuges on new sites. It also downblends any nuclear fuel it holds that exceeds its civilian needs. The P5+1 suspends unilateral nuclear sanctions and sanctions on civilian goods, while initiating nuclear technology cooperation with the Islamic Republic.
4. Iran ratifies the IAEA measures it implemented in step 2, and puts new enrichment site construction on hold until all issues with the IAEA are resolved. The P5+1 lift all sanctions.

This may reflect the substance of the Russian "step-by-step" plan. If it does, there are several major hurdles. First is the need for the United States to cease pushing regime change and lift its sanctions. While there is no American law that openly promotes the fall of the Islamic Republic (such laws have been applied to other nations in the past, especially Iraq), a case can be made that the United States has had a de facto policy of regime change for decades. Thinkers left and right alike have a tendency to couch their arguments about appropriate measures against Iran in terms of what is least likely to alienate or oppress an alleged liberal democratic majority that will ultimately arise, overthrow the government, and implement a much more responsible foreign policy. Even the most sober analysts sometimes exhibit this tendency. Assuring Iran that the United States does not have a policy of regime change is thus not a matter of reversing some "Iran Liberation Act." It would require a major shift in the mentality of the vast majority of the American foreign policy elite—something which cannot be legislated. Progress on the nuclear issue would provoke such a change, but in Mousavian's conception this runs into a chicken-egg problem, as Western assurances are required to initiate that progress. However, even if the West manages a shift against regime change, Iran will not likely be satisfied—its leaders have lived through decades of tension with foreign powers and many, especially in the conservative factions, will be profoundly skeptical of a Western change of heart.

This issue is entangled in the plan's call for sanction relief. Even as tensions over Iran's nuclear program have peaked in recent months, new sanctions laws have prominently referenced concerns about human rights issues in Iran. The step-by-step plan does not and should not refer to Iran's internal politics. If it is carried through, there is no reason to believe that the Iranian people will be freer. The president will thus have to convince Congress to back his initiative, which will be difficult given the intensity of concerns about Iran. A parallel problem may arise in the European Union, as continuing human rights concerns in Iran will remain a sticking point. The regime will likely feel a need to show off its conservative credentials after cooperation with the West, so a domestic demonstration—perhaps death sentences for gays or a crackdown on dissenters—may make some Europeans very uneasy about pushing to normalization with the mullahs.

The plan's first step, halting 20 percent enrichment in exchange for Tehran Research Reactor (TRR) fuel and cuts to the toughest sanctions, is realistic, especially if this is Tehran's initial negotiating position. The proposal essentially turns back the clock to 2008 or 2009. However, because Iran has been enriching since then, the West will likely demand additional assurances, such as careful controls on the TRR fuel, and may also make a more limited offer—such as refusing to provide TRR fuel but lifting sanctions, or vice versa. It is more likely still that the West will seek Iranian concessions from the next several steps before turning back the sanctions clock, reducing chances of Iranian assent.

The second step, tighter IAEA controls in exchange for cuts to UN sanctions and a recognition of Iran's right to enrich, will be tougher. Iran might be quite willing to concede here, although it does profess worries that the IAEA monitoring regime is passing information to Western intelligence agencies (in fact, information is flowing the other direction). However, the West will find this step very unappealing. Recognition of an Iranian right to enrichment is inevitable if there is to be a peaceful settlement, but this is a very tough pill to swallow. The West retains deep concerns about the direction of Iran's nuclear program and the trustworthiness of the Iranian government, and recognition of Iran's right to enrichment will require a major reduction in those concerns; completing the first step will be some assurance, but certainly not enough. Iran currently enriches more than it needs for civilian purposes, and the West will surely wish to keep Iran from locking in this risky status quo.

The third step, ceasing to make new centrifuge sites while down-blending excess enriched uranium, is challenging for Iran. The latter element requires Iran to overcome a measure of its deep distrust of the United States, because getting rid of extra uranium will dramatically reduce the viability of the weaponization option. The former element can only be verified by proving a negative—that there are no new centrifuge sites within massive Iran. Inspectors could thus become quite intrusive, and would certainly need access to sensitive military sites like Parchin. The West must make an improbable move—lifting sanctions on civilian goods—in return. Restoring Iran's access to aviation parts risks restoring Iran's air forces, and Iran's neighbors to the east and west suffer from very weak air defenses. Even small gains could make a big difference and increase dependence on American air power.

The final step, in which Iran holds back its nuclear program until all outstanding issues are resolved while the West cuts all sanctions, is a pipe dream and cannot be achieved anytime soon. As discussed, sanctions are going to be very difficult for the West to lift without significant Iranian progress on unrelated issues like human rights, and such progress is highly unlikely. It is also tough to see Iran resolving all issues with the IAEA. There is no good evidence that Tehran has decided to weaponize. However, Iran's nuclear program has always had a weaponization element, which makes great strategic sense. Iran's leaders would have to either end their nuclear program or undergo a culture shift to a nuclear program focused on energy production.

Russia has reversed its position on Iranian sanctions numerous times.[36] After the release of a 2011 United Nations report on the Iranian nuclear program Russia resisted calls for additional sanctions. Deputy foreign minister Gennad M. Gatilov said, "The world community will see all additional sanctions against Iran as an instrument of regime change in Tehran. . . . This approach is unacceptable to us, and the Russian side does not intend to consider such a proposal. " Russia went on to criticize the IAEA report saying it was intentionally politicized.[37] They also responded harshly to mentions of either an American or Israeli strike on Iran.

The NATO intervention in Libya may have ended hopes of deeper cooperation with Russia on Iran. The Russians felt that they stuck their necks out by backing a strong Security Council resolution against Gaddafi's actions. When NATO used the resolution to justify a de facto regime change operation rather than a narrow humanitarian defense of Benghazi, Moscow felt it had been taken advantage of. The operation, and subsequent lobbying for action in Syria and Iran, seems to match the top two external threats listed in Russia's defense strategy of the previous year:

- "The desire to endow the force potential of the North Atlantic Treaty Organization (NATO) with **global functions** carried out **in violation of the norms of international law** and to move the military infrastructure of NATO member countries closer to the borders of the Russian Federation, including by expanding the bloc;
- The attempts to **destabilize the situation in individual states** and regions and to **undermine strategic stability**."

Russia has a fear that foreign powers—in particular NATO—will conspire to encircle it, starve it of influence, and provoke "color revolutions" against its government. Libya may seem distant, but NATO's willingness to act without clear legal support and outside its home region to remove a leader who had lately been a force for stability is a very troubling sign in the eyes of Russian strategists. Moscow is delaying action on Syria because it wants no repeats of NATO's resounding Libya victory, especially not against its key allies. Arms sales to the regime suggest Russia wants Syria to be the high water mark of the revolutionary surge. Given the growing weakness of Damascus, Moscow would be wise to improve the defenses of its remaining friends. This could make an attack against Iran tougher. If the West ends up intervening in Libya, Syria, and Iran, panic will tear through the halls of the Kremlin, and Russia will become more aggressive in defense of its interests.

CHINA

China has been wary of sanctions against Iran and generally supportive of its right to some form of nuclear program. Although China has acquiesced to pressure to support UN resolutions against Iran's nuclear program, as one of Iran's top trading partners, China has often refused to support sanctions against Iran.[38]

China supports Iran's right to a peaceful nuclear program and supports negotiations as opposed to sanctions or military action.[39] Since 2000, China has made attempts to evade sanctions and sell dual-use materials to Iran that can be used in manufacturing weapons including nuclear missiles. In 2009, several Chinese companies were found to be shipping dual-use materials including aluminum sheets.[40] In 2010, a Taiwanese company announced that it had completed a deal through a Chinese company to send more dual-use materials and technology to Iran in violation of sanctions.[41] In March 2011, the United States expressed concern that Iran might still be working with Chinese companies to acquire technology that could be used in the production of nuclear weapons.[42]

In response to the November 2011 IAEA report, Chinese Foreign Ministry spokesman Hong Lei called for "dialogue and cooperation."[43] The IAEA released a resolution expressing "serious concern that Iran continues to defy the requirements and obligations contained in the relevant

IAEA Board of Governors and U.N. Security Council Resolutions" and fears that the program has military dimensions.[44]

Because they are major trading partners it is difficult to see China as an advocate or partner in any military action against Iran under any circumstances. China has pushed back against, violated, or minimally complied with many of the sanctions measures.[45] However, despite its official resistance to sanctions and the occasional complicity of Chinese companies in violations, China has reduced its imports of Iranian oil by hundreds of thousands of barrels per day.[46] However, China imports more than five million barrels each day, so cuts to Iran are a fraction of its needs. It is possible that China's cuts are merely intended to avoid negative attention. It's also possible that they're temporarily cutting purchases to put pressure on Iranian sellers to lower prices—they, and the general difficulty Iran has had with selling its oil, have created an allegedly steep discount. However, the cuts are at odds with broader Chinese energy policy. With a rapidly growing economy and increasingly eager domestic consumers, most forecasts have Chinese energy consumption growing consistently for at least the next two decades. To accommodate this, the government has pushed for aggressive expansion in every energy sector. In recent months, however, Chinese domestic oil production has fallen by several hundred thousand barrels per day.[47] Combined with imports lost to sanctions, the Chinese oil market has had to find new sources for 467,000 barrels per day (bpd) just to keep intake level. (Imports have surged to record highs in response.) In this context, the Iran decision is puzzling. It appears that China does not expect these sanctions to go on forever, or at least that it feels the affected oil volume is not worth enough (about U.S. $7.5 billion per year) to risk damaging relations with the United States and the rest of the Iran sanction coalition. The shift of Chinese imports away from Iran is not merely a symbolic gesture, but it's also not a sea change.

THE ARAB STATES

The Gulf Cooperation Council

The Gulf Cooperation Council (GCC), a group of six Gulf states including Saudi Arabia, the United Arab Emirates, Kuwait, Bahrain, Qatar, and Oman, has served as the anchor of non-Iranian regional influence since the fall of Saddam Hussein. However, there is a diversity of opinion within its ranks—Oman has positioned itself as a neutral broker between Iran and the rest of the world, and with the United Arab Emirates has significant economic ties to the Islamic Republic; Saudi Arabia has called for American intervention and Bahrain has blamed Iran-sponsored Shia activism for its recent unrest. In general, GCC leaders have worked to head off any challenges to the traditional monarchical order (hence their fears over the Arab Spring and their bid to expand the alliance to include the other Arab monarchies, Jordan and Morocco) and have pushed against Shia, democratic, and revolutionary movements. Iran is thus an intrinsic threat to the GCC states—it is a Shia, nominally democratic power with ties to a menagerie of radical groups and its own revisionist streak, and it does not even call their alliance by its chosen name (Iranian sources call it the [P]GCC, for Persian Gulf Cooperation Council). Iran also enjoys a strategic location, superior geography, and a larger and more rounded economy than its rivals across the Gulf. Their key strength—massive oil revenue—is also their greatest weakness. They are absolutely the weaker side of the dyad.

Saudi Arabia

Saudi Arabia supports efforts to constrain the Iranian nuclear program. It has pledged support for sanctions or force, if deemed appropriate. Saudi Arabia also plans to make up for any oil shortfall caused by sanctions on Iran's oil industry.[48] As the last surviving non-Iranian power in the Gulf region, Saudi Arabia has the most to lose from a nuclear Iran. Prince Turki al Faisal, a prominent Saudi diplomat and senior member of the royal family, has vowed that if Iran succeeds in acquiring nuclear weapons, Saudi Arabia will also pursue a nuclear program.[49] Saudi Arabia would be willing to abandon the NPT if it isn't serving Arab interests and has proven ineffective in controlling the spread of nuclear weapons to Iran.[50] Leaked cables demonstrate that King Abdullah has privately pushed for a U.S. military strike on Iran—he told an American envoy that the United States should "cut the head off the snake"—but publicly the government has been more moderate in its views, calling for sanctions but never directly for military action.[51]

The Saudi-Iranian relationship has been a cold war for many years, with Saudi- and Iranian-backed factions grappling in Lebanon, Iraq, Syria, and elsewhere. Places with large Shia factions are especially contested. This rivalry has led some in Saudi Arabia to believe that if Iran gets the bomb, it will be pointed at Riyadh and not Tel Aviv.

This rivalry has been most salient of late in the Syrian conflict. The Assad regime has been in an alliance with Iran for three decades. This alliance was built on common interests, enemies, and traits. The two aim to hinder the regional goals of the United States and Israel, and have thwarted peace-building plans in Iraq, Palestine, and Lebanon. Riyadh has accordingly been a strong advocate of regime change in Syria, and has provided support to rebel forces. It also has its hands involved in burying the Shia-dominated opposition to the Bahraini monarchy. The fall of the Al Khalifa family would give Iran a foothold right next to the critical Saudi oil zones.

Saudi Arabia is so eager to see Iran's nuclear facilities destroyed that, according to an anonymous United States defense source from the area, it has quietly given Israel permission to pass over a narrow strip of Saudi airspace should they bomb Iran's nuclear facilities. They have arranged tests to ensure the safety of Saudi forces. According to the source, this was all done with the agreement of the State Department.[52] However, with the end of the American presence in Iraq, the Israelis are unlikely to fly over the kingdom—it is much further.

Following the foiled assassination plot against the Saudi ambassador to the United States, rather than advocating a military response, retired government official and influential royal family member Prince Turki Al-Faisal said:

> Such an act I think would be foolish and to undertake it I think would be tragic. . . . If anything it will only make the Iranians more determined to make an atomic bomb. It will rally support for the government among the population, and it will not end the program. It will merely delay it if anything. . . . An attack on Iran I think will have catastrophic consequences. The retaliation by Iran will be worldwide.[53]

Despite his assertion that military action would be foolish, he maintains that Saudi Arabia "fully supports tightening of the sanctions, assertive diplomacy and concerted action via the United Nations."[54] In response, Saudi Arabia authored a UN Resolution condemning terrorism and attacks on diplomats, specifically the plot against the Saudi ambassador to the United States.[55] The European Union expressed solidarity by sanctioning five Iranians related to the attempted assassination plot.[56] Furthermore, the United States recently completed an arms deal with Saudi Arabia that will give them $30 billion in fighter jets and other weaponry.[57]

In the event that Iran does gain nuclear weapons, Saudi Arabia has plans to build their own nuclear weapons with the help of Pakistan. Saudi Arabia helped fund Pakistan's nuclear program, reportedly under the agreement that Pakistan would return the favor.[58] Saudi Arabia is not equipped with the technology or expertise to develop its own nuclear weapons without outside assistance, and Pakistan is the most likely source given their expertise and close relationship with Saudi Arabia.[59]

The United Arab Emirates

Although the United Arab Emirates and Iran share strong bilateral relations based mostly on economic benefits and trade, growing tension between the two has deteriorated those relations and resulted in an unprecedented advocacy by Emirati officials for a military attack on Iran. Tension arose because of UAE's increasing support for the sanctions against Iran, Iran's meddling in Bahrain's affair to support the Shia opposition, Iran's threats to close Gulf oil shipment lanes at the Strait of Hormuz, and above all Iran's new plans to turn the disputed islands of the strait into an Iranian tourist draw.

In an interview with the *Washington Times* in July 2010, Yousef Al-Otaiba, Emirati ambassador to the United States, publicly announced his country's support for an attack on Iran if sanctions fail to stop the country's nuclear ambitions. Al-Otaiba stated, "The benefits of bombing Iran's nuclear program outweigh the short-term costs such an attack would impose." Al-Otaiba also explained the dangers of a nuclear Iran at length: "I think despite the large amount of trade we do with Iran, which is close to $12 billion . . . I am willing to absorb what takes place at the expense of the security of the UAE."[60]

The hostility is fueled by the UAE's long disagreement with Iran over the sovereignty of the three disputed islands of Abu Musa, Greater Tunb, and Lesser Tunb, which the shah seized in 1971 during the British withdrawal. The three islands occupy a very strategic location at the inner mouth of the Strait of Hormuz. Both countries claim the ownership of the three islands; the UAE has taken the issue to the UN Security Council. Emirati officials renewed their claim after Ahmadinejad made a surprise visit to Abu Musa in April 2012. UAE foreign minister Sheikh Abdullah bin Zayed Al Nahyan called the visit a "flagrant violation" of UAE sovereignty.

In the Iranian narrative, the islands were stolen by British imperialists and their weak colonial puppets to prevent the rise of any rivals for control of the Gulf. Holding the islands is thus a mark of Iran overcoming its colonizers and becoming a regional power. To the Arabs, the islands symbolize Iran's quest for dominance, and their seizure by Iran is nothing more than an act of looting done while the police were out of town. The Iranians have made stark threats to those who would interfere with their control over the islands; the GCC has announced it regards Iran's presence as a "transgression of the sovereignty of, and interference in the domestic affairs of all member states."[61]

The United States had also recently intervened and showed its support to UAE over the Islands dispute—an unusual move as America is typically careful to avoid involvement in territorial disputes. President Obama met with UAE crown prince Mohammed bin Zayed Al-Nahyan in late June, 2012. President Obama and the crown prince issued a joint statement calling for peaceful resolution of the dispute. The United States "strongly supports the UAE's initiative to resolve the issue through direct negotiations, the International Court of Justice, or another appropriate international forum," the statement said. Obama and Prince Nahyan also pledged to conduct more military exercises and training and to identify future defense equipment sales as security tensions rise in the Gulf in the absence of diplomatic progress on ending Iran's nuclear program. In November 2011, the United States announced a plan to sell the UAE a military package including 4,900 Joint Direct Attack Munitions among an array of other weapons. Theodore Karasik of the Institute of Near East and Gulf Military Analysis in Dubai detailed the UAE's defensive needs following the IAEA report:

> There is a complete reanalysis of the need of the UAE and what kinds of weapon systems they need the most to achieve their strategic goals in an international coalition. The GCC states at this time are united against Iranian pursuit of a nuclear weapon [but] they are not united on the political and economic ties.[62]

For over a decade, Dubai has been Tehran's most important window to the world's economy and has welcomed one of the largest Iranian Diaspora communities in the world. UAE and Iran have a long history of strong trade relations that have benefited both countries for years and which have been increasing steadily reaching around $12 billion in 2007. Re-export business between the two countries—goods sent to the UAE for shipment to Iran, and Iranian goods sent to the UAE for shipment to other countries—totaled 31.9 billion dirhams ($8.7 billion) in the first nine months of 2011.[63] However, the UAE's trade relations with Iran suffered greatly from the sanctions imposed on Iran. Minister for Economy Sultan bin Saeed al-Mansouri stated that "trade with Iran was always with consumable items. . . . We should not really stop that. The issue is with the financial transactions . . . regarding that, it has been affected. . . . If you want to export 20 tons of rice, the financial system does not allow you to do that." The IMF warned that the loss of Iran as a trading partner could cut 0.7 percent off Emirati GDP.

After the global financial crisis of 2008, Dubai's economic markets were collapsing and Abu Dhabi, the largest of the emirates, "bailed out heavily indebted Dubai to the tune of $10 billion, giving Abu Dhabi both economic and political clout over Dubai."[64] This allowed Abu Dhabi to be much more assertive in its security policies and to essentially be the only voice dealing with Iran. Under the direction of Abu Dhabi, the UAE has purchased large amounts of sophisticated weaponry from the United States in an effort to provide some deterrence against any "imperial" ambitions Iran may have. The UAE was the first country the United States allowed to procure the Terminal High Altitude Air Defense System, although experts question its utility against Iranian missiles. Despite these weapons purchases, the UAE is still hesitant to completely oppose Iran, and its open economy makes enforcing sanctions difficult.[65] Instead, the UAE wants firmer security commitments from the United States.[66]

Kuwait

In Kuwait the internal political debate is mainly about maintaining stability, sovereignty, and independence; Iran threatens all three. Kuwaiti forces recently arrested an Iranian spy network working for the IRGC and charged with gathering information on Kuwaiti military installations.[67] Kuwait has a Shia minority population which the government has accused of being loyal to Iran, though much of the Shia population sees Iran as a place of shared religious beliefs and an ancestral home, but not a place that they are loyal to.[68]

Like most countries in the region, Kuwaiti Emir Sheikh Sabah al Ahmad Al Sabah stated that the disagreement over Iran's nuclear program should be resolved through "dialogue, peaceful means and adherence to the principles of international legitimacy."[69] After years of dealing with military conflicts on its own borders with Iraq, Kuwait does not want to see another armed conflict and denounces military strikes on Iran. Kuwait has said that any nuclear power used for "inhuman purposes" would not be tolerated.[70] Not all members of the Kuwaiti government, however, are against Iranian nuclear capabilities. Following the release of the 2011 IAEA report, a Kuwaiti member of parliament was sued for money-laundering for the Iranian nuclear program. He was accused by a former employee and expatriate of using a company he is prominently involved with as a way to support the Iranian nuclear program and help Iran evade sanctions.[71]

Despite a rocky political relationship, the two countries have a budding economic relationship. Iran reported that Iran-Kuwaiti trade totaled $213 million in 2010. Iran's then commerce minister Mehdi Gazanfari praised the relationship, saying that "the establishment of a joint trade council between Iran and Kuwait will play an effective role in strengthening relations and increasing the level of trade between the two countries." He continued saying that Kuwaiti-Iranian trade has the potential to increase to as much as $500 million per year.[72] In October 2011, the Speaker of Kuwait's National Assembly, Jassem Mohammad al Kharafi, acknowledged the political turmoil between the states caused by the IRGC spying scandal but addressed the opportunity for positive growth with Iran, "We accept any differences between our country and Tehran but we are keen not to leave any disagreement without reaching a solution that serves our nations and peoples."[73] But despite the overtures made by the Iranians to strengthen trade ties with Kuwait, bilateral trade between the two countries only totaled 0.6 percent of Kuwait's total trade—well behind the UAE (1.5 percent), Saudi Arabia (2.4 percent), and the United States (10.4 percent).[74] Kuwait has abided by the UN sanctions, but it has also opened positive trade relations with Iran.[75]

Kuwait has a deep connection with the United States—the United States led the push to liberate Kuwait in 1991, and in return Kuwait allowed the United States to operate through its territory during the Iraq War. The United States retains 15,000 soldiers in Kuwait, and has proposed to sell the Kuwaiti government $4.2 billion of Patriot air and missile defense systems.[76]

Bahrain

Bahrain sees Iran as a major threat to its national security and sovereignty. Iran has conquered Bahrain in the past and has occasionally laid claim to the islands.[77] Bahrain's Sunni rulers oversee a Shia majority that they fear is loyal to Iran, and they see an Iranian hand in the protests that have rocked their country.[78]

Bahrain has opposed the use of its territory as a launching point for any intervention. Bahrain's Minister of Foreign Affairs, Shaikh emphasized that "the presence of a U.S. naval base in Bahrain does not mean that Manama will allow its use to launch an attack on any country . . . Bahrain's lands will be used only to defend the country in line with the joint Gulf Cooperation Council action."[79] The shaikh's words were clearly designed to rule out any possibility of a U.S. attack on Iran launched from Bahrain. Despite these warnings to the West, the shaikh warned Iran that Bahrain would respond with force to an Iranian attack.

Though Bahrain has officially opposed the use of American bases on its territory for action against Iran, behind the scenes the story has been different. A 2009 wire published by Wikileaks reported that King Hamad told then CENTCOM head David Petraeus that "[Iran's nuclear] programme must be stopped. The danger of letting it go on is greater than the danger of stopping it."[80] Prince Mohammed Bin Zayed also urged the United States not to allow Iran to continue its nuclear program uncontested.[81]

Despite urging tough action against Iran, Bahrain has been highly supportive of Iran's right to a peaceful nuclear program. Bahrain released a public statement that said, "Bahrain has consistently made clear its support for the right of all states to the peaceful civilian use of nuclear energy, transparently and in accordance with the relevant international framework and safeguards . . . Bahrain has made clear on a number of occasions that the Islamic Republic of Iran is no exception to this right."[82] In remarks to the 2010 International Institute for Strategic Studies (IISS) Manama Dialogue, FM Al Khalifa emphasized the right of all countries to peaceful nuclear programs, noting that the GCC and Iran each were engaging in nuclear research. He argued that the root of the problem was disagreements over enrichment that could be resolved through the creation of an international fuel bank.[83]

Popular protests in Bahrain have impacted its Iran policy. In a recent GCC meeting, Bahrain and other countries accused Iran of meddling in the affairs of Bahrain by instigating and aiding the protests.[84] Despite the brutal crackdown against the protestors, the ruling Sunni royal family is split on how to deal with the uprising. Conservatives led by army commander Khalifa Bin Ahmed and Prime Minister Sheikh Khalid Bin Ahmed are vehemently against any concessions to the protesters. They accuse Iran of being the acting force behind the uprising. In contrast,

Crown Prince Salman Bin Hamad has shown a greater willingness to engage with protesters.[85]

The remarkably transparent Bahrain Independent Commission of Inquiry (BICI), tasked by the Bahraini government with investigating the events around the protests, was unable to reach a clear ruling on Iranian involvement in the protests, noting that the evidence the government released did not successfully link Iran to "specific incidents." The report explains:

> It is the position of the [Government of Bahrain] that the alleged involvement by Iran during the events of February and March 2011 is part of a continuous policy of Iranian interference in the domestic affairs of Bahrain. . . . The Government of Bahrain has contended that the Iranian Government employed a variety of media outlets to influence the progression of demonstrations in Bahrain during the events of February and March 2011 and to broadcast what is described as false information about developments in Bahrain. . . . The evidence presented to the Commission by the Bahraini government on the involvement by the Islamic Republic of Iran in the internal affairs of Bahrain does not establish a discernable link between specific incidents that occurred in Bahrain during February and March 2011 and the Islamic Republic of Iran.[86]

The government claims that the BICI was unable to find evidence because it is classified and cannot be released. In light of the threat of instability caused by mass protests, Bahrain has reason to exaggerate claims of a coalition between Shi'a and the Iranian government in order to shore up their legitimacy while simultaneously undermining the legitimacy of the opposition movement. Beyond that, in an attempt to divide the opposition and maintain control of the kingdom, the Bahraini government has portrayed the uprising as a Shi'a movement against their Sunni neighbors in order to build support for crackdowns in the Sunni community.[87] Iranian backing would deepen Sunni worries.

Following the release of the 2011 IAEA report and the attempted assassination of the Saudi Arabian ambassador to the United States, Bahrain made similar unsubstantiated allegations against Iran. According to the Bahraini government, forces thwarted a terrorist plot by a group associated with Iran. The attacks were reportedly intended for the Saudi Arabian Embassy and the Gulf Causeway between Bahrain and Saudi Arabia.[88] Tensions between Bahrain and Iran grew.

In spite of the likely falsehood of at least some of the Bahraini government's allegations, it is hard to imagine Iran has not taken any action in Bahrain, for Iran has enough reasons to act that its choices might be called overdetermined. The Islamic Republic was founded by the popular overthrow of a conservative monarchy, and it retains elements of this revolutionary ideology. It has consistently opposed many of the Gulf monarchies as the antithesis of the ideals of the Islamic Revolution.

Government repression in Bahrain has become a major theme in the Iranian media. A revolutionary Bahrain would also be a stiff challenge to Iran's local enemies—the GCC would risk becoming moribund if it retained an anti-GCC member, regional Shia populations (such as those in Saudi Arabia's Eastern Province) could be invigorated, and Saudi Arabia would suddenly have an unfriendly neighbor on its doorstep. Iran also aims to increase its regional influence and decrease that of the United States; the fall of the U.S. Navy base in Bahrain would meet this goal. Further, Iran has often tried to use Shia populations as a pathway for its influence.

Saudi Arabia has already shown the willingness to provide military support to keep its allies in the Bahraini royal family in power. Most of Saudi Arabia's oil lies in the Eastern Provinces, which have a large Shia population. If Bahrain falls to a democratic regime, Saudi Arabia fears a similar threat to its own kingdom.[89] Tensions are elevated because Gulf monarchs fear that Iran will seek to promote uprisings by Shia groups. This is an unconfirmed fear, but one which contributes to the calculations of the Bahraini and Saudi kingdoms.

Qatar

Qatar has maintained strong security relations with the United States, allowing the presence of American bases and importing American arms. However, Qatar and the United States engage in surprisingly little trade,[90] and Doha has been accused of hesitation in its pursuit of terrorists in order to not appear too closely allied with the United States[91] and avoid angering key figures. It has also hosted representatives of numerous radical groups in an effort to become a regional power broker. These attempts to straddle the line between a needed ally in the United States and a pro-independence state have not always worked out to Qatar's benefit. In a recent meeting between a Qatari emir and the Iranian president, Qatar was reportedly threatened, "[If Syria is attacked,] the first missile [in retaliation] will fall on you."[92] Similarly, in 2007, Iranian Admiral Ali Shamkhani said that if its nuclear sites are attacked, it will not only strike U.S. bases in the region but also "strategic targets such as oil refineries and power stations" in Qatar, Bahrain, and the other Gulf States.[93] As part of its efforts to fortify and protect GCC states against such attacks by Iran, the United States is considering selling Qatar bunker-busting bombs.[94]

Oman

Oman has a close relationship with Iran. This relationship includes commitments to hold joint military exercises, a security pact, formal trade relations, and discussions on sharing oil and gas reserves in the Strait of

Hormuz. Oman has been particularly supportive of the Iranian nuclear program and has not expressed any concerns publicly.[95] The official position of Oman, as stated on its Ministry of Foreign Affairs website:

> The sultanate hopes Washington will engage in a "direct dialogue" with Teheran to resolve the crisis over the Iranian nuclear program. The sultanate has no reason not to believe Iran's assurances that its program has purely civilian purposes. This region, no doubt, does not want to see any military confrontation or any tension.[96]

Along the same lines, Oman has made it very clear that it will not participate in a war between Iran and the West. In a joint press conference with the Pakistani foreign minister, the foreign minister of Oman stated that neither Oman nor Pakistan would support any military actions against Iran and its potential nuclear facilities.[97]

Despite its refusal of support for any military action against Iran, Oman serves a valuable role in U.S.-Iranian relations. Due to its friendly relationship with both Iran and the United States, Oman often acts as a mediator between the two countries. For example, Oman was critical in negotiating the release of American hikers captured hiking into Iranian territory from Iraq, even going so far as to pay their bail and provide transit. One regional diplomat likened their role to that of the Swiss or Swedes.[98] Although Oman would be of no help during any military strike on Iran, it could prove vital as a mediator in negotiations.

Other Arab States

Given that many of the countries in the greater Middle East are still dealing with the aftermath of the Arab Spring, it is unclear what role they are able to play in the Iranian nuclear situation. The several states have varying relations with Iran.

Iraq

Iraq will likely do all it can to stay neutral in the event of a military strike on Iran. Iraq is approximately 60 percent Shi'a. There are three main political parties within the Shi'a population: Dawa, the Islamic Supreme Council of Iraq, and the Sadrists. The Dawa Party, the party of current prime minister al Maliki, is highly nationalistic. They are skeptical of external involvement in Iraqi government whether it is by Iran or the West. Dawa won the support of some Sunni and Kurds who felt threatened by the other parties with closer ties to Iran. One such party is the ISCI, or the Islamic Supreme Council of Iraq. They are closely aligned with the Shi'a middle class, and receive significant funding from Iran. Though they are very close with Iran, the ISCI is also receptive to U.S. involvement. They voted against the withdrawal of U.S. troops. The final

Shi'a political faction is the Sadrists. This is the party of the highly religious lower classes and consequently has a lot of influence in the Shi'a urban area of Iraq.[99] The Sadrists were deeply skeptical and sometimes militant toward the American presence in Iraq, and have backed the Assad regime in Syria.

According to November 2011 reports, the decision of the Iraqi government not to allow U.S. troops to remain in Iraq beyond the agreed-upon date was likely influenced by Iran. Al Maliki advisor Saad Yousef Al-Mutalabi said of the situation, "It is taking Iran into consideration. We understand that there is a certain sensitivity. And we do not want an excuse for the Iranians to intervene in Iraq on the pretext that you have American troops."[100] Now that U.S. troops have been withdrawn from Iraq, a power struggle has broken out between Al-Maliki and his rivals. Maliki has recently accused the leaders and representatives of rival parties of supporting terrorism and has used the security forces under his control to either detain them or force them to flee.

Egypt

Egypt and Iran have had uneasy diplomatic relations since Egypt signed a peace treaty with Israel in 1978. After the shah was overthrown in 1979, he and his family were allowed to live in Cairo. Egyptian support of Iraq in the Iran-Iraq War only furthered the animosity between the two countries.[101]

In 2007, while seeking to further diplomatic ties with Iran, the Egyptian government opposed economic sanctions or military action against Iran.[102] However, in 2008 Egypt announced that it supported the international community in its efforts to stop Iran from developing a nuclear weapon. In fact, a leaked cable dated from 2010 reported that Egyptian leaders said that the Islamic Republic "is going to take us to war."[103] Despite showing an awareness of the threat of violence in the region, Egypt maintained that military action should not be used against Iran.

In the 2011 elections, the Muslim Brotherhood's Freedom and Justice Party and the Salafist al-Nour party received the most votes.[104] However, the new Egyptian government is still in transition which makes it difficult to discern what the political landscape will look like months and years from now. But the interim government has been taking action that appears to be much friendlier to Iran than previous regimes were. For example, Iranian naval vessels were allowed to use the Suez Canal for the first time since 1979.[105]

Iran hailed the election of the Brotherhood's Muhammad Morsi to the presidency, and has made regular overtures to him for restored relations. However, Morsi has remained quiet on Iran, and worries of a pro-Iranian turn under Islamist governance appear to have been quite overstated. Iran's attempts to approach Morsi have taken on a pathetic air—Ahmadinejad phoned Morsi to invite him to attend the Non-Aligned Movement (NAM) summit that Tehran hosted in late 2012, and then publicized plans to send his chief of staff, Hamid Beqaei, to extend the invitation in person. *Al-Hayat*, a major Arabic newspaper based in London, cited a source close to the president's office when reporting that Morsi would be sending Prime Minister Hesham Kandil or Foreign Minister Mohamed Kamel Amr instead of attending himself.[106] Morsi and his office did little to assuage these rumors, choosing instead to play hard to get. Despite this apparent snub, it was announced in late August 2012 that President Morsi would in fact travel to Tehran and attend the summit at the end of the month, a move than was seen as perhaps signaling a shift in Egyptian policy and approach towards Iran.[107] In fact, Morsi criticized Iran during his remarks before the NAM summit when he openly backed a regime change in Syria: "Our solidarity with the struggle of the Syrian people against an oppressive regime that has lost its legitimacy is an ethical duty as it is a political and strategic necessity."[108] This and further disagreements over Syria suggest that a grand rapprochement is not realistic in the immediate future. Egypt will not back Iran's nuclear program to the point of exertion.

Yemen

Yemen's official position on Iran's nuclear program may change depending on the outcome of the present unrest. The Saleh government's position was that Iran has a right under international law to a peaceful nuclear program but not to a nuclear weapons program.[109] But with the fall of Saleh and the transfer of power to his deputy, Abd-Rabbu Mansour Hadi, things may change.

While the United States has provided substantial economic and military aid to Yemen in recent history for counterterrorism purposes, Yemen was never a proactive ally against Iran. The United States considered Yemen an ally against terrorism during President Saleh's regime, but even Yemen's counterterrorism policies came under question because well known militants were treating Yemen as a safe haven. Yemen is in the midst of violent internal conflict and therefore will not be a significant player in the near future. However, the Yemenis are certainly no friends of Iran's, as Iran is believed to be providing the Houthi insurgency—a Zaidi Shia movement—with arms.[110]

Syria

Syria is Iran's closest state ally in the region. Ever since the Iran-Iraq war in 1980–1988 (when Syria chose to ally with non-Arab Iran against Saddam Hussein and the United States), Syria and Iran have had a strategic alliance based on common enemies rather than a common ideology, and extending into multiple aspects of cooperation comprised of diplomatic, military, and economic interactions. Iranian patronage is key to the survival of the Assad regime in the face of the uprising and internal conflict in Syria. Although Iran may question Assad himself (and Iran does certainly question the tactics he has used against the internal uprising), Iran clearly intends to ensure the survival of a pro-Iranian Alawite regime in Syria if at all possible. Iran has defended the Assad regime to the hilt, providing technical, economic, and military assistance and amplifying its rhetoric. After an assassin's bomb killed several members of the regime's inner circle and Western reactions were muted, Majlis Speaker Ali Larijani argued that the West believes that there are good and bad assassinations—implicitly linking the Syrian attack to the killings of nuclear scientists in Iran. There are, however, rumblings of discontent within Iran as the Assad regime's position weakens. Liberal elements had long seen Tehran's strong support of the Arab Spring (the Islamic Awakening, in its parlance) but branding of the Syrian protests as terrorism—even before they had become violent—as hypocritical. As the regime's crackdown grew bloodier and bloodier, these voices grew louder. Once the regime's grip grew unsteady, some figures, including the conservative Larijani and figures close to former guard head Mohsen Rezaei, began hinting at support for a pragmatic solution. However, these voices remain a minority within the political elite, and Larijani couched his remarks in much more familiar rhetoric.

Syria supports Iran's nuclear program, including a right to enrichment, and has engaged in nuclear proliferation of its own, apparently with North Korean aid. The true question is how Iran will conduct itself should Assad fall, a prospect that looks increasingly likely. Syria is Iran's main ally in the region, and is a transportation route for Iranian weapons to reach Hezbollah. Syria and Hezbollah are vital to Iran's ambitions in the greater Middle East—they allow Iran to exert influence on the peace process, to directly threaten Turkey and Israel, to enclose Iraq, and to appear in the Mediterranean. With American forces to Iran's east and the anti-Iranian Gulf monarchies to the South, Iran's best opportunities lie to the west. The fall of Syria would cost Iran some of its ability to wage asymmetric war, and would push Iran's borders back much closer to home. Iran will be weakened and less secure. How would this impact Iran's nuclear program? On the one hand, Tehran could see a narrative of enemy advances towards it and decide that nuclear weapons or a more advanced breakout option offer the regime security against a growing threat. On the other, Tehran could see its attempts to revise the regional order coming to naught, and decide that reaching an understanding with the great powers is a necessity, at least in the medium term.

Jordan

Amman and Tehran have historically had bad relations. Jordan supported the shah during the Iranian revolution and backed Saddam Hussein in the Iraq-Iran War, and has a peace treaty with Israel.[111] The deep mutual hostility between the region's conservative Sunni monarchs and Iran's radical Shia republicans is certainly present, and it is compounded by Iran's connections to radical Palestinian groups. Some among Jordan's hosts of Palestinian refugees are a potential vector for Iranian influence.

In December 2011, King Abdullah II met with Ahmadinejad and expressed his desire to improve Jordanian-Iranian trade relations using "practical steps."[112] However, in a leaked cable Jordanian officials expressed deep concerns to U.S. officials, suggesting that Iran is "an octopus whose tentacles reach out insidiously to manipulate, foment, and undermine the best laid plans of the West and regional moderates." They argued that Iran is likely to use talks as a delaying tactic and to boost its prestige as a resistance power. The former president of the Jordanian Senate, Zeid Rifai, told American officials that the choice was stark: "Bomb Iran, or live with an Iranian bomb."[113] Despite the close proximity of the two states, Jordan and Iran have practically no trade relations, very poor political relations, and a history of political conflict and distrust. Jordan also has a strong relationship with the United States and a growing partnership with the GCC. With those two facts in consideration, Jordan would likely be a quiet ally in the event of a strike.

Lebanon

Before, during, and since the Lebanese civil war, the country's political makeup has experienced foreign influences. While the current Lebanese government shows a distinct inclination towards Iran, not all political factions share this predilection. Former Lebanese prime minister Rafiq Hariri (well known for his post–civil war reconstruction efforts and assassination by Syrian government-linked parties) was a close business partner and ally of the Saudi royal family,[114] while his son, Saad (a Saudi citizen), headed the previous government. Contrasting the Hariris has been Hezbollah, supported by Iran and Syria and, more recently, "leaders" of the ruling coalition, known as the March 8 Alliance. Indeed, before experiencing the current violent unrest within its borders, Syria constituted the "land bridge" between Iran and Lebanon, often used for the trafficking of arms to Hezbollah.[115] That said, the relationship between Iran and its proxy in Lebanon is not status quo. Sanctions against the regime in Tehran have seriously affected the economy, to the extent that Iran reportedly is unable to honor its usual $350 million in aid in 2012 due to financial hardship.[116] However, as long as Iran continues to back

Hezbollah financially or militarily, the relationship will remain important.

Lebanon, not unlike other countries, has voiced support for Iran's right to a *peaceful* nuclear program. Indeed, during its term membership on the UN Security Council, Lebanon abstained from Resolution 1929, which imposed further sanctions against Iran.[117] Though Lebanese government sought to characterize this abstention as a rejection of the resolution, many Iran supporters in Lebanon condemned the action.[118] And while official Lebanese-Iranian trade relations are not particularly strong, the two countries have frequently held meetings to establish and further their economic cooperation including seventeen trade agreements in 2010[119] and a $50 million energy memorandum of understanding in 2011.[120]

Of further concern, Hezbollah has become increasingly competent with regard to its intelligence/counterintelligence abilities in partnership with Iran. In late 2011, both Hezbollah and Iran succeeded in discovering two separate CIA informant networks working within their respective countries. In the case of Hezbollah, the group was able to leverage its political power to acquire U.S.-provided technology to discover the informants' identities and arrest them.[121] That the two counterintelligence efforts occurred at the same time should not be misconstrued as simply coincidence, but rather further demonstrates the close ties between the Hezbollah and its approved government in Lebanon, and the Iranian government.

It is very likely that Lebanon would vehemently oppose any strikes on Iranian nuclear facilities. That said, there have been mixed signals sent from both the elected government and Hezbollah. President Michel Suleiman stated in April 2012 that Lebanon would not strike Israel in the event of an Israeli strike against Iran,[122] while Hezbollah leader Sheikh Hassan Nasrallah addressed followers in February 2012, saying that Tehran would not direct Hezbollah to act should Israel strike Iran. He did not, however, rule out the possibility of Hezbollah retaliation.[123]

OTHER REGIONAL COUNTRIES

Turkey

Turkey is a growing regional power and a centrist force in Middle Eastern politics. Though a NATO member, Turkey has conducted a healthy amount of trade with Iran. In 2010, as Iran was considering the prospects of opening some of its companies up to public trading, Turkey announced that it wanted to triple its total investment in Iran from $10 billion within half a decade.[124] Turkey and Iran then announced a trade deal worth $30 billion between the two countries in February 2011.[125] In response to this deal, Ahmadinejad proclaimed his gratitude for Turkey's support of its nuclear program, and added that both countries should stand up against the pressure from Western powers to influence or effect unwanted change.[126] Because of this economic partnership, there have been several reports of Turkey sheltering Iranian banks that funnel money into the Iranian nuclear program, and some speculate that they act as a method of providing access to European markets for Iranian funds.[127] However, Turkey's president, Abdullah Gul, has insisted that Turkey is abiding by the terms of sanctions.[128] Turkey is a growing power in the region and has taken on the role of mediator in nuclear discussions.[129]

In 2010 Turkey and Brazil signed a nuclear deal with Iran, allowing Iran to enrich their uranium to higher levels than the standard set by international law, though the deal was blocked by the United States.[130] In June 2010, Turkey voted against UN Security Council Resolution 1929 imposing more sanctions on Iran's nuclear program and military activities.[131] Later that June, Turkey called for Iran to negotiate with the global powers over a nuclear-fuel deal.[132] However, Turkey remains economically engaged with Iran and therefore does not support further sanctions.

Despite Turkey's growing economic ties to Iran, there remains conflict and competition between the two countries over regional dominance. In September 2011, Turkey agreed to house an early detection warning radar system as part of the NATO defense shield[133]—a move that, not surprisingly, angered Iran. Ahmadinejad responded by criticizing Turkey for establishing a defense shield aimed at "defending the Zionist regime,"[134] while former commander of the IRGC Maj. Gen. Yahya Rahim Safavi was quoted in early 2012 as saying that "Turkey must radically rethink its policies on Syria, the NATO missile shield and promoting Muslim secularism in the Arab world, or face trouble from its own people and neighbors."[135] In 2011, Iran threatened to strike the NATO defense shield in Turkey should Israel launch an attack.[136]

Beyond disagreements over policy between Turkey and Iran, the two countries compete over influence in the Caspian region, particularly in Azerbaijan. In a gesture of goodwill and openness, both Iran and Turkey cancelled visa requirements for citizens of Azerbaijan. Azerbaijan has maintained a close relationship with Turkey and a hot-and-cold relationship with Iran (as will be expanded upon later).[137] Although there is no open animosity over Azerbaijan,[138] there is tension over who will have the most influence in that country.

Turkey has ties to the West as well as Iran and the Muslim world. Turkey sees itself as crucial in bridging this divide and facilitating a solution to the Iranian nuclear problem.[139] Turkey is unlikely to challenge Western powers in the event of a military strike on Iran, but it would not directly contribute to the efforts. Turkey abides by UN sanctions but has balked at supporting harsher unilateral sanctions. Ultimately, Turkey, like many other countries with a financial stake in Iran, desires regional stability and prosperity above all else.

India

India's Iran policy is widely considered realist. India imports a significant share of its oil from Iran, and has repeatedly entertained constructing transnational hydrocarbon pipelines through the Islamic Republic. It also has attempted to cultivate Iran as a check on Pakistani and Saudi ambitions, and has resisted unilateral sanctions on Iran. India switched to a barter regime that would avoid U.S. sanctions while allowing it to continue to purchase Iranian oil, although the Indian government likely perceives the barter regime as a favorable trade. At the same time, it has accepted and complied with UN sanctions.[140]

India has been developing stronger economic ties with Iran through its investment in the Port of Chabahar. The Port of Chabahar, located in the southeast corner of Iran, is a designated free trade zone, serving as a main trade route for goods destined for and leaving from landlocked Central Asian countries. India has been financing both the port and highways inland to Afghanistan and the rest of Central Asia—an effort to bypass the nearby, Chinese-funded port of Gwadar in Pakistan, which was intended to serve a similar purpose. In return for this investment, India gains preferential access to the quickly growing energy sectors of Central Asia.[141] This newly developing economic link between India and Iran only furthers India's desire to limit economic sanctions on Iran and maintain stability in the region.

Despite these evolving economic partnerships and investments, India has been somewhat at odds with Iran in recent times. Due to banking sanctions on Iran, India struggled to pay Iran about $5 billion for previous oil purchases for much of 2011. After Iran threatened to cut India off entirely in the mid-late summer, India was able to pay Iran using Turkey as an intermediary—a position Turkey values. Although India was ultimately able to pay Iran, Saudi Arabia was prepared to sell India its own product supplement supplies lost due to sanctions. The episode demonstrated the continuing importance of Iran's economic influence in the region.[142] Ties have also been strained by the attack on an Israeli diplomat in Delhi in early 2012, an attack for which Iran was accused by Israel. The ensuing investigation linked Iran to the incident, and the attack places India in a difficult situation—pulled in one direction by regional balances and its reliance on Iranian crude oil purchases, and in the other direction by purchases of arms from Israeli firms,[143] Western states, and Iran's failure to respect Indian sovereignty in the New Delhi bombing.

India has a budding economic relationship with Saudi Arabia. India's approximately 160 million Muslims have a religious connection with the holy sites of Mecca and Medina, which they can travel to on state-subsidized *hajj* flights.[144] Furthermore, 1.5 million Indian workers constitute Saudi Arabia's largest expatriate community. Saudi Arabia agreed to support India's bid for observer status in the Organization of Islamic Conference, and is India's largest supplier of foreign oil and India is Saudi Arabia's fourth largest consumer of oil. With India's booming economy likely to double its oil consumption over the next twenty years, the states will be seeing more of each other in the future.[145]

Given all of the economic investments India has in both Iran and Saudi Arabia, India has a strong vested interest in maintaining regional peace and stability. However, a nuclear Iran would also upset the regional balance of power. Following the 2011 IAEA report, an Indian official publicly stated that a nuclear Iran would be harmful to regional security.[146] Despite stating its opposition to Iranian nuclearization, India has not instituted new sanctions. But, it worked on a resolution with other IAEA board members criticizing Iran for its non-compliance and nuclear program.[147] It is unlikely that India would aid a military strike on Iran, but likely that it would support other efforts to ensure that Iran does not gain nuclear weapons as long as those efforts do not damage India's economic interests.[148] New rounds of sanctions imposed by the United States and designed to cripple Iran's central bank have been denounced by India. They are currently looking for ways to continue trade with Iran while abiding by the law.[149]

Pakistan

Pakistan does not traditionally do a lot of trade with Iran because of Iran's close economic relationship with India, its support of the northern anti-Taliban alliance in Afghanistan, Pakistan's close relationship with Saudi Arabia, and Pakistan's Baluchistan region acting as a base from which the Jundullah operate. However there have been attempts by both countries to improve trade relations. In September 2011, they announced a proposed economic partnership that would bolster Pakistan's struggling energy sector and provide it with another ally in the effort to stabilize Afghanistan.[150] Furthermore, Pakistan and Iran established the Pak-Iran gas pipeline project to expedite the transfer of Iranian gas into Pakistan. The United States urged Pakistan to open up to India rather than Iran, but Pakistan has shunned that recommendation. U.S. ambassador to Pakistan Cameron Munter tried to warn Pakistan following the 2011 IAEA report that Iran would not be a stable trading partner, but Pakistan opted to continue with the pipeline.[151] Secretary of State Hillary Clinton reiterated this point in March 2012, saying that the pipeline construction, joint or Iranian in nature, would still be a violation of the Iran sanctions law.[152]

Speaker of the National Assembly Fahmida Mirza explained that "Pakistan attaches great importance to its relations with Iran and has a strong desire to further consolidate the existing political and economic ties,"[153] and has stated opposition to sanctions against Iran.[154] Pakistani elements are widely believed to have greatly contributed to Iran's nuclear development program. In fact, Pakistan's most prominent nuclear scientist, A. Q. Khan, was found guilty of helping Iran establish a nuclear program, though he was soon pardoned by President Pervez Musharraf. Evidence collected by prosecutors shows that Khan aided in the construction of a covert Iranian nuclear enrichment facility between 1989 and 1996, although Khan claimed he discontinued services in 1991 after three years.[155] It is unlikely that A. Q. Khan could have sold nuclear technology to Iran without any segments of the Pakistani military or government knowing.[156] In statements made to prosecutors, A. Q. Khan and his assistants claimed that senior Pakistani general Mirza Aslam Beg was consulted and approved of all nuclear sales to Iran between 1989 and 1991, although General Beg denies this. The 2011 IAEA report corroborated the story that A. Q. Khan supplied Iran with much of its nuclear weapons technology.[157] In 2005, Pakistan acknowledged that Khan supplied Iran with nuclear enrichment technology, but denied having knowledge of it at the time.[158]

Afghanistan

The Afghan government has been linked to proposals for a nuclear-free region and world.[159] While this may appear to be an anti-Iranian position, the truth is more ambiguous—Iran has also been a strong advocate of these proposals, which it uses to draw attention to Israeli and Western nuclear arsenals. Kabul seems to be setting a course between Iran and America, announcing that its territory would not be used for an attack and accepting Iranian money while also retaining large levels of American troops—counter to Iranian wishes. Iran's behavior toward Afghanistan has been much more complicated. In the Qajar period, Iran made numerous attempts to capture Heart. In 1998, during Taliban rule, Iran massed tens of thousands of troops on the Afghan border after the execution of several Iranian diplomats and a journalist.[160] Iran also provided political and logistical support to the American invasion.[161] Since the Taliban removal, however, Iran has made large contributions to the reconstruction of Afghanistan.[162]

After the United States removed the Taliban from political power, Iran began a policy of investment in Afghanistan while simultaneously opposing the actions of the International Security Assistance Force. Such investment has clearly aimed at securing Iranian interests in the region. Iranian benefits from this "benevolent" action include limits to the inflow of refugees, a slowing of cross-border drug trafficking, and the strengthening of ties with the Afghan Shi'a population. One 2009 estimate placed Iranian investment in humanitarian assistance in Afghanistan since 2011 at $500 million, not a trivial sum.[163] But while the Iranian government has acted outwardly in a "benevolent" manner, the IRGC and its Qods Force has sought to arm the Taliban, expand Shi'ism and Iranian culture, and undermine the Afghan political structure through bribery and political sabotage.[164]

Iran has begun to hedge its bets in Afghanistan, building ties to the Taliban, considering providing them weapons, and allowing them to open offices in Zahedan, near Iran's border with Pakistan and Afghanistan. This appears to be an alliance of convenience. Both the Taliban and Iran want American influence in Afghanistan to decrease, but they retain deep ideological differences. Together with Iran's concern for the Afghan Shia, Iran-Taliban friendship is likely to be loose, and is likely to run into difficulties after American withdrawal deprives them of their central common interest.

Azerbaijan

Azerbaijan has shown support of the United States' position on Iran's nuclear program. In March 2008 Azeri customs impounded ten tons of nuclear materials headed from Russia to Iran's nuclear site at Bushehr. Although the materials were eventually released, the Azeri actions helped the U.S. intelligence community track their origins.[165] Azerbaijan has an atypical relationship with Iran because Azerbaijan's population is majority Shi'a and 16 percent of Iranians are ethnically Azeri—including former prime minister and leading opposition figure Mir Hossein Mousavi and Supreme Leader Ali Khamenei.[166]

The nature of Azerbaijan's relationship with Iran is formed by the close ties between Azerbaijan and Israel. Within the country, there is a significant Jewish Azeri population, in the region of 25,000.[167] Former Knesset member Yosef Shagal described the situation and benefits in plain language, stating that "the stronger the connection between Baku and Jerusalem, the more weakened Iran will be."[168] Iran, unsurprisingly, opposes this close relationship with Israel, particularly in light of the material support Tel Aviv has shown Baku—in February of 2012, Azerbaijan purchased $1.6 billion worth of weapons systems from state-owned Israel Aerospace Industries, and total annual trade between the two countries is $4 billion.[169] Tensions between Azerbaijan and Iran worsened in May 2012 when Tehran recalled its ambassador in Baku after protests outside the Iranian embassy, which allegedly included religious insults directed towards Iranian clerics.[170]

As Azerbaijan's energy production grows and its relationship with Israel expands, its role as an important regional player will also grow. Azerbaijan publicly opposes any military action that could destabilize the region.[171] However, leaked comments by the Azeri president Ilham Aliyev described the Israel-Azerbaijan relationship as being "nine-tenths . . .

below the surface." Some senior U.S. diplomats and intelligence officials posit that Israel has negotiated access to Azeri airfields from which some form of strike could be taken against Iran, though officials from both Israel and Azerbaijan deny these appraisals.[172]

Turkmenistan

Turkmenistan, recovering from sixteen years of the bizarre autocratic rule of Saparmurat Niyazov, has been expanding its international ties and opening itself to new relationships. Throughout this, it has pursued an avowedly neutral foreign policy with such enthusiasm that neutrality is even proclaimed in the Turkmen national anthem. Ashgabat has accordingly kept its head low throughout the Iran nuclear crisis.

Of Turkmenistan's five main industries and export areas, the largest is natural gas, accounting for 50 percent of its economy.[173] Though Turkmenistan shares a long border with Iran near the major city of Mashhad, the two states do not do large amounts of trade. Ashgabat only supplies 5 percent of the natural gas used in Iran.[174] Turkmenistan's natural gas industry has grown in recent years in anticipation of the construction of the Trans-Afghanistan Pipeline (TAPI), which the Asian Development Bank (financing the construction) hopes to be operational by 2016 or 2017.[175] Set to have the capacity to shift 108 billion cubic feet (bcf) of gas per year and deliver to Afghanistan, Pakistan, and India, Turkmen officials see the pipeline as a means of diversifying its natural gas customer base.[176] Additionally, 2010 saw the completion of a direct pipeline between Iran and Turkmenistan, which, along with an Iran to Kazakhstan via Turkmenistan railway, will solidify the relationship between the two countries.[177] One analysis put forward assumes that the increased use of this pipeline, and increasing economic interest in Turkmenistan by Western countries, could limit Iran's ability to influence Turkmenistan based on their economic ties.[178] That said, approximately 1.3 million ethnic Turkmen live in Iran, making a complete severance of the link between the two countries highly unlikely.[179]

Turkmenistan also maintains a positive relationship with the United States. The United Nations has built a monitoring station capable of detecting any environmental changes caused by nuclear tests in Turkmenistan along the Iranian border, angering Iran.[180] A leaked U.S. cable revealed rumors that Turkmenistan and Russia were using a nuclear cleanup conducted by Russia as an alternative way of smuggling nuclear materials into Iran, though Turkmenistan denied the charge and it lacked the ring of truth. Border guards did locate small arms that Iranian diplomats had been attempting to smuggle out of the country.[181]

Turkmenistan is playing both sides of the Iranian nuclear issue. Turkmenistan has been cooperating with Western countries in helping to monitor Iran, while simultaneously reassuring Iran that Turkmenistan respects its right to a peaceful nuclear program.[182] Turkmenistan would not support a military strike on Iranian nuclear facilities, as support would violate its neutrality; it also has an agreement with Tehran forbidding either country to allow its territory to be used against the other.[183]

North Korea

North Korea has a history of selling nuclear technology to other countries,[184] and has proved to be an avid supporter of Iran's nuclear program, offering aid through technology and materials. In August 2011, North Korea reportedly gave Iran software that can make calculations key to nuclear weapon design.[185] Tehran and Pyongyang also have a long history of cooperation on ballistic missiles, with several Iranian missiles (including the famous Shahab-3 family) derived from North Korean designs, and possibly some technology flowing in the opposite direction.

Following the 2011 IAEA report, more reports of cooperation between Iran and North Korea have emerged. The South Korean news media has quoted several anonymous diplomatic sources that say "hundreds of North Korean engineers and scientists have been working at nuclear facilities in Iran."[186] Japanese news source Sankei Shimbun reported that ten North Korean scientists had been working closely with the Iranians on their nuclear program in exchange for Iranian "financial aid" to North Korea. North Korea will not be supportive of any military action against Iran, and it would be likely to attempt to sell weapons to Iran during a conflict. This could lead to increased tension with the United States, which could spill into U.S.-China or U.S.-Russia relations depending on how the great powers respond to North Korean arms transfers through their territory.

CONCLUSION

The above review of the positions of the key international players regarding Iran's nuclear program suggests that while there are a few overt supporters of a potential Iranian nuclear weapon, a majority of states (including those bitterly opposed to Iran's overall policies) accept that under the terms of the Nuclear Nonproliferation Treaty (NPT), Iran is permitted to develop its nuclear power sector, provided it complies with all inspection procedures of the NPT. There is less consensus on Iran's rights to enrich uranium beyond fuel grade (approximately 3 percent). Even the United States' position on this has fluctuated over the years. What is clear is that most Iranians, including those who despise the regime, believe that Iran has the right to enrich and should be treated like other members of the NPT. This is one of the reasons a solution to this problem is so difficult to attain.

NOTES

1. Peter Crail, "History of Official Proposals on the Iranian Nuclear Issue," Arms Control Association, 2009, www.armscontrol.org/factsheets/Iran_Nuclear_Proposals.

2. "U.S., U.K. and Canada Sanction Iran," *United Press International—Special Reports*, July 8, 2011, www.upi.com/Top_News/Special/2011/07/08/US-UK-and-Canada-sanction-Iran/UPI-83241310132448/.

3. "Report: Iran aAuthorities behind Attack on U.K. Embassy," *Haaretz*, Dec. 1, 2011, www.haaretz.com/news/diplomacy-defense/report-iran-authorities-behind-attack-on-u-k-embassy-1.399006.

4. Riazat Butt, "William Hague Calls for Tougher Sanctions against Iran," *Guardian*, Dec. 1, 2011, www.guardian.co.uk/world/2011/dec/01/william-hague-calls-tougher-sanctions-iran.

5. Alistair MacDonald, "U.K. Defense Chief Cites Iran's Nuclear Risk," *Wall Street Journal*, Oct. 4, 2011, http://online.wsj.com/article/SB10001424052970203791904576610920375866818.html.

6. Justin Cohen, "Exclusive Ed Miliband Interview, Part Two," *Jewish News*, Feb. 24, 2011, www.totallyjewish.com/news/national/?content_id=15827.

7. "UK's Clegg Fears Military Conflict with Iran," Associated Press, Feb. 2, 2012, news.yahoo.com/uks-clegg-fears-military-conflict-iran-200111721.html.

8. Seumas Milne, "War on Iran Has Already Begun: Act Before It Threatens All of Us," *Guardian*, Dec. 7, 2011, www.guardian.co.uk/commentisfree/2011/dec/07/iran-war-already-begun.

9. "Iran Nuclear Crisis: France Wants 'Stricter' Sanctions," BBC News, Jan. 3, 2012, www.bbc.co.uk/news/world-middle-east-16389858.

10. CNN Wire Staff, "France Condemns Iran Nuclear Move as 'Provocation,'" CNN, July 19, 2011,http://articles.cnn.com/2011-07-19/world/iran.nuclear.centrifuges_1_iran-nuclear-move-nuclear-activities-nuclear-program?_s=PM:WORLD.

11. "Sarkozy Says Iran Nuclear Bid Could Provoke Preemptive Military Action," *Al-Arabiya News*, Aug. 31, 2011, http://english.alarabiya.net/articles/2011/08/31/164882.html.

12. DPA, "France: Iran Risks Attack if It Continues to Develop Nuclear Program," *Haaretz*, Sept. 28, 2011, www.haaretz.com/news/diplomacy-defense/france-iran-risks-attack-if-it-continues-to-develop-nuclear-program-1.387192.

13. "Royal: Iran's Nuclear Activity Endangers Israel," *European Jewish Press*, Nov. 6, 2006, www.ejpress.org/article/11482.

14. Indira A. R. Lakshmanan, "Germany Wouldn't Join Military Action to Halt Iran Nuclear Aims," *Bloomberg*, Jan. 12, 2011, www.bloomberg.com/news/2011-01-12/germany-wouldn-t-join-military-action-to-halt-iran-nuclear-aims.html.

15. "Berlin Says US and France Guilty of Hypocrisy," *Spiegel International*, Sept. 24, 2007, www.spiegel.de/international/world/0,1518,507443,00.html.

16. David Wroe, "Iran: Germany's Special Friend." *Global Post*, Jan. 22, 2011, www.globalpost.com/dispatch/germany/110122/iran-nuclear-program-talks.

17. "Germany Bows to International Pressure over Bank," *Spiegel International*, Apr. 4, 2011, www.spiegel.de/international/world/0,1518,757276,00.html.

18. Judy Dempsey, "In Response to Iran's Nuclear Program, German Firms Are Slowly Pulling Out," *New York Times*, Feb. 2, 2010, www.nytimes.com/2010/02/03/business/global/03sanctions.html?adxnnl=1&adxnnlx=1316444782-IRUisOV8wMHQsC9fkufvCw.

19. Deborah Cole, "Brazil, Germany Clash on Iran Nuclear Sanctions," *Agence France-Presse*, March 10, 2010, www.google.com/hostednews/afp/article/ALeqM5g2kb3E9JqYyb59mx1mNbf_kTMbog.

20. Annika Folkeson, "World Powers React to U.N. Nuclear Report," *The United States Institute of Peace*, Nov. 11, 2011, http://iranprimer.usip.org/blog/2011/nov/11/world-powers-react-un-nuclear-report.

21. Josh Halliday, "Wikileaks: US Advised to Sabotage Iranian Nuclear Sites by German Think-Tank," *Guardian*, Jan. 18, 2011, www.guardian.co.uk/world/2011/jan/18/wikileaks-us-embassy-cable-iran-nuclear.
22. "EU to Slap New Sanctions on Iran's Officials and Firms," BBC News, Dec. 1, 2011, www.bbc.co.uk/news/world-europe-15984216.
23. "Report: Iran Authorities behind Attack on UK Embassy," *Haaretz*, Dec. 1, 2011, www.haaretz.com/news/diplomacy-defense/report-iran-authorities-behind-attack-on-u-k-embassy-1.399006.
24. DCA, "Germany Probing Alleged Iran Plot to Attack US Bases on Its Soil," *Haaretz*, Dec. 1, 2011, www.haaretz.com/news/diplomacy-defense/germany-probing-alleged-iran-plot-to-attack-u-s-bases-on-its-soil-1.398987.
25. "Die Weiterverbreitung von Massenvernichtungswaffen und ihrer Trägermittel stellt potenziell die größte Bedrohung der globalen Sicherheit und damit eine der größten politischen Herausforderungen für die internationale Staatengemeinschaft dar," *Wei ßbuch 2006*, 20.
26. "Für die internationale Gemeinschaft kommt es darauf an [. . .] den Iran von einer konstruktiven Lösung im Atomkonflikt zu überzeugen." *Wei ßbuch 2006*, 55.
27. "Iran: EU Bilateral Trade and Trade with the World," DG Trade, March 21, 2012, trade.ec.europa.eu/doclib/docs/2006/september/tradoc_113392.pdf.
28. Ralph Winnie, "Iran: Russia's Strategic New Partner," Russia Beyond the Headlines, March 24, 2010, http://rbth.ru/articles/2010/03/24/240310_iran.html.
29. Lionel Beehner, "Russia-Iran Arms Trade," The Council on Foreign Relations, Nov. 1, 2006, www.cfr.org/iran/russia-iran-arms-trade/p11869.
30. Beehner, "Russia-Iran Arms Trade."
31. "Iran Protests Cancelled S-300 Delivery," *Claremont Institute: MissileThreat*, Oct. 11, 2010, www.jpost.com/IranianThreat/News/Article.aspx?id=183608.
32. Andrew Kramer, "As Its Arms Makers Falter, Russia Buys Abroad," *New York Times*, Mar. 12, 2010, www.nytimes.com/2010/03/13/business/global/13ruble.html?pagewanted=all.
33. "Bushehr Nuclear Plant Goes on Stream," Fars News Agency, Sept. 12, 2011,http://english.farsnews.com/newstext.php?nn=9006200182.
34. Ariel Farrar-Wellman, "Russia-Iran Foreign Relations," Iran Tracker, Aug. 2, 2010, www.irantracker.org/foreign-relations/russia-iran-foreign-relations.
35. Mousavian, "Real Solutions to Nuclear Deadlock with Iran," *Boston Globe*, Mar. 31, 2012.
36. Associated Press, "Russia Calls for Courage on Iranian Nuke Program," *Jerusalem Post*, July 15, 2010, www.jpost.com/Headlines/Article.aspx?id=181526.
37. Ellen Barry, "Russia Dismisses Calls for New U.N. Sanctions on Iran," *New York Times*, Nov. 9, 2011, www.nytimes.com/2011/11/10/world/europe/russia-dismisses-calls-for-new-un-sanctions-on-iran.html?ref=nuclearprogram.
38. Robert Frasco and Ariel Farrar-Wellman, "China-Iran Foreign Relations," Iran Tracker, July 13, 2010,www.irantracker.org/foreign-relations/china-iran-foreign-relations.
39. "China Renews Call for Negotiated Solution to Iran's N. Issue," Fars News Agency, June 24, 2011,http://english.farsnews.com/newstext.php?nn=9004030993.
40. Glenn R. Simpson and Jay Solomon, "Fresh Clues of Iranian Nuclear Intrigue," *Wall Street Journal*, Jan. 16, 2009, http://online.wsj.com/article/SB123206759616688285.html.
41. Frasco and Farrar-Wellman, "China-Iran Foreign Relations."
42. Indira Lakshmanan, "U.S. Concerned Chinese Companies May Be Aiding Iran Nuclear Weapon Effort," *Bloomberg*, Mar., 10, 2011,www.bloomberg.com/news/2011-03-10/u-s-concerned-chinese-companies-may-be-aiding-iran-nuclear-weapon-effort.html.
43. Annika Folkeson, "World Powers React to U.N. Nuclear Report," *The United States Institute of Peace*, Nov. 11, 2011, http://iranprimer.usip.org/blog/2011/nov/11/world-powers-react-un-nuclear-report.

44. Matthew Lee, "Iran Nuclear Program: Russia, West Agree on Iran Text," *Huffington Post,* Nov. 17, 2011, www.huffingtonpost.com/2011/11/17/iran-nuclear-program-text_n_1099121.html.

45. Nidhi Verma, " India, Iran to Settle Some Oil Trade in Rupees-Source, " Reuters, www.reuters.com/article/2012/01/20/india-iran-idUSL3E8CK3C120120120.

46. "China's Iran Crude Imports Drop 45% in February," *Bloomberg,* Mar. 21, 2012, www.businessweek.com/news/2012-03-21/china-s-iran-crude-imports-drop-45-percent-in-february.

47. Javier Blas, "China Faces Crude Oil Output Challenge," *Financial Times,* Mar. 28, 2012, www.ft.com/cms/s/0/e1550712-78b3-11e1-9f0f-00144feab49a.html?ftcamp=published_links/rss/markets/feed//product#axzz1qWfaYHBq.

48. Jay Solomon, "Saudi Suggest 'Squeezing' Iran over Nuclear Ambition," *Wall Street Journal,* June 22, 2011,http://online.wsj.com/article/SB10001424052702304887904576400083811644642.html?KEYWORDS=Saudi+Suggests+'Squeezing'+Iran+Over+Nuclear+Ambitions.

49. Turki Al-Faisal is often used by the Saudi regime to test public reactions to language and stances that may be unpopular. Because he not extremely close to power, if his remarks cause significant backlash, it is easy for the Saudi regime to back off. He also tends to have a pessimistic outlook. See Jason Burke, "Riyadh Will Build Nuclear Weapons if Iran Gets Them, Saudi Prince Warns," *Guardian,* June 29, 2011, www.guardian.co.uk/world/2011/jun/29/saudi-build-nuclear-weapons-iran.

50. Tariq Khaitous, "Issue Brief: Egypt and Saudi Arabia's Policies toward a Nuclear Iran," The Nuclear Threat Initiative, Dec. 2011,www.nti.org/e_research/e3_96.html.

51. Ian Blak and Simon Tisdall, "Saudi Arabia Urges US to Attack Iran to Stop Nuclear Programme," *Guardian,* Nov. 28, 2010, www.guardian.co.uk/world/2010/nov/28/us-embassy-cables-saudis-iran.

52. Hugh Tomlinson, "Saudi Arabia Gives Israel Clear Skies to Attack Iranian Nuclear Sites," *Times,* June 12, 2010,www.timesonline.co.uk/tol/news/world/middle_east/article7148555.ece.

53. Reuters, "Saudi Prince Warns Against Any Attack on Iran," MSNBC.com, Nov. 15, 2011, www.msnbc.msn.com/id/45312130/ns/world_news-mideast_n_africa/t/saudi-prince-warns-against-any-attack-iran/#.TtOkZLKP641.

54. Reuters, "Saudi Prince Warns Against Any Attack on Iran."

55. "Iran Criticizes Saudi Arabia UN Resolution," CNN.com, Nov. 17, 2011, www.cnn.com/2011/11/16/world/meast/un-saudi-iran/index.html.

56. "EU Sanctions Five Iranians over Saudi Ambassador Plot; Ashton Says Iran Nuclear Talks Could Resume Soon," Al-Arabiya.net, Oct. 21, 2011, www.alarabiya.net/articles/2011/10/21/172989.html.

57. Jason Ukman, "U.S., Saudi Arabia Strike $30 Billion Arms Deal," *Washington Post,* Dec. 29, 2011, www.washingtonpost.com/blogs/checkpoint-washington/post/us-saudi-arabia-strike-30-billion-arms-deal/2011/12/29/gIQAjZmhOP_blog.html.

58. Yossi Melman, "In Face of Iran Threat, Saudi Arabia Mulls Nuclear Cooperation with Pakistan," *Haaretz,* Sept., 8, 2011,www.haaretz.com/print-edition/features/in-face-of-iran-threat-saudi-arabia-mulls-nuclear-cooperation-with-pakistan-1.383153.

59. Pervez Hoodbhoy, "The Bomb: Iran, Saudi Arabia, and Pakistan," South Asian News Agency, www.sananews.net/english/2012/01/the-bomb-iran-saudi-arabia-and-pakistan/.

60. Eli Lake, "UAE Diplomat Mulls Hit on Iran's Nukes," *Washington Times,* July 6, 2010,www.washingtontimes.com/news/2010/jul/6/uae-ambassador-endorses-bombing-irans-nuclear-prog/?page=2.

61. "GCC Slams Iran Provocation," *Khaleej Times,* April 18, 2012, www.khaleejtimes.com/kt-article-display-1.asp?xfile=/data/government/2012/April/government_April25.xml&section=government.

62. Claire Ferris-Lay, "US Prepares Military Package for UAE against Iran," Arabian Business, Nov. 13, 2011, www.arabianbusiness.com/us-prepares-military-package-for-uae-against-iran-429723.html.

63. Martina Fuchs, "Major UAE Currency Houses Halt Iran Rial Business," *Daily Star* (Lebanon), March 16, 2012, www.dailystar.com.lb/Business/International/2012/Mar-16/166830-major-uae-currency-houses-halt-iran-rial-business.ashx#axzz28vi4jqdJ.

64. Karim Sadjadpour, "The Battle of Dubai," *The Carnegie Papers* 10 (2011), http://carnegieendowment.org/files/dubai_iran.pdf.

65. Sadjadpour, "The Battle of Dubai."

66. Sadjadpour, "The Battle of Dubai."

67. Bachara Nassar Charbel, "GCC-Iran Relations: Trail of Tensions," Middle East Online, June 4, 2010, www.middle-east-online.com/English/?id=39390.

68. Lindsey Stephenson, "The Political Underpinnings of Kuwaiti Sectarian Polemics," *Jadaliyya,* May 4, 2011, www.jadaliyya.com/pages/index/1449/the-political-underpinnings-of-kuwaiti-sectarian-p.

69. Layelle Saad, "UAE Wants Sanctions on Iran to End," *Gulf News,* Dec. 7, 2010,http://gulfnews.com/news/gulf/uae/general/uae-wants-sanctions-on-iran-to-end-1.724970.

70. "Kuwait Opposes Military Strikes against Iran," AFP via Iran Focus, June 3, 2007, www.iranfocus.com/en/index.php?option=com_content&view=article&id=11457:kuwait-opposes-military-strike-against-iran&catid=4:iran-general&Itemid=26.

71. Bill Bowers, "Kuwait MP Accused of Role in Iranian Nuclear Program," *Arab Times*. Nov. 27, 2011, www.arabtimesonline.com/NewsDetails/tabid/96/smid/414/ArticleID/176577/reftab/36/Default.aspx.

72. "Iran, Kuwait Trade Value Hits $213m," *Mehr News,* Feb. 4, 2011, www.mehrnews.com/en/newsdetail.aspx?NewsID=1245743.

73. "Kuwait Speaker, MP's Praise Ties with Iran," Kuwait News Agency, Oct. 2, 2011, www.kuna.net.kw/NewsAgenciesPublicSite/ArticleDetails.aspx?id=2193812&Language=en.

74. DG Trade Statistics, "Kuwait: EU Bilateral Trade and Trade with the World," *European Commission: Trade,* June 8, 2011, http://trade.ec.europa.eu/doclib/docs/2006/september/tradoc_113408.pdf.

75. Will Fulton and Ariel Farrar-Wellman, "Kuwait-Iran Foreign Relations," *American Enterprise Institute: Iran Tracker,* Aug. 1, 2011, www.irantracker.org/foreign-relations/kuwait-iran-foreign-relations.

76. Brian Murphy, "America's Uneasy Gulf Allies Adding to Arsenals," Associated Press, July 30, 2012, news.yahoo.com/americas-uneasy-gulf-allies-adding-arsenals-180605065.html?_esi=1.

77. Iran officially abandoned its claim in the Pahlavi era, but some Iranian neoconservatives have attempted to renew it.

78. "Shut Up the Shias," *Economist,* Sept. 9, 2010, www.economist.com/node/16994636.

79. "Bahrain Says It Will Not Be Used as a Launchpad to Attack Iran," Kingdom of Bahrain Ministry of Foreign Affairs, Aug. 21, 2010,www.mofa.gov.bh/Default.aspx?tabid=1037&language=en-US.

80. "US Embassy Cables: Bahrain King Says Iranian Nuclear Programme Must Be Stopped," *Guardian,* Nov. 28, 2010, www.guardian.co.uk/world/us-embassy-cables-documents/232927.

81. Meir Javedanfar, "Wikileaks Awkward Reading for Iran," *Diplomat,* Jan .17, 2011,http://the-diplomat.com/2011/01/17/wikileaks'-awkward-reading-for-iran.

82. Habib Toumi, "Bahrain Ambassador Denies Making Anti-Iran Statement," *Gulf News,* Nov. 8, 2010, http://gulfnews.com/news/gulf/bahrain/bahrain-ambassador-denies-making-anti-iran-statement-1.708079.

83. It is worth noting that FM Al Khalifa was speaking immediately before Turkish FM Davutoglu! Sheikh Khalid Al Khalifa, "First Plenary Session—Sh Khalid Al Khalifa," The International Institute for Strategic Studies, Dec. 4, 2010, www.iiss.org/conferences/the-iiss-regional-security-summit/manama-dialogue-2010/plenary-sessions-and-speeches/first-plenary-session/sh-khalid-al-khalifa/.

84. Mahmood Rafique, "Iran Is Poking Its Nose into GCC Internal Affairs: Shaikh Khalid," *TwentyFour-Seven News*, May 3, 2011, http://twentyfoursevennews.com/gcc/headline/iran-is-poking-its-nose-into-the-gcc-countries-internal-affairs-shaikh-khalid/.

85. Patrick Cockburn, "Power Struggle Deepens Divisions among Bahraini Royal Family," *Independent*, Sept. 27, 2011, www.independent.co.uk/news/world/middle-east/power-struggle-deepens-divisions-among-bahraini-royal-family-2361462.html.

86. Mahmoud Cherif et al., "Report of the Bahrain Independent Commission of Inquiry," The Bahrain Independent Commission of Inquiry, Nov. 23, 2011, http://files.bici.org.bh/BICIreportEN.pdf.

87. Karen Leigh, "How Bahrain's Government Is Dividing the People," *Time*, March 23, 2011, www.time.com/time/world/article/0,8599,2064934,00.html.

88. Associated Press, "Bahrain Says Terror Suspects Linked to Iran's Revolutionary Guard," *Guardian*, Nov. 14, 2011, www.guardian.co.uk/world/2011/nov/14/bahrain-terror-iran-revolutionary-guard?newsfeed=true.

89. Barbara Stark, "Saudi Arabia, Unseen Participants at Bahrain talks, Prefers Negotiation Not Violence," *Al Arabiyya*, July 5, 2011, www.alarabiya.net/articles/2011/07/05/156179.html.

90. Christopher M. Blanchard, "Qatar: Background and U.S. Relations," Congressional Research Service, June 6, 2012, www.fas.org/sgp/crs/mideast/RL31718.pdf.

91. "The Secret Alliance: Cables Show Arab Leaders Fear a Nuclear Iran," *Spiegel* International, Dec. 1, 2010, www.spiegel.de/international/world/0,1518,731877,00.html.

92. "Lebanese Sources Close to Hizbullah: Washington Asks Tehran for Negotiations on Iraq, Afghanistan; Iran Demands Comprehensive Settlement Including Syria, Bahrain; Ahmadinejad to Qatari Emir: If Syria's Attacked, 'The First Missile Will Fall on You,'" *New Middle East News*, Sept. 14, 2011, http://nmen.org/lebanese-sources-close-to-hizbullah-washington-asks-tehran-for-negotiations-on-iraq-afghanistan-iran-demands-comprehensive-settlement-including-syria-bahrain-ahmadinejad-to-qatari-emir-if-syria/.

93. "Iran Missile Chronology," Nuclear Threat Initiative, Aug. 2011, www.nti.org/media/pdfs/iran_missile.pdf?_=1316474223.

94. Tzvi Ben Gedalyahu, "US-Israel-Qatar 'Bunker Bomb Axis' against Iran?," *Israel National News*, Nov. 16, 2011, www.israelnationalnews.com/News/News.aspx/149795#.TtPoC7KP640.

95. Kenneth Katzman, "Oman: Reform, Security, and US Policy," Congressional Research Service, Aug. 26, 2011, www.fas.org/sgp/crs/mideast/RS21534.pdf.

96. "Oman's Positions," Oman Ministry of Foreign Affairsm www.mofa.gov.om/mofanew/index.asp?id=2.

97. "Use of Force against Iran on Nuclear Isuue to Be Opposed: Pakistan, Oman," *PakTribune*, April 4, 2006, http://paktribune.com/news/Use-of-force-against-Iran-on-nuclear-program-issue-to-be-opposed-Pakistan-Oman-139600.html.

98. Tim Lister, "Oman in 'Honest Broker' Role Again as US Seeks Freedom of Iran Hikers," CNN, Sept. 15, 2011, www.cnn.com/2011/09/15/world/meast/oman-iran-hikers/index.html?iref=allsearch.

99. Matthew Duss and Peter Juul, "The Fractured Shia of Iraq: Understanding the Tensions within Iraq's Majority," Center for American Progress, Jan. 2009, www.americanprogress.org/issues/2009/01/pdf/shia_elections.pdf.

100. Gabriel Gatehouse, "Iran 'Influenced' Iraq over US Troops Exit," BBC News, Nov. 14, 2011, www.bbc.co.uk/news/world-middle-east-15724404.

101. Will Fulton, Ariel Farrar-Wellman, and Robert Frasco, "Egypt-Iran Foreign Relations," *AEI: IranTracker*, Aug. 11, 2011, www.irantracker.org/foreign-relations/egypt-iran-foreign-relations.

102. Tariq Khaitous, "Egypt and Saudi Arabia's Policies toward Iran's Nuclear Program," Nuclear Threat Initiative—Issue Brief, Dec. 2007,www.nti.org/e_research/e3_96.html.

103. Ian Black and Simon Tisdall, "Saudi Arabia Urges U.S. Attack on Iran to Stop Nuclear Programme," *Guardian*, Nov. 28, 2010,www.guardian.co.uk/world/2010/nov/28/us-embassy-cables-saudis-iran.

104. "Results of Egypt's People's Assembly Election," Carnegie Endowment for International Peace, http://egyptelections.carnegieendowment.org/2012/01/25/results-of-egypt's-people's-assembly-elections.

105. "Egypt Allows Iranian Warships 'Can Use Suez Canal,'" BBC News, Feb. 18, 2011, www.bbc.co.uk/news/world-middle-east-12493614.

106. Yoel Goldman and Gave Fisher, "Morsi Set to Skip Non-Aligned Movement Conference in Iran," *Times of Israel*, Aug. 3, 2012, www.timesofisrael.com/morsi-to-skip-non-aligned-movement-conference-in-iran-reports-london-based-paper/.

107. "Egypt's Morsi to Make Historic Trip to Tehran," *Al-Jazeera*, Aug. 19, 2012, www.aljazeera.com/news/middleeast/2012/08/2012818182526548301.html.

108. "Morsi Criticises Syria at Tehran Meeting," *Al-Jazeera*, Aug. 30, 2012, www.aljazeera.com/news/middleeast/2012/08/20128308579560767.html.

109. Will Fulton and Ariel Farrar-Wellman, "Yemen-Iran Foreign Relations," The American Enterprise Institute: IranTracker, Aug. 10, 2011,www.irantracker.org/foreign-relations/yemen-iran-foreign-relations.

110. "Iran Backing Houthi Rebels, U.S. Claims," UPI, March 15, 2012, www.upi.com/Top_News/Special/2012/03/15/Iran-backing-Houthi-rebels-US-claims/UPI-92521331825597/.

111. Will Fulton, Ariel Farrar-Wellman, and Robert Frasco, "Jordan-Iran Foreign Relations," The American Enterprise Institute: IranTracker, Aug. 11, 2011, www.irantracker.org/foreign-relations/jordan-iran-foreign-relations.

112. Associated Press, "Jordan's King Wants Improved Ties with Iran," Fox News, Dec. 12, 2010, www.foxnews.com/world/2010/12/12/jordans-king-wants-improved-ties-iran/.

113. "US Embassy Cables: Jordan Wary of US Engagement with Iran," *Guardian*, Nov. 28, 2010, www.guardian.co.uk/world/us-embassy-cables-documents/200230. Ian Black and Simon Tisdall, "Saudi Arabia Urges U.S. Attack on Iran to Stop Nuclear Programme," *Guardian*, Nov. 28, 2010, www.guardian.co.uk/world/2010/nov/28/us-embassy-cables-saudis-iran.

114. "Biography: Mr. Rafic Hariri," Rafic Hariri: The Official Website of the Former Prime Minister of Lebanon, www.rhariri.com/general.aspx?pagecontent=biography.

115. "Bashar al Assads Syria Is Now in Death Spiral," *Telegraph*, July 21, 2012, www.telegraph.co.uk/news/worldnews/middleeast/syria/9417495/Bashar-al-Assads-Syria-is-now-in-a-death-spiral.html

116. "Iran Cutting Financial Aid to Hezbollah—Report," *Daily Star*, Oct. 12, 2011, www.dailystar.com.lb/News/Politics/2011/Oct-12/151111-iran-cutting-financial-aid-to-hezbollah-report.ashx#axzz1alhXsNyA.

117. United Nations Security Council, "Security Council Imposes Additional Sanctions on Iran, Voting 12 in Favor to 2 Against with 1 Abstention," United Nations Security Council 6335th Meeting, June 9, 2010, www.un.org/News/Press/docs/2010/sc9948.doc.htm.

118. "Iran's Allies Condemn Lebanon's Abstention," *Ya Libnan*, June 10, 2010, www.yalibnan.com/2010/06/10/irans-allies-condemn-lebanons-abstention/.

119. "Lebanon and Iran Ink 17 Trade Agreements," *Daily Star*, Oct. 14, 2011, www.dailystar.com.lb/Business/Lebanon/Oct/14/Lebanon-and-Iran-ink-17-trade-agreements.ashx#axzz1Tn8U4PlG.

120. "Lebanon, Iran Sign a $50 Million MOU," *Ya Libnan*, July 20, 2011, www.yalibnan.com/2011/07/20/lebanon-iran-sign-a-50-energy-mou/.

121. Mark Hosenball, "Hezbollah, Iran Uncover CIA Informants," Reuters, Nov. 21, 2011, www.reuters.com/article/2011/11/21/us-cia-hezbollah-idUSTRE7AK2MQ20111121.

122. Roi Kais, "'Lebanon Won't Attack Israel in Case of Strike on Iran,'" Ynetnews.com, Apr. 21, 2012, www.ynetnews.com/articles/0,7340,L-4218850,00.html.

123. Alexandra Sandels, "Nasrallah: Tehran Won't Order Hezbollah Strikes if Israel Attack," *Los Angeles Times*, Feb. 8, 2012, http://latimesblogs.latimes.com/world_now/2012/02/nasrallah-iran-aid-syria-lebanon-shiite-sunni-assad-khamenei-islam-hezbollah.html.

124. Thomas Grove, "Turkey's PM Tells Businessmen to Boost Iran Trade," Reuters, Sept. 16, 2010, www.reuters.com/article/2010/09/16/turkey-iran-trade-idUSLDE68F18F20100916.

125. "Reports: Iran, Turkey Sign Trade Pact Potentially Worth $30 Billion," CNN, Feb. 7, 2011, http://articles.cnn.com/2011-02-07/world/iran.turkey_1_trade-pact-minister-ali-akbar-salehi-turkey?_s=PM:WORLD.

126. "Iran, Turkey Seek to Boost Economic Ties," Radio Free Europe Radio Liberty, Feb. 14, 2011, www.rferl.org/content/iran_turkey/2308840.html. "Turkish Premier Voices Support for Iran Nuclear Position," Press TV, March 29, 2012, www.presstv.ir/detail/233685.html.

127. Louis Charbonneau, "Special Report—Tracking Iran's Money Trail to Turkey," Reuters, Sept. 20, 2010, http://uk.reuters.com/article/2010/09/20/uk-iran-banks-turkey-idUKTRE68J1R720100920.

128. Lally Weymouth, "Turkey's President on Its Relations with Iran, Israel and the US," *New York Times*, Sept. 22, 2010, www.washingtonpost.com/wp-dyn/content/article/2010/09/21/AR2010092105114.html?sid=ST2010092604067.

129. Peter Kenyon, "Turkey Emerges as Mediator in Iran Nuclear Debate," NPR, May 6, 2010, www.npr.org/templates/story/story.php?storyId=126506964.

130. Joe Klein, "Dealing with Tehran: The Return of Diplomacy," *Time*, May 20, 2010, www.time.com/time/magazine/article/0,9171,1990793,00.html.

131. United Nations Security Council, "Security Council Imposes Additional Sanctions on Iran," June 9, 2010, www.un.org/News/Press/docs/2010/sc9948.doc.htm.

132. Marc Champion, "Turkey Asks Iran to Return to the Negotiating Table," *Wall Street Journal*, June 30, 2010, http://online.wsj.com/article/SB10001424052748703374104575336853114123616.html?mod=WSJ_WSJ_US_World.

133. Thom Shanker, "US Hails Deal with Turkey on Missile Shield," *New York Times*, Sept. 15, 2011, www.nytimes.com/2011/09/16/world/europe/turkey-accepts-missile-radar-for-nato-defense-against-iran.html.

134. Associated Press, "Iran Criticized Turkey over Missile Defense Shield," Al Arabiya News, Oct. 5, 2011, www.alarabiya.net/articles/2011/10/05/170229.html.

135. Soner Cagaptay, "Next Up: Turkey vs. Iran," *New York Times*, Feb. 14, 2012, www.nytimes.com/2012/02/15/opinion/next-up-turkey-vs-iran.html.

136. "Iran Says Could Target Turkey Missile Shield," Reuters, Nov. 26, 2011, www.reuters.com/article/2011/11/26/us-iran-turkey-missiles-idUSTRE7AP0PE20111126.

137. Giorgi Lomsadze, "Azerbaijan, Iran and Turkey's Diplomatic Love Triangle," Eurasianet, July 20, 2011, www.eurasianet.org/node/63918.

138. Fulya Ozerkan, "Turkey Seeks Thaw in Iran-Azeri Ties," *Hurriyet Daily News*, Apr. 12, 2011, www.hurriyetdailynews.com/n.php?n=turkey-seeks-thaw-in-iran-azerbaycan-ties-2011-04-12.

139. "Turkey's Gul Urges Diplomacy on Iran," Press TV, Sept. 23, 2010, http://edition.presstv.ir/detail/143739.html.

140. Sumit Ganguly, "India's 'Realist' Iran Policy," *Diplomat*, Aug. 27, 2012, http://thediplomat.com/indian-decade/2012/08/27/indias-realist-iran-policy/. "India Bans Iran Nuclear-Related Trade," *Asian Defense News*, Apr. 4, 2011, www.asian-defence.net/2011/04/india-bans-iran-nuclear-related-trade.html.

141. Christophe Jaffrelot, "A Tale of Two Ports," *YaleGlobal* online, Jan. 7, 2011, http://yaleglobal.yale.edu/content/tale-two-ports.

142. AFP, "India to Make Oil Payment to Iran via Turkey," *Al Arabiya News*, July 31, 2011, www.alarabiya.net/articles/2011/07/31/160155.html.

143. Amol Sharma and Diksha Sahni, "New Delhi Attack Tests India's Relations with Iran," *Wall Street Journal*, Feb. 15, 2012, http://online.wsj.com/article/SB10001424052970204883304577222412053171078.html.

144. "India," *CIA World Factbook*, Sept. 27, 2011, https://www.cia.gov/library/publications/the-world-factbook/geos/in.html.
145. Harsh V. Pant, "Saudi Arabia Woos China and India," *The Middle East Quarterly*, Fall 2009, 45–52, www.meforum.org/1019/saudi-arabia-woos-china-and-india.
146. Indrani Bagchi, "Nuclear Iran Not in India's Interest," *Times of India*, Nov. 18, 2011, http://articles.timesofindia.indiatimes.com/2011-11-18/india/30414678_1_nuclear-iran-nuclear-programme-iaea-decision.
147. Bagchi, "Nuclear Iran Not in India's Interest."
148. Ariel Farrar-Wellman, "India-Iran Foreign Relations," The American Enterprise Institute: IranTracker, June 25, 2010, www.irantracker.org/foreign-relations/india-iran-foreign-relations.
149. Nidhi Verma, " India, Iran to Settle Some Oil Trade in Rupees-Source, " Reuters, www.reuters.com/article/2012/01/20/india-iran-idUSL3E8CK3C120120120.
150. Michael Kugelman, "Tilting Toward Tehran?," *Foreign Policy*, Sept. 15, 2011, http://afpak.foreignpolicy.com/posts/2011/09/15/tilting_toward_tehran.
151. "Shun Iran Pipeline, Open Up to India: US to Pakistan," *Economic Times*, Nov. 15, 2011, http://articles.economictimes.indiatimes.com/2011-11-25/news/30441080_1_pipeline-project-pak-iran-pakistan-and-iran.
152. Alex Rodriguez, "Pakistan's Iran Pipeline Plan further Strains Ties with U.S.," *Los Angeles Times*, March 8, 2012, http://articles.latimes.com/2012/mar/08/world/la-fg-pakistan-iran-pipeline-20120309.
153. "Fehmida for further Boosting Pakistan, Iran Economic Ties," Associated Press of Pakistan, Feb. 5, 2011, www.app.com.pk/en_/index.php?option=com_content&task=view&id=95802&Itemid=2.
154. Anne Tang, "Pakistan Opposes Sanctions on Iran: Speaker," English.news.cn, Feb. 4, 2010, http://news.xinhuanet.com/english2010/world/2010-02/04/c_13163962.htm.
155. "Weapons of Mass Destruction: AQ Khan and His Network," Global Security, www.globalsecurity.org/wmd/world/iran/khan-iran.htm.
156. "The Nuclear Network of A.Q. Khan: A Hero at Home, a Villain Abroad," *Economist*, June 19, 2008, www.economist.com/node/11585265.
157. "Pakistan, N. Korea Aided Iran's Nuclear Program," YnetNews.com, Nov. 8, 2011, www.ynetnews.com/articles/0,7340,L-4145336,00.html.
158. "Weapons of Mass Destruction: AQ Khan and His Network," Global Security, www.globalsecurity.org/wmd/world/iran/khan-iran.htm.
159. "Policy Areas: Weapons of Mass Destruction," Ministry of Foreign Affairs, Afghanistan, www.mfa.gov.af/policyarea.asp#wmd.
160. Harsh V. Pant, "Pakistan and Iran's Dysfunctional Relationship," *Middle East Quarterly* 16, no. 2 (Spring 2009): 43–50, www.meforum.org/2119/pakistan-and-irans-dysfunctional-relationship.
161. Suzanne Maloney, "Tehran and Washington: A Motionless Relationship?," The Brookings Institute, www.brookings.edu/~/media/research/files/articles/2011/11/iran%20maloney/11_iran_maloney.
162. "Background Note: Afghanistan," U.S. Department of State, Dec. 6, 2010, www.state.gov/r/pa/ei/bgn/5380.htm.
163. George Gavrilis, "Harnessing Iran's Role in Afghanistan," Council on Foreign Relations, June 5, 2009, www.cfr.org/iran/harnessing-irans-role-afghanistan/p19562.
164. Majidyar Kagan et al., "Iranian Influence in the Levant, Egypt, Iraq, and Afghanistan," The American Enterprise Institute and The Institute for the Study of War, May 2012, www.understandingwar.org/sites/default/files/IranianInfluenceLevantEgyptIraqAfghanistan.pdf.
165. Michael Rubin, "Boxed In: Containing a Nuclear Iran," Middle East Forum, Oct. 2008, www.meforum.org/1986/boxed-in-containing-a-nuclear-iran.
166. "Middle East: Iran," *CIA World Factbook*, Sept. 27, 2011, https://www.cia.gov/library/publications/the-world-factbook/geos/ir.html.

167. "Azerbaijan," The Jewish Virtual Library, www.jewishvirtuallibrary.org/jsource/vjw/Azerbaijan.html.

168. Anna Zamejc, "The Blooming Friendship between Azerbaijan and Israel," Radio Free Europe Radio Liberty, March 9, 2010, www.rferl.org/content/The_Blooming_Friendship_Between_Azerbaijan_And_Israel/1978312.html.

169. Sheera Frenkel, "What's the Israel-Azerbaijan Connection?," *Christian Science Monitor*, Apr. 26, 2012, www.csmonitor.com/World/Middle-East/2012/0426/What-s-the-Israel-Azerbaijan-connection.

170. David M. Herszenhorn, "Iran Recalls Its Ambassador from Azerbaijan," *New York Times*, May 22, 2012, www.nytimes.com/2012/05/23/world/middleeast/after-protests-iran-recalls-ambassador-from-azerbaijan.html.

171. "Azerbaijan Says Opposes Military Solution of Iranian Nuclear Dispute," *Azer-News*, Arp. 26, 2010, www.azernews.az/en/Nation/32087-Azerbaijan_says_opposes_military_solution_of_Iran_nuclear_dispute.

172. Mark Perry, "Israel's Secret Staging Ground," *Foreign Policy*, March 28, 2012, www.foreignpolicy.com/articles/2012/03/28/israel_s_secret_staging_ground?page=full.

173. "Background Note: Turkmenistan," U.S. Department of State, Jan. 23, 2012, www.state.gov/r/pa/ei/bgn/35884.htm.

174. Ariel Cohen, James Phillips, and Owen Graham, "Iran's Energy Sector: A Target Vulnerable to Sanctions," The Heritage Foundation, Feb. 14, 2011,www.heritage.org/research/reports/2011/02/irans-energy-sector-a-target-vulnerable-to-sanctions.

175. "TAPI Pipeline to Be Online by 2017, Predicts ADB," Universal Newswires, March 4, 2011, www.universalnewswires.com/centralasia/viewstory.aspx?id=3453.

176. Marat Gurt, "Turkmenistan Agrees Trans-Afghan Pipeline Gas Deals," Reuters, May 23, 2012, www.reuters.com/article/2012/05/23/us-gas-turkmenistan-idUSBRE84M0NJ20120523.

177. Ariel Farrar-Wellman and Robert Frasco, "Turkmenistan-Iran Foreign Relations," The American Enterprise Institute: IranTracker, July 8, 2010, www.irantracker.org/foreign-relations/turkmenistan-iran-foreign-relations. "Turkmenistan Opens New Iran Gas Pipeline," BBC News, Jan. 6, 2010, http://news.bbc.co.uk/2/hi/asia-pacific/8443787.stm.

178. Martha Brill Olcott, "International Gas Trade in Central Asia: Turkmenistan, Russia, and Afghanistan," The Baker Institute for Public Policy Energy Forum, May 2004,http://iis-db.stanford.edu/pubs/20605/Turkmenistan_final.pdf.

179. Jim Nichol, "Turkmenistan: Recent Developments and U.S. Interests," Congressional Research Service, May 26, 2011, www.fas.org/sgp/crs/row/97-1055.pdf.

180. JPost Staff and Associated Press, "Iran: UN Monitoring Station a Spy Post," *Jerusalem Post*, Sept. 12, 2009,www.jpost.com/IranianThreat/Article.aspx?id=162699.

181. Catherine A. Fitzpatrick, "US Cables on Turkmenistan, Iran Surface in Wikileaks," Eurasianet, Nov. 29, 2010,www.eurasianet.org/node/62453.

182. "Iran's Nuclear Is Just for Peaceful Purposes, Turkmen President Says," Ahluhl Bayt News Agency, Aug. 2, 2011,http://abna.co/data.asp?lang=3&Id=225002.

183. Saparmuart Niyazov and Mahmud Ahmadinezhad, "Joint Communiqué of Presidents of Turkmenistan and Iran," http://presidentniyazov.tripod.com/id62.html

184. Fredrik Dahl, "Analysis: West Fears Possible Iran-North Korea Nuclear Links," Reuters, Sept. 17, 2011, www.reuters.com/article/2011/09/17/us-nuclear-iran-northkorea-idUSTRE78G2HD20110917.

185. Dahl, "Analysis: West Fears Possible Iran-North Korea Nuclear Links."

186. "North Korea and Iran: 'Evil' Nuclear Fusion?," *RussiaToday*, Nov. 16, 2011, http://rt.com/news/iran-korea-nuclear-cooperation-413/.

Military Section Appendixes

Appendix B: Study of Costs of a U.S. Strike on Iran

The United States would bring to bear a more diverse, advanced set of assets than Israel. Its attack would be more effective, but it would also be much more expensive. Consider, for instance, the opening days of the U.S. intervention in Libya. This operation had many things in common with a potential strike on Iran—it included extensive operations against Libya's air defense and command and control networks, and a high operational tempo. However, it had many differences—chiefly, the substantial contributions of allied forces and the extreme degradation of the opponent's ability to resist. The United States will be unable to count on international support, much less assistance, for a strike on Iran, and it will face an enemy that, while it is not the picture of readiness, is far more capable than Gaddafi's disorganized and poorly equipped military. This is a sobering thought when one realizes that the first nine days of the Libyan operation cost a reported $550 million. This is more or less the ideal length for an American campaign against Iran—enough to hit a large number of targets related to the Iranian nuclear and missile programs and seriously damage Iran's air defenses, navy, and military command structures. Of course, the United States could engage in some sort of midsize, one-time strike to send a signal to Iran. This would be more expensive than the Israeli strike but less expensive than other options. Iran could entangle the United States in a more protracted conflict, or engage in infrequent destructive behavior requiring military measures in response. We will consider the cost of a brief American campaign, and then discuss the various contingencies that could result.

A ONE-WEEK WAR

The most obvious sources for cost estimation would be the most recent major air campaigns against an enemy putting up significant resistance—the 1991 Gulf War, the 1999 air war in Serbia, and the 2011 Libya intervention. The full cost of the Gulf War air campaign is difficult to estimate, though we do know that U.S. aerial and missile forces expended $2.2 billion of munitions.[1] The costs of the other operations were as follows:

Operation	*Duration*	*Cost ($)*
Noble Anvil (Serbia)	78 days	1.775 billion
Odyssey Dawn (Libya), opening phase	9 days	550 million

The high cost of the early phase of operations in Libya was driven by the use of 184 Tomahawk cruise missiles, which cost roughly $1.4 million each. A U.S. campaign in Iran would likely include the use of as many, if not more, Tomahawks, plus large numbers of air-launched cruise missiles which cost roughly as much. (For reference, the Gulf War saw the launch of 298 Tomahawks and thirty-five air-launched cruise missiles, costing $380 million in total.[2]) The Libya operation also featured an opening salvo against key air defense sites by B-2 Spirit bombers dropping guided bombs. This single three sortie mission cost $4.7 million. A campaign against Iran would require heavy usage of the B-2 due to its ability to deliver heavy weapons like the GBU-28 or even the new fifteen-ton Massive Ordnance Penetrator[3] that would be needed to destroy hardened and buried targets like covert nuclear facilities.

An attack on Iran would also presumably see the use of both land- and sea-based resources, while the Libya operation has been almost entirely land-based. We would thus have to add the costs of operations conducted from the two carrier battle groups likely to be in the area. A single carrier group costs roughly $2.7 billion to operate for a year.[4] A one-week presence by two carrier groups would thus cost $106 million, ignoring the costs of munitions expended. We will factor this cost into our calculations, for the presence of *two* carrier groups in the area is not guaranteed under normal operating conditions, and naval air support would still be needed for operations in Iraq and Afghanistan. It is quite reasonable to suppose that the United States would deploy additional carrier groups to the region in the event of hostilities, or accrue significant costs in rebalancing its forces to adjust for the increased needs in the Gulf.

Additionally, an attack will likely include significant measures to hinder Iran's ability to retaliate—its missile facilities and its various naval assets. This would have to be done fairly soon after the initiation of operations to prevent closure of the Strait of Hormuz or ballistic missile launches. This will require the use of further munitions and will reinforce the need for a very high operational tempo. The navy will need to maintain some of its additional presence in the area of Iran for a while after the attack to deter Iranian retaliation and to assist in preventing suspicious Iranian vessels from entering the strait, where they might lay mines.

There is a significant possibility that the United States will lose some aircraft during the operation. Replacing these aircraft can add significantly to the expenses of an operation. Basing operational tempo and loss rates in the 1991 Gulf War, we will assume that in seven days, 17,500 sorties will be flown at a loss rate of 0.5847 aircraft per 1,000 sorties and 0.7385 seriously damaged aircraft per 1,000 sorties.[5] This leads to an anticipated 10.2 aircraft lost and 12.9 aircraft damaged.

We thus arrive at the following estimates of cost for a brief war with Iran:

Item	*Cost (millions of $)*	*Notes*
Naval Operations	106	Two carrier groups for one week
Tomahawk, CALCM, and other cruise missiles	531.6	Cost for 300 Tomahawks and 100 other missiles
Sustained Naval Presence	424	One carrier group for eight weeks
B-2 Operations	28.4	Five three-sortie attacks, using a total of 60 GBU-28s and 120 JDAMs
Munitions	662.2	Usage adjusted from Gulf War[6]
Air operations	945	Assumes sortie length of 4.5 hours and sortie cost of $12,000 per hour.[7]
Subtotal	**2,697.2**	
Aircraft losses	535.8	Assumes aircraft cost of $50 million, and that all damage incidents cost $2 million.
Total	**3,233**	

Not all costs of aircraft loss or of the operation as a whole will necessarily be felt by the taxpayer. The air force has money budgeted to cover replacing lost aircraft, and defense budgets typically include delegation of authority to shuffle several billion dollars within the budget to cover the cost of contingencies.[8] There are, of course, indirect costs to such a transfer—for instance, training activities being defunded.

ADDITIONAL COSTS OF SUSTAINED CONFLICT

There are three scenarios for continuing conflict, each with its own costs; the scenarios are not necessarily mutually exclusive.

Scenario One: Brief Retaliatory Strike

Given Iran's extensive ties to terrorism and the likelihood that the Iranian people would expect their government to at least partially follow through on its decades of bellicose rhetoric, it is quite reasonable to expect some form of violent response to a strike. Depending on the nature of this response, American policymakers may feel it is appropriate to retaliate. The facilities of the IRGC, and in particular its Qods Force, would be the most natural targets for this operation. The damage to Iran's defenses from the initial strike would make retaliation easier.

The targets would require no more than a few precision-guided munitions to destroy, making it a fairly simple operation. Assuming that the United States would attack ten targets with two rounds each, we arrive at a cost of:

Item	*Cost (millions of $)*
Munitions	10.0
Air operations	2.7
Total[9]	**12.7**

Scenario Two: Clearing Hormuz

The Iranians have repeatedly stated their ability and willingness to seal the Strait of Hormuz if they are attacked. This would be an extraordinary step that would cause serious damage to the global economy and force urgent military effort to clear the strait of mines and missile threats. This would entail large numbers of strike aircraft patrolling Iranian coastal areas looking for minelaying craft and antiship missile launchers, AWACS/JSTARS and similar aircraft to coordinate them, and minesweepers to clear the mines.[10] Estimates typically project mineclearing taking less than forty days, while estimates for air operations vary greatly (and note that some suggest that the threat of missile attacks on the navy's limited number of mineclearing vessels would force them to wait until the missile threat is reduced, delaying the reopening of the strait and further harming the global economy). We will be charitable and assume a fifteen-day air campaign and a thirty-day mineclearing campaign.

The mineclearing campaign will consist of ten of the navy's fourteen *Avenger*-class mine countermeasures vessels (four of which are already deployed in Bahrain). Minesweepers from other nations would likely join in the hunt. We will also assume some specialized aviation assistance.

Item	*Cost (millions of $)*	*Notes*
Avenger-class vessels	5.91	10 ships for 30 days, based on inflation-adjusted FY1996 annualized operating costs
MH-53E Sea Dragon	48	Ten aircraft flying eight hours per day for 30 days.[11]
Total	**53.9**	

The air warfare campaign will consist of antimissile patrols, coordinating aircraft, and antiship/antisubmarine patrols.

Item	*Cost (millions of $)*	*Notes*
Anti-missile strike patrols	64.8	Fifteen aircraft in the air at all times for fifteen days.[12]
JSTARS/ AWACS aircraft	27.3	Based on $24,000 per flying hour cost for E-3 AWACS and $52,000 per flying hour cost for JSTARS,[13] assuming one of each on station at all times for fifteen days.
P-3 naval patrol/ASW	16.2	At $22,500 per flying hour, with two on station at all times for fifteen days.[14]
Antiship strike patrols	34.5	Eight aircraft in the air at all times for fifteen days.
Munitions	33.4	200 guided bombs, 50 anti-radiation missiles
Total	**176.2**	
Total, Including Demining	**230.1**	

Scenario Three: Warfare

It is quite possible that Iran's response to an attack would be severe enough to merit a continuation of major air operations against Iran, with the goal of seriously degrading its conventional forces, eliminating its aerial, naval, and missile forces, crippling military industry and command and control, and possibly even destabilizing the rule of the mullahs. This would entail a continuation of the air campaign in more or less the same fashion as it had been carried out in the initial strikes. Munitions costs would rise, as there would be significantly more use of general purpose bombs and air to surface missiles as the United States engages Iran's military. Beyond that, however, cost profiles would likely remain more or less the same for several weeks, though cruise missiles and B-2s would likely see little use as Iran's air defenses would be a much lesser threat. One week of these operations would cost:

Item	*Cost (millions of $)*	*Notes*
Naval operations	106	Two carrier groups
Munitions	494.1	See usage table[15]
Air operations	945	Identical operational tempo, though with more strike missions and fewer combat air patrols. Sustaining a high tempo over an extended period may require more units to enter the theater, which would impose additional costs not counted here.
Subtotal	**1,545.1**	
Aircraft losses	535.8	Loss rates are presumed to be the same.
Total	**2,080.9**	

After perhaps six weeks of these operations, the damage to Iran's fixed assets would be so severe that targets would be harder and harder for American pilots to find. The United States would have achieved total air supremacy, and Iranian airspace might even be considered safe for the operation of high-value assets like the E-8 JSTARS. The remnants of Iran's militaries would now be in hiding. Operations like Noble Anvil and Odyssey Dawn have shown that enemy forces can sustain this posture for extended periods of time with low attrition rates, and the Iranians have likely taken particular care to prepare for this scenario. Iranian retaliatory actions may continue. The United States may thus find it very difficult to extract itself from air operations and may continue at a lowered operational tempo indefinitely. The cost profile for one week of these lower-tempo operations is estimated as follows:

Item	*Cost (millions of $)*	*Notes*
Naval operations	106	Two carrier groups still needed.
Munitions	121.1	See usage table.[16]

Air operations	432	Operational tempo: 8,000 sorties/week (from 1,7500 sorties/week in major operations)
Subtotal	**659.1**	
Aircraft losses	190.4	Loss rates downgraded to 0.45 aircraft lost and 0.65 aircraft damaged per 1000 sorties.[17]
Total	**849.5**	

SCENARIOS FOR SUSTAINED CONFLICT

Based on these figures, we can construct a few scenarios for a sustained conflict, and estimate their costs.

Scenario 1: Iran Sues for Peace

The United States swiftly responds to Iran's retaliation. Within weeks, the mullahs realize that the damage to their repressive apparatus is becoming severe enough to jeopardize their continued rule of the country. They approach the United States through back channels and offer favorable terms. The United States, eager to avoid creating another chaotic black hole in the Middle East, accepts the offer.

Item	*Number of Weeks*	*Cost (millions of $)*
Initial Attack	1	3,233
High Tempo Operations	3	6,242.7
Low Tempo Operations	0	0
Total		**9,475.7**

Scenario 2: Collapse

U.S. airstrikes cause high casualties in the Iranian militaries, but are particularly effective in preventing effective command and control. The militaries fragment as an anti-IRGC faction of the Artesh attempts a coup. Iran descends into chaos, and the United States drops its operational tempo as it attempts to influence outcomes in its favor rather than winning by force.

Item	*Number of Weeks*	*Cost (millions of $)*
Initial Attack	1	3,233
High Tempo Operations	3	6,242.7

Low Tempo Operations	3	2,548.5
Total		**12,024.2**

Scenario 3: Defeat in Detail

The Iranian military and state structures hold together even as the United States achieves its military objectives. After several weeks, it becomes clear that Iran has been dealt an incapacitating blow, but that political change will not result. The United States ceases operations in Iranian airspace (though Iran's defenses are now so weak that it can regain access at will) and returns to a containment posture against a crushed, but angry, Islamic Republic.

Item	*Number of Weeks*	*Cost (millions of $)*
Initial Attack	1	3,233
High Tempo Operations	6	12,485.4
Low Tempo Operations	6	5,097
Total		**20,815.4**

Scenario 4: Entanglement

The United States destroys the Iranian militaries' fixed assets and heavy weapons. However, repeated acts of terrorism and asymmetric attacks make it politically difficult to draw down operations. This, coupled with growing bureaucratic inertia, traps the United States in sustained lower-tempo operations against Iran for months.

Item	*Number of Weeks*	*Cost (millions of $)*
Initial Attack	1	3,233
High Tempo Operations	6	12,485.4
Low Tempo Operations	26	22,087
Total		**37,805.4**

FOLLOW-UP STRIKES

Most experts agree that an attack on Iran's nuclear program, however successful, would not end Iran's desire for the bomb—it would be likely, in fact, to make it more urgent, as Iranian leaders would have had their nation's vulnerability demonstrated before the world. There is thus a consensus that sometime within a decade of an attack, another round of counterproliferation strikes would be needed. This cycle could even repeat itself ad infinitum—Israeli experts have allegedly compared follow-up strikes to "mowing the lawn." Future strikes would be different from the first round. Large, crucial targets like the enrichment halls at Natanz would be replaced by smaller, dispersed, and hidden/hardened targets. Heavy penetration munitions like the GBU-28 and MOP may again be in demand. However, Iran will likely have ordered the departure of the IAEA in the wake of the first attacks, so the United States would be entirely dependent on its own intelligence apparatus for identification of targets. Total destruction of the renewed nuclear program would be an unrealistic goal—only a further delay is attainable. A new round of attacks would probably cost less than the initial attacks by a significant margin, as there would be fewer targets and less risk to American pilots, as Iran's air defenses would not have recovered from the first blow.[18] The expenses of containing Iran's retaliation, however, would likely be similar, as the reconstruction of, for instance, a mass flotilla of suicide boats would be well within Iran's means. This second strike may cost $2 billion or less in today's dollars, though as before there would be risk of escalation and entanglement.

NOTES

1. Eliot A. Cohen, *Gulf War Air Power Survey* (*GWAPS*), vol. 5 (Washington, DC: Office of the Secretary of the Air Force, 1993), 554.
2. Cohen, *GWAPS*, 5:554.
3. It is difficult not to look at the very existence of the MOP project and see Iran.
4. Inflation-adjusted, from figures in "Navy Carrier Battle Groups: The Structure and Affordability of the Future Force," United States General Accounting Office, Feb. 1993, http://archive.gao.gov/d36t11/148427.pdf.
5. Numbers derived from Cohen, *GWAPS*, 5:651. Note that the loss rates are for combat sorties, whereas the operational tempo of 2,500 sorties per day is derived from overall sorties. However, as discussed in the section on the costs of an Israeli airstrike, loss rates for peacetime military aviation are comparable.
6. Weapons usage rates are assumed to be roughly the same as during the Gulf War (taken from Cohen, *GWAPS*, 5:553–54), although AAM usage rates are slightly higher, and use of anti-armor missiles is significantly lowered. Use estimated as follows:

Munition	Number	Total Cost (millions of $)
GBU-28	60	9
Other guided bomb	1500	83.7
Air to air missile	150	50
Air to ground missile	600	250
Anti-radiation missile	600	269.5

Note that the use of anti-radiation missiles, which can be very expensive, can be higher depending on employment tactics. In some conflicts, the missiles were regularly fired unaimed with the hope that a radar will begin emitting while they are in flight; this can dramatically increase use rates. More recent models of the missiles are designed to reduce unaimed fire.

7. The sortie length is based on back-of-the-envelope estimations of time needed for aircraft to reach targets in Iran. Cost per hour varies significantly per aircraft—recent-model F-16s cost about $9,000 per hour to operate, while an F-15E costs $19,500. These numbers are taken from the March 30, 2011, Congressional Research Service report, *Operation Odyssey Dawn (Libya): Background and Issues for Congress*.

8. In 2010, this transfer authority covered $4.5 billion. Congressional Research Service, *Operation Odyssey Dawn (Libya)*, 26.

9. Presumed strike package composition: two strike aircraft, four TARCAP, four SEAD, aircraft averaging $12k per hour to operate and flying 4.5 hour missions. Each strike package hits two of the ten targets. Munitions used: two guided bombs per strike aircraft, plus one anti-radiation missile per SEAD aircraft. No air to air missiles are factored in, as the IRIAF would be seriously weakened in the initial campaign and would find it difficult to respond. These calculations do not include any involved naval vessels or support like tankers, EW, or AWACS aircraft.

10. Some authors have suggested that an invasion of the coastal areas would be necessary to accomplish the mission of protecting Hormuz. This would be far more expensive than any of the options presented here.

11. Cost per flying hour is $20,000, based on information from Craig Hooper, "What's Strangling the CH-53K?," Defense Tech, Apr. 29, 2010, http://defensetech.org/2010/04/29/whats-strangling-the-ch-53k/.

12. Based on estimates from Talmadge, "Closing Time," 109, again using $12,000 per flying hour figure.

13. As seen in William Matthews, "Toward a 10-Year Airship," *Defense News*, May 11, 2009, www.airshipvision.eu/fichiers/Strato-DARPA-US.pdf.

14. Calculated from Paul P. Lawler, "Cost Implications of the Broad Area Maritime Surveillance Unmanned Aircraft System for the Navy Flying Hour Program and Operation and Maintenance Budget," Naval Postgraduate School, Dec. 2010.

15. Usage table:

Type	Number expended	Total cost (millions of $)
Guided bomb	1500	83.7
Unguided bomb	1500	5.4
Air to air missile	10	4.1
Air to ground missile	1000	176.4
Anti-radiation missile	500	224.5

16. Usage table:

Type	Number expended	Total cost (millions of $)
Guided bomb	500	27.9
Unguided bomb	100	0.3
Air to air missile	0	0
Air to ground missile	400	70.5
Anti-radiation missile	50	22.4

17. Given the improvements in electronic warfare since 1991 and Iran's highly outdated air defenses, air losses could drop much lower (although peacetime loss rates would be about 0.31 aircraft per 1,000 sorties at the sortie lengths involved, so we would still expect some losses). However, even with air defense systems that can endanger aircraft operating at altitude knocked out, effectively targeting Iran's ground

forces would require some operations within range of numerous, easy-to-hide Short Range Air Defense Systems (SHORADS).

18. Assuming, of course, that outside powers like Russia were not so disgusted by the first attack that they provided Iran with advanced air defense systems.

Appendix C: Dynamics and Costs of an Israeli Strike

There are two sorts of missions that we can expect to see the Israelis carrying out. In the initial hours of a conflict with Iran, they will focus heavily on hitting as many targets as possible in the shortest amount of time, denying Iran the opportunity to react or hide key assets. They will seek to put as many aircraft in Iranian airspace at once as they can, and most of these aircraft will return as soon as they have hit their targets. As the conflict wears on, the Israelis may seek to maintain an aerial presence in Iran to interfere with Iran's efforts at self-defense, reconstruction, and retaliation. They will seek to keep as many aircraft as they can on patrol over Iran, twenty-four hours a day. We will call these two options a burst attack and sustained patrols.

BURST ATTACK

The bottleneck in a burst attack is the number of aircraft that can be refueled by the entire Israeli tanker force in a short period of time, short enough that they can take part in a combined operation. The Israelis would send up all—or perhaps all but one—of their tankers and as many aircraft as they could support.

The most important aircraft in the raid would be the IAF's twenty-five F-15Is. With their more powerful armament, they will be vital in attacking buried targets like the enrichment facilities of Natanz and Fordow, and will likely all be used in the initial sortie. They burn fuel at a higher rate than the F-16I and will thus require more from the tankers at the first refueling, but they also carry enough that most should be able to complete their mission and return home without needing a second refueling. Once the F-15Is have had their time at the trough, the tankers will still have an enormous amount of fuel available, which can supply F-16Is to round out the strike force. These have some ability against buried targets, but will also focus on suppressing Iran's air defenses, destroying its fighters, and hitting key infrastructure.[1] Some will likely remain with the tankers to keep Iranian fighters away.

We make the following informed assumptions about the performance of Israel's aircraft. We will use them to calculate Israel's capabilities.[2]

Aircraft	*Performance*	*Notes*
KC-707	Burns 11,725 pounds of fuel per hour when cruising, burns about 14,000 pounds in the first hour of flight as it climbs to altitude	Based on publicly available estimates, notes on engine performance, and public remarks by pilots and aviation enthusiasts
	Holds about 190,000 pounds of fuel at takeoff	
	Provides fuel to Israeli fighters at 3,000 pounds per minute	Based on similar performance by American tankers; can offer fuel at faster rates, but fighters and other small aircraft are unable to safely receive it.
	Does not operate in enemy airspace, but not totally risk-averse	Based on media remarks by relevant IAF personnel
F-15I	Burns 9,000-15,000 pounds of fuel per hour	Low figure delivers a combat radius consistent with public estimates; high figure top of a range gleaned from remarks by pilots
	Holds 30,500 pounds of fuel at takeoff	Assumed load of two external fuel tanks. This is not necessarily the maximum amount of fuel the aircraft can carry—it can take on more once off the ground.
F-16I	Burns 4,500-7,500 pounds of fuel per hour	Low end consistent with open-source figures, high end extrapolated from F-15I performance
	Holds 18,000 pounds of fuel	Assumes use of two 600-gallon non-jettisonable fuel tanks.

With these assumptions, the Israelis can easily refuel their entire fleet of twenty-five F-15Is. Depending on whether they hold one tanker in reserve or take a slight risk and send all eight out, they will be able to support a minimum of thirty-five to forty F-16Is (though cautiousness about fuel availability might lead them to actually send out fewer aircraft). This number is likely sufficient to hit most key nuclear targets; two or three return strikes certainly are.

SUSTAINED PATROL

The bottleneck in a sustained patrol is the rate at which aircraft can be redeployed into action on return from a mission. Combat aircraft sometimes land, rearm, refuel, and take off again for the battlefield, but they cannot do this indefinitely. The physical shock of landing, the forces of flight, the complexity of the modern aircraft, and simple wear and tear combine to ensure that a returning aircraft will need hours of maintenance in order to safely go back into combat. Pilots will need to be briefed on their next mission, and at some point they need to rest. We can estimate the total ground time required between sorties, and then use this to find the total number of sorties each aircraft can fly in a day. Using this, the length of the patrols, and the number of aircraft available, we can estimate the size of the twenty-four-hour patrol.[3]

We estimate based on these parameters, and an assumed four-hour loiter time on its refueling track, that each KC-707 can fly no more than 1.74 sorties per day.[4] They would support F-16Is flying ninety-minute patrols and F-15Is flying forty-five-minute patrols over Iran's nuclear zone.[5] We thus arrive at the following maximum twenty-four-hour patrol sizes by aircraft type:

Aircraft	*Sortie Rate*	*Fleet Size*	*Patrol Length*	*Maximum Patrol Size*
KC-707	1.74	8	4 hours	2.31
F-15I	2.03	25	45 minutes	1.58
F-16I	1.83	100	90 minutes	11.43

However, the KC-707s will not carry enough fuel to supply patrols of those sizes. Consider these tables of the net amount of fuel that will be brought onto station during a twenty-four-hour period, and the amount that will be demanded in the same time.[6]

24-Hour Total Supply (pounds of fuel)	
Maximum (newly arrived)	2,126,976
Minimum (after 4 hours)	1,474,128

24-Hour Total Demand (pounds of fuel)[7]	
F-15I	913,500
F-16I	1,647,000
Total	**2,560,500**

Thus, Israel's tanker fleet will be a key limiting factor in efforts to sustain aerial patrols over Iran. The Israelis thus have a limited ability to sustain air power over Iran—they can only keep a few aircraft in the fight, and they must cover a massive area—Iran's military core is about 198,000 km^2, roughly the size of Kyrgyzstan or South Dakota.[8] They would be unable to exercise absolute control in this airspace and would certainly be harassed by Iran's weak air forces. Worse, they would not cover the Gulf coast, meaning Iran would be free to cause as much trouble in Hormuz as it pleased. The United States would almost certainly be drawn into the conflict because of this.

What would prompt Israel to use this suboptimal option? Area patrols like this may become necessary if Iran begins launching missiles at Israel in the wake of a strike, with aircraft hunting for Iranian launchers. Coalition patrols in the 1991 Gulf War were famously inept at destroying Iraqi Scud missiles, despite the major effort they made to hunt them and their frequent claims of success. Technology and weaponry have improved significantly since then, but it is questionable that such a small number of aircraft could effectively cover such a large area even with the best technology. The choice to operate a twenty-four-hour patrol would thus likely be made by political leaders failing to resolve the crisis or hoping to appear they are doing something, rather than due to expected effectiveness.

A sustained crisis with Iran could also push the conflict toward twenty-four-hour Israeli presence, with aircraft operating close to their maximum operational tempo as they repeatedly fly to Iran to bomb a range of political, military, and nuclear sites. These missions would likely be shorter, allowing the Israelis to reach higher sortie rates across aircraft types.

REPEATED BURST ATTACKS

After a first wave of strikes, it is not likely that the Israelis will immediately shift to the sustained attack plan or stop attacking altogether. The first wave will not be large enough to destroy all of Iran's key nuclear sites. They will likely launch a second wave attack as soon as they can, and may continue this pattern for days. Mass air raids pose more of a problem for air traffic control, yet are better able to suppress Iran's air defenses and overwhelm its attempts to protect itself. The rate of these raids will be determined by the maximum sortie rates of the involved aircraft. Because these missions are shorter than patrol missions, they will be able to sustain slightly higher sortie rates for long periods. We estimate them as follows:

Aircraft	*Sortie Rate*	*Aircraft per Sortie*
KC-707	2.15	8
F-15I	2.27	25
F-16I	2.27	43–53

The KC-707 fleet again limits Israel's operational tempo, though by a tiny amount. At this rate, the Israelis will be able to launch maximum mass attacks on Iran about every eleven hours and ten minutes with large airstrikes. For shorter periods, they can cut that time to perhaps seven hours. Three major concerns could cut this tempo or force operations to a halt. The first is Israel's fuel supplies, which we will discuss shortly. The second is pilot fatigue—depending on the number of aircrews per airframe the Israelis have, this rate might not be sustainable in the long run. The third is aircraft losses. It is unlikely that the Iranians will manage to down a significant number of Israeli aircraft if the Israelis are using massed attacks. However, the "loss" of a tanker or two due to maintenance issues would reduce strike package sizes and decrease the margin for error.

FUELING THE FIGHT

Repeatedly sending dozens of aircraft to faraway targets consumes immense amounts of fuel. Can Israel, with its limited fuel infrastructure and storage capacity, sustain its air operations for long periods, or will it begin to run out of gas? Israeli jet fuel usage by attack type (without counting drones, intelligence aircraft, etc.) is at minimum:

Attack Type	*Daily Consumption*	*Barrels per day of fuel*
Repeated Bursts	5,130,935 pounds	17,965
Sustained Patrols	6,114,468 pounds	21,409

Note that these numbers are not barrels of crude oil—they are barrels of refined oil products, in this case jet fuel. Israel will thus need intake of crude sufficient to make that much jet fuel, and refinery capacity sufficient to convert the crude, or it will have to import the fuel itself (hardly guaranteed, if the international community is angry enough about a strike). As of 2010 it consumed about 24,500 barrels of kerosene (the base of aviation fuel) per day under normal conditions.[9] When refined, a barrel of crude oil is separated into a number of products, including about 4.1 gallons of kerosene per barrel.[10] At that rate, Israel needs to import 251,000 barrels per day to meet its current nonmilitary needs.

Israel can produce 35,000 barrels of kerosene per day, 21,000 at the Oil Refineries Limited facility in Haifa[11] and 14,000 at the Paz facility in

Ashdod. After normal nonmilitary fuel consumption is accounted for, this leaves 10,500 barrels. This is not enough to cover either sustained military option on a permanent basis; Israel would have to rely on stores of pre-made jet fuel. Moreover, Israeli refineries tend to reduce operations or shut down for safety during wars, so Israel's jets may be drawing from unreplenished stores if Iran retaliates.

During the 2006 war in Lebanon, the Israeli Air Force averaged 1,426 flight hours per day. During the 2008–2009 war in Gaza, it averaged 897 flight hours per day.[12] In both conflicts, the IAF was reportedly operating well below capacity; in both, there were not reports of jet fuel shortages (though during the 2006 war, the United States provided the Israelis with some). Assuming that the average flight hour burns 5,000 pounds of fuel,[13] the Israelis would have been consuming 25,000 barrels of aviation fuel per day over Lebanon and 15,700 over Gaza. During the Lebanon war, oil tankers stopped docking in Israel, and refineries shut down. Israel was forced to draw from its semi-secret reserves.[14] There are no publicly available figures on how big this reserve is, or even where it is located. We thus cannot weigh in on how long it can sustain a military campaign, though it is certain that it is a finite period, likely a few months at most. Other fuel reserves are likely not substantial—the Ben Gurion International Airport reserves, for instance, would cover about one day of combat.

THE THREAT OF FUEL SHORTAGES

In addition to the air assault's strain on its fuel supplies, Israel will certainly want to conduct major patrols over itself, Palestine, and Lebanon to counter retaliation. These will create a much smaller strain on Israel's fuel supplies, but will add to an unsustainable condition. During the 2006 Lebanon War, the IAF averaged about thirty sorties each day to prevent Hezbollah UAVs from entering Israel.[15] Assuming that the IAF would keep up a similar level of operations to shield itself during a conflict with Iran, it would burn at least an additional 1,800 barrels of jet fuel per day.

The worst case scenario is that Iran could get its allies to attack Israel. A combined wave of rocket and terror attacks from Hezbollah and Iran-friendly Palestinian groups like Islamic Jihad (PIJ), while not necessarily likely, could force the IAF to conduct air operations on multiple fronts. By straight addition, this would lead to the following minimum daily jet fuel usage rates:

	Air assault on Lebanon	*Air assault on Gaza*	*Both*
Burst attacks on Iran	44,765 barrels	35,465 barrels	60,465 barrels

Sustained patrols over Iran	48,209 barrels	39,909 barrels	63,909 barrels

All of these use rates exceed Israel's daily jet fuel production capacity even if all jet fuel is being used for military purposes. It's likely that these figures substantially overestimate Israel's *actual* fuel consumption in the event of such a crisis. Both the Lebanon and Gaza air wars included major operations in support of invading ground troops, including the delivery of paratroopers behind enemy lines, close air support missions, and evacuation of wounded soldiers. It's entirely possible that sustained attacks from Hezbollah or Gaza would lead to an Israeli ground intervention, but they'd be unlikely to launch that invasion immediately, as it would be a costly and unpopular decision. They also wouldn't necessarily have to wage full air wars simultaneously against both Gaza and Hezbollah even if both were attacking with all their might. Though their rocket attacks create fear and place pressure on the Israeli government, actual casualty rates have been low. The Israelis have a history of prosecuting multi-front wars sequentially—holding on the first front, fighting to victory on the second, and only then attacking the first—even when the price of this strategy must be paid in blood.

Even so, there remains a significant chance that that multi-front war would rapidly bleed Israel's stores of jet fuel. Here is how long (in days) a one million barrel jet fuel reserve would last with and without refineries operating, and with no civilian jet fuel use; analysts who believe Israel's reserves to be greater or smaller can scale these numbers as they see fit.[16]

Days of Fuel without Refineries or Crude Imports

	Air Assault on Lebanon	*Air Assault on Gaza*	*Both*	*Neither*
Repeated burst attacks	22.3	28.1	16.5	55.6
Sustained patrols	20.7	25	15.6	46.7

Days of Fuel with Refineries and Crude Imports

	Air Assault on Lebanon	*Air Assault on Gaza*	*Both*	*Neither*
Repeated burst attacks	102.4	2150.5	39.2	∞
Sustained patrols	75.7	203.7	34.5	∞

The Israelis thus have some cause for concern if they become entangled on multiple fronts, especially since the more fronts are open, the less likely it is that Israel can safely operate its refineries or import oil. Everyone knows that Israel can only keep up a high tempo of operations for so long, but fuel shortages could significantly shorten that period. Israel can likely destroy Iran's key nuclear sites within a few days at most. However, if Iran takes retaliatory action, or if the Israelis have decided on a broader scope of targets, Jerusalem may soon find itself forced to cut tempo significantly regardless of danger. It could find itself at the mercy of an American decision to launch an emergency resupply mission.

NOTES

1. These aircraft will also be prepared to take a number of other actions when things go wrong, replacing lost aircraft, initiating search and rescue, etc.

2. Note that Israeli mission planners will likely, like American planners, use modestly complex computer programs to design their mission and estimate their needs. The work that follows does not benefit from such software, so it should be taken with a grain of salt.

3. We will use the figures, formulas, and methods found in the appendixes of Eric Stephen Gons, *Access Challenges and Implications for Airpower in the Western Pacific* (Santa Monica, CA: Pardee RAND Graduate School, 2010). Gons estimates that ground time is always at least three hours (due to the need to taxi, refuel, and rearm) plus 0.68 times the flight time (due to accumulating maintenance needs). These figures, combined with flight time, add up to a turnaround time for the aircraft in question. Divide 24 (the length of the day) by the turnaround time to find the maximum number of sorties per airframe per day. The maximum number of sorties might actually be lower, as the aircrew also has limits. However, keeping more aircrews than airframes can allow the true maximum to be approached, even when mission durations are pushing aircrews to endurance.

4. This long sortie allows the tanker to refuel a patrol both before and after its time in Iran's airspace, and provides about twenty-four minutes of extra time in case of difficulties.

5. The F-15I must fly shorter patrols due to its higher fuel consumption. Note that these patrols are measured by time over Iran's nuclear areas, not over Iran—transit time is not counted. Both patrol lengths allow the patrolling aircraft twenty to thirty minutes more fuel than they would need even if they had to wait several minutes before fueling when returning to the refueling tracks, and had refueled first on their way out (this adds an additional half hour to time between refuelings).

6. We provide a maximum and minimum number for the supply so that the reader can see the amount of fuel the tankers will burn over the course of their four hour patrols—they will slowly reduce their refueling capability.

7. We use the minimum figure for fuel demand here, so the maximum figures used in other calculations would yield an even smaller patrol.

8. We interpret this core area as a polygon extending from Tehran to Tabriz, south to Kermanshah, and east to Esfahan. This area includes key nuclear, missile, and military facilities that would be highly relevant to any Iranian action against Israel.

9. Does not include military consumption. See "Ministry of National Infrastructures Fuel and Gas Administration Data Indicate a 15% Decrease in Fuel Oil Consumption during 2010," Israeli Ministry of National Infrastructures Spokesperson's Office, March 2011.

10. "What a Barrel of Crude Oil Makes," Texas Oil and Gas Association, www.txoga.org/articles/308/1/WHAT-A-BARREL-OF-CRUDE-OIL-MAKES.

Note that the claimed maximum kerosene outputs of Israel's two refineries, in relation to their crude oil inputs, suggests they can wring more kerosene from a barrel of crude—up to 6.1 gallons, in the case of the Ashdod facility. The necessary crude intake might thus be less than 251,000 barrels.

11. Prospectus, Oil Refineries Limited, section 7-31, www.orl.co.il/financialReports/eng_0011007.pdf.

12. Benjamin S. Lambeth, *Air Operations in Israel's War against Hezbollah* (Santa Monica, CA: RAND Project Air Force, 2011).

13. This may be aggressive—a substantial portion of flying hours in both wars were by helicopters, which do not burn fuel as quickly as jets.

14. Amiram Barkat, "Turkey Cannot Block Israel's Oil Supply," Globes: Israel's Business Arena, Sept. 2011, www.globes.co.il/serveen/globes/docview.asp?did=1000685052&fid=1724.

15. Lambeth, *Air Operations*.

16. The one million barrel reserve would put Israel on comparable footing to the United States, where stocks of jet fuel have historically hovered between twenty and thirty-five days of ordinary usage. A one million barrel jet fuel reserve would give Israel forty days of ordinary usage.

Economic Section Appendixes

Appendix D: Hydrocarbon Production of Gulf States in 2011

Bahrain
Net Oil Exports: 3 kbd
Oil Exports to U.S.: 2 kbd
Refinery Capacity: 262 kbd

Iran
Net Oil Exports: 2.4 mmbd
Oil Exports to U.S.: nominally 0
Refinery Capacity: 1.4 mmbd
Natural Gas Exports: 0.034 tcf

Iraq
Net Oil Exports: 1.7 mmbd
Oil Exports to U.S.: 450 kbd
Refinery Capacity: 598 kbd

Kuwait
Net Oil Exports: 2.1 mmbd
Oil Exports to U.S.: 182 kbd
Refinery Capacity: 889 kbd

Qatar
Net Oil Exports: 1 mmbd
Oil Exports to U.S.: 10 kbd
Refinery Capacity: 200 kbd
Natural Gas Exports: 3.3 tcf

Saudi Arabia
Net Oil Exports: 7.3 mmbd
Oil Exports to U.S.: 1 mmbd
Refinery Capacity: 2 mmbd

United Arab Emirates
Net Oil Exports: 2.3 mmbd
Oil Exports to U.S.: 40 kbd
Refinery Capacity: 781 kbd

Appendix E: Hydrocarbon-Related Critical Foreign Dependencies Near Iran

One of the most eye-catching documents betrayed to Wikileaks was a list of American "critical foreign dependencies," that is, facilities around the world crucial to America's interests. Many of these are oil and natural gas facilities in the greater Middle East.

Note that many of these facilities have physical or supply-chain connections, so the loss of multiple facilities will not necessarily be purely additive—for instance, the daily production of all the Saudi facilities listed is 19 million barrels per day, which is significantly greater than actual Saudi production, because the facilities represent different stages of petroleum production and processing.

Note that Iran's Khark Island oil terminal, plus the Strait of Hormuz, are listed as critical foreign dependencies. The Bab al Mandab and Suez Canal are also listed; Iran's capacity to act in these areas should be investigated. There is also a Rafael weapons plant in Israel that could become a target.

Abqaiq stabilization facility (KSA): 5 million barrels per day, 7 million capacity
As-Safaniya oil field and processing center (KSA): 1.2 million barrels per day
Baku-Tbilisi-Ceyhan Pipeline (Azerbaijan): 1 million barrels per day capacity
Basra terminal (Iraq): 1.5 million barrels per day capacity
Das Island LNG terminal (UAE)
Jabal az-Zannah oil terminal (UAE)
Mina al Ahmadi terminal (Kuwait): 2 million barrels per day capacity
Qatif Junction (KSA): "All of Saudi Arabia's oil," destruction would stop production for "months"
Qatif Project (KSA): 800k barrels per day
Ras al Juaymah terminal (KSA): 3 million barrels per day capacity
Ras Laffan natural gas and gas-to-liquid plant (Qatar): World's largest plant of its kind

Ras Tanura terminal (KSA): 6 million barrels per day capacity, loss predicted to provoke an $80-$100 spike from a $40/bbl initial crude price.

Ras at Tanaqib processing center (KSA)

Sangachal Terminal (Azerbaijan): 1.2 million barrels per day capacity

Shaybah oil field and gas/oil separation plant (KSA): 1 million barrels per day

Appendix F: Scenarios for Loss of Oil after an Attack on Iran

The following is a list of possible impacts on oil markets in the aftermath of an American or Israeli strike on Iran. Sets of actions are grouped; it is possible that events from multiple groups could occur at the same time (for instance, the initial panic could be followed by a moderate Iranian campaign against the Strait of Hormuz, attacks on Azerbaijani oil facilities, and a general war). The only action guaranteed to occur is the initial panic; all others will depend on Iranian perceptions, choices, and capabilities.

Initial Panic: News that an attack was underway on Iran's nuclear program would cause an immediate panic in global oil markets regardless of whether Iran takes any kind of action in retaliation. Any signs that the campaign is continuing, or that Iran is going to retaliate, could expand the impact of this panic.

Production Loss: None

Minimal Iranian Actions in Hormuz: Reports of Iranian actions of any form in Hormuz, ranging from threatening behavior by speedboats to isolated mine hits or missile launches, would broaden the initial panic as investors suspect that Iran is beginning to launch a campaign against Hormuz.

Production Loss: None long term; sinking a tanker could cause the loss of one to two million barrels on that particular day and would drive up insurance rates (figures estimate increased price per barrel of oil due to shipping insurance ~$1.20; Tanker War impact $2.45–$2.85, translating to a $0.02–$0.07 increase in gas prices)

Moderate Campaign against Hormuz: Iran could mount a sustained and damaging, but not crippling, attack on shipping in Hormuz. This would not be enough to stop shipping, and in its lighter forms it might not even significantly reduce it. Oil prices would climb, however, due to both speculation and rising insurance rates.

Production Loss: 4.25 million barrels per day (based on Lehman Bros. estimates of worst point of Tanker War—25 percent reduction in shipping)

Attempts to Stop Traffic: Iran's most aggressive option against Hormuz is to attempt to make it completely unsafe to pass. The most important tool in this campaign would be mines. Iran has two to three thousand mines in its arsenal, though its ability to deploy them all in a crisis is in doubt—dedicated minelaying vessels, for instance, would quickly be targeted by American air patrols, and might even be destroyed in the initial air campaign. However, Iran could plausibly deploy several hundred of the mines on short notice, and that could seriously endanger shipping. If Iran is obviously attempting to mine the strait, impact on oil prices could be extremely severe; the decisive defeat of this attempt would presumably calm markets.

Production Loss: As much as full capacity (17 million barrels) for the days of combat, gradual return to normal afterwards (could take days or weeks).

Any successful minelaying would likely reduce traffic for a time. This scenario is a failed Iranian attempt to close the strait, so Iran would likely expend significant amounts of its arsenal in just a few days, meaning the net impact may be smaller than either a sustained moderate antishipping campaign or a brief stoppage of traffic.

Brief Stoppage: There is not a consensus that Iran would actually be able to stop traffic. However, if they were successful, the global daily production of oil would drop by tens of millions of barrels. It's likely that within a few days enough mines would be cleared to allow traffic to move again, though the percentage of ships affected by Iranian operations could still be as high as ten percent, which could reduce the strait's throughput and significantly drive up oil and shipping insurance prices.

Production Loss: 17.4 million barrels of oil per day for three and a half days or more, gradual return to normal afterwards (could take days or weeks).

Sustained Stoppage: Iran could mine the strait and then use its arsenal of antiship missiles to harass the vessels attempting to clear the mines. The United States has a fairly small set of mineclearing vessels, so it may be wary of putting them in harm's way. The worst-case scenario is that the strait is impassable and the United States waits for Iran's missiles to be destroyed before clearing the mines. Experts suggest that the clearance of the strait could take as much as three and a half months in these circumstances. More than 1.5 billion barrels of oil would flow through the strait during a period of that length. The impact of this loss could be extreme.

Production Loss: 17.4 million barrels of oil per day for up to 112 days (likely less)

Light Attacks on Gulf Oil Facilities: Iran can, using missiles, saboteurs, and commandos, do damage to the various oil facilities—refineries, pipelines, ports, production fields—found in the greater Gulf area. It is reasonable to suspect that Iran would engage in at least minimal attacks on oil facilities. This could reduce export capacity of the affected states for up to a few months, and the news that attacks of any kind were occurring would also likely cause price spikes.

Heavier Attacks on Gulf Oil Facilities: Iran could mount a larger-scale campaign on the oil facilities, possibly putting some out of commission. This could reduce exports by millions of barrels per day for an extended period and seriously hinder the ability of states like Saudi Arabia to make up for production losses elsewhere. (See appendix B for list of major Gulf oil facilities.)

Partial Stoppage of Iranian Oil: If Iran takes significant retaliatory action, the United States could selectively target Iranian oil facilities as it did during the Tanker War. This could partly reduce Iran's net oil production.

Total Stoppage of Iranian Oil: Severe actions by Iran could prompt the destruction of its oil facilities. Iran could also stop its oil production unilaterally to punish the world for harming it. Experts are divided on whether Saudi Arabia could make up for this loss in production. Iran could live off of its currency reserves for a substantial period—perhaps up to a year and a half—before it would need to restart production.

Production Loss: 2.3 million barrels per day. If Iran shuts down its facilities, this could be restarted quickly; if the facilities are destroyed, it will take longer.

Actions against Kurdistan: There has been speculation that Israel could leverage its ties in Iraqi Kurdistan to gain the right to use Kurdish facilities for a number of purposes during a strike. This could prompt Iranian retaliation against Kurdish oil facilities, or possibly even Iranian attempts to incite Arab-Kurdish conflict in disputed areas like Kirkuk.

Production Loss: 50k barrels per day

Actions against Azerbaijan: There has been even more speculation that Israel could use its extensive cooperation with Azerbaijan to get access to Azeri facilities for use in an attack, and Azerbaijan's close relationship with Israel might make it a target even if it is not directly involved in a strike. Azerbaijan has significant oil and natural gas facilities, and its border in the resource-rich Caspian Sea is disputed by Iran. A conflict in this area, or attacks on Azeri oil facilities, could have serious economic consequences and could create difficulties for long-term regional pipeline projects as well as pipelines already in existence, like that running from Baku, through Tbilisi, to Ceyhan on Turkey's Mediterranean coast.

Production Loss:

Baku-Tbilisi-Ceyhan Pipeline: 1 million barrels per day capacity (U.S. "critical foreign dependency")
Sangachal Terminal: 1.2 million barrels per day capacity (U.S. "critical foreign dependency")
Baku-Supsa Pipleline: 145k+ barrels per day
Baku-Novorossiysk Pipeline: ~100k barrels per day
Possible political fallout on regional pipeline deals

Actions against Israel

Production loss:

Askelon-Eilat Pipeline: 400k barrels per day Mediterranean to Red Sea, 1.2 million barrels per day Red Sea to Mediterranean

Warfare: There is a possibility that warfare could break out between Iran and the striking state. Such a confrontation would have significant potential for escalation and could include regular Iranian actions against any number of the targets discussed above, or terrorism around the world. The economic impacts of this could be substantial.

Mitigating Factors: If the world has some warning—say, an extended political debate—before intervention, states might build their oil stocks, and speculation could drive up prices before the action, cushioning the spike when an attack actually occurs. This would not, however, be able to eliminate the impact of even a brief stoppage of Hormuz.

While all of the possible negative impacts on the world's oil markets *could* happen at once, it is unlikely that they all will. Additionally, there are some experts that doubt Iran will be maximally aggressive in its targeting of oil, as it has a great deal to lose from a disruption—oil revenues make up about 60 percent of the Iranian government's overall revenue.

Appendix G: The Rise of Emerging Markets in the Global Economy

The dynamics of global output as measured by gross domestic product (GDP) and growth measured by yearly percentage increases in GDP have changed significantly since the beginning of the globalization period, as have the sectors in which global growth is taking place. Over the past two and a half decades, the percentage of world growth that has taken place in advanced economies, which are grouped together in the Organisation for Economic Co-operation and Development (OECD), has declined, while the percentage of growth that takes place in EMEs has increased.[1] As of 2009, the EMEs generated 39.06 percent of world GDP, with Brazil, India, and China (BIC) accounting for 22.57 percent of all output.[2] In comparison, advanced economies accounted for 56.98 percent of all output, with the United States accounting for 23.58 percent.[3] This distribution is in contrast to the period from 1960 to 1972, when advanced economies accounted for 80.3 percent of growth while emerging market countries accounted for just 16.6 percent of growth.[4]

Changing shares of global output

	1960 – 1972	*2008 – 2009*
Emerging market economies	16.6%	39.06%
Brazil, India, and China		22.57%
Advanced economies	80.3%	56.98%
United States		23.58%

As a reflection of these changes, the distribution of world GDP growth has changed as well. From 1960 to 1972, advanced economies grew at a rate of 7.18 percent, while EMEs grew at a rate of 3.71 percent.[5] In contrast, from 2008 to 2009, advanced economies grew at a rate of 0.17 percent, while EMEs grew at 2.34 percent. Furthermore, with global growth of 11.6 percent from 1960 to 1972 and of 2.73 percent from 2008 to 2009, growth accounted for by advanced economies from 1960 to 1972 was approximately 62 percent and EMEs was 31.98 percent, while from 2008 to 2009 advanced economies accounted for 6.22 percent and EMEs accounted for 89 percent.[6] In other words, EMEs are growing at a pace much faster than advanced economies. This trend is evident even in the period preceding the crisis years. From 1986 to 2007, world growth was 6.18 percent, EME growth was 2.43 percent and advanced economy growth was 3.53 percent.[7] EMEs thus composed 39.32 percent of growth and advanced economies composed 57.12 percent of growth. Though not the stark difference of the crisis years, these figures still do indicate the rate of growth of emerging markets is still increasing relative to that of developed economies.

Changing patterns of GDP growth

	1960 – 1972	*1986 – 2007*	*2008 – 2009*
Emerging market economies	3.71%	2.43%	2.34%
Advanced economies	7.18%	3.53%	0.17%

Changing shares of growth

	1960 – 1972	*1986 – 2007*	*2008 – 2009*
Global growth	11.6%	6.18%	2.73%
Emerging economies' share	31%	39.32%	89%
Advanced economies' share	62%	57.12%	6.22%

The distribution of global growth has been shaped by changes in sectoral composition of these EMEs. From 1960 to 1972, agriculture in EMEs composed 21.59 percent of GDP, while from 1986 to 2008, it composed 11.78 percent, with the share of industry growing to 34.19 percent from 27.93 percent, and services to 54.03 percent from 50.48 percent.[8] In comparison, the share of agriculture in advanced economies went from 3.5 percent to 1.9 percent, with services going to 66.63 percent from 62.9 percent and industry declining to 28.14 percent from 33.6 percent.[9] These changes have been combined with both the decline of exports as a percentage of the growth of advanced economies to 5.72 percent in the period from 1986 to 2007 from 7.95 percent in the period 1960–1972 and the rise of exports in EMEs from 5.17 percent to a tremendous 11.72 percent, and also the decline of the growth of investment in advanced economies to 2.46 percent from 5.93 percent and its doubling in EMEs to 1.34 percent from .73 percent.[10] These changes suggest that the growth in emerging market countries has been driven by exports, especially in the manufacturing and service sectors.

Changing economic composition (share of GDP)

		1960 – 1972	*1986 – 2008*
Emerging market economies	*Agriculture*	21.59%	11.78%
	Industry	27.93%	34.19%
	Services	50.48%	54.03%
Advanced economies	*Agriculture*	3.5%	1.9%
	Industry	33.6%	28.14%
	Services	62.9%	66.63%

Changing role of exports in growth

	1960 – 1972	*1986 – 2007*
Emerging markets	5.17%	11.72%
Advanced economies	7.95%	5.72%

Changing investment growth

	1960 – 1972	*1986 – 2007*
Emerging markets	0.73%	1.34%
Advanced economies	5.93%	2.46%

NOTES

1. Eswar Prasad and M. Kose, *Emerging Markets Resilience and Growth Amid Global Turmoil* (Washington, DC: Brookings Institution Press, 2010), 30.
2. Kose and Prasad, *Emerging Markets*, 30.
3. Kose and Prasad, *Emerging Markets*, 30.
4. Kose and Prasad, *Emerging Markets*, 30.
5. Kose and Prasad, *Emerging Markets*, 35.
6. Kose and Prasad, *Emerging Markets*, 35.
7. Kose and Prasad, *Emerging Markets*, 35.
8. Kose and Prasad, *Emerging Markets*, 38
9. Kose and Prasad, *Emerging Markets*, 35
10. Kose and Prasad, *Emerging Markets*, 35.

Select Bibliography

MILITARY SECTION

Albright, Brannan, and Stricker. "The Physics Research Center and Iran's Parallel Military Nuclear Program." Institute for Science and International Security, 2012.

Albright, David, and Corey Hinderstein. "The Iranian Gas Centrifuge Uranium Enrichment Plant at Natanz: Drawing from Commercial Satellite Images." Institute for Science and International Security, March 14, 2003. www.isis-online.org/publications/iran/natanz03_02.html.

Al-Rodhan. "The Impact of the Abqaiq Attack on Saudi Energy Security." CSIS Burke Chair, Feb. 27, 2006.

Arasli. "Obsolete Weapons, Unconventional Tactics, and Martyrdom Zeal: How Iran Would Apply Its Asymmetric Naval Warfare Doctrine in a Future Conflict." George C. Marshall European Center for Security Studies Occasional Paper Series No. 10. Apr. 2007.

Baglole, Joel. "GBU-39 Bomb: Bang for the Buck." About US Military. http://usmilitary.about.com/od/afweapons/a/gbu39bomb.htm.

Bahgat, Gawdat. "Nuclear Proliferation: The Case of Saudi Arabia." *Middle East Journal* 60, no. 3 (Summer 2006): 421–43.

"Bahrain Targets Shia Religious Sites." *Al Jazeera English*, May 14, 2011. http://english.aljazeera.net/video/middleeast/2011/05/2011513112016389348.html.

Barkat, Amiram. "Turkey Cannot Block Israel's Oil Supply." Globes, Sept. 2011. www.globes.co.il/serveen/globes/docview.asp?did=1000685052&fid=1724.

Board on Environmental Studies and Technology. *Acute Exposure Guideline Levels for Selected Airborne Chemicals*. Vol. 4. 2004. www.nap.edu/openbook.php?record_id=10902&page=273.

Bolkcom, Christopher. "Military Suppression of Enemy Air Defenses (SEAD): Assessing Future Needs." Congressional Research Service, 2006.

Brannan, Paul. "Satellite Imagery Narrows Qom Enrichment Facility Construction Start Date." Institute for Science and International Security, Nov. 5, 2009. http://isis-online.org/isis-reports/detail/satellite-imagery-narrows-qom-enrichment-facility-construction-start-date/.

Butt, Yousaf. "Are Sanctions a Fatwa on Iran?" *National Interest*, Jan. 12, 2012. http://nationalinterest.org/commentary/are-sanctions-fatwa-iran-6363.

Carnegie Endowment for International Peace. "Gates on Iran." Dec. 7, 2006. www.carnegieendowment.org/2006/12/07/gates-on-iran/xh1.

Carter. "Military Elements in a Strategy to Deal with Iran's Nuclear Program." CNAS, June 2008.

Carter, Sara A. "Iran Missile Test Points to Dangerous 2012 in Dealing with Tehran." *Washington Examiner*, Jan. 2, 2012.

"CBU-75 Sadeye." Federation of American Scientists Military Analysis Network, 1999. www.fas.org/man/dod-101/sys/dumb/cbu-75.htm.

"CBU-87/B Combined Effects Munition (CEM)." Federation of American Scientists Military Analysis Network, 1999. www.fas.org/man/dod-101/sys/dumb/cbu-87.htm.

Cheng et al. "Global Oil Choke Points." Lehman Brothers, Jan. 18, 2008.

Cirincione, Joseph. "Bombs Won't 'Solve' Iran." Carnegie Endowment for International Peace Issue Brief, May 11, 2005.
Clawson and Eisenstadt. "The Last Resort: Consequences of Preventive Military Action against Iran." WINEP, 2008.
Congressional Research Service. "Iran: US Concerns and Policy Responses." Apr. 18, 2011.
Cooper and Harrison. "Selected Options and Costs for a No-Fly Zone over Libya." Center for Strategic and Budgetary Analysis Backgrounder, March 2011.
Cordesman. "Iran, Oil, and the Strait of Hormuz." CSIS Burke Chair, March 26, 2007.
Cordesman and Steitz. "Iranian Weapons of Mass Destruction: Iran's Nuclear Weapons Programs: Works in Progress?" CSIS Burke Chair in Strategy (Draft), Nov. 6, 2008.
"Covert Action." *Crisis Guide: Iran*. Council on Foreign Relations Multimedia Project. www.cfr.org/interactives/CG_Iran/index.html#/analyzing-the-options/.
Crist. "Gulf of Conflict: A History of U.S.-Iranian Confrontation at Sea." Washington Institute Policy Focus #95, June 2009.
DeLeon, Jenkins, Kellen, and Krofcheck. *Attributes of Potential Criminal Adversaries of U.S. Nuclear Programs*. Santa Monica, CA: RAND Corporation, 1978.
Dwyer, Devin. "Cost of Libya Intervention $600 Million for First Week, Pentagon Says." ABC News, March 28, 2011. http://abcnews.go.com/Politics/libya-us-intervention-fly-zone-gadhafi-cost-taxpayers/story?id=13242136.
"F-16 Armament: AGM-65 Maverick Air-to-Ground Missile." F-16.net,www.f-16.net/f-16_armament_article4.html.
"Factsheets: AGM-45 'Shrike' Anti-Radiation Missile." U.S. Air Force, 2007. www.hill.af.mil/library/factsheets/factsheet.asp?id=5797.
"First F-16I Sufa Ready for Delivery to Israel." F-16.net, Nov. 26, 2003. www.f-16.net/news_article912.html.
Friedman, George. "Rethinking American Options on Iran." STRATFOR, Aug. 2010.
Freilich. "Decision Time in Jerusalem." *Journal of International Security Affairs* 18 (Spring 2010): 55–64.
Fuhrmann and Kreps. "Targeting Nuclear Programs in Times of War and Peace." Belfer Center Discussion Paper 2009-11; Harvard Kennedy School, Oct. 2009.
"GBU-57/B Massive Ordnance Penetrator (MOP)." Global Security, 2011. www.globalsecurity.org/military/systems/munitions/mop.htm.
Gerecht. "Should Israel Bomb Iran?" *Weekly Standard*, July 2010.
Gerecht. "To Bomb, or Not to Bomb: That Is the Iran Question." *Weekly Standard*, Apr. 2006.
Gholz. "Threats to Oil Flows through the Strait of Hormuz: Implications for American Grand Strategy." LBJ School Hormuz Working Group, March 2007.
Glasstone and Dolan. *The Effects of Nuclear Weapons*. 3rd ed. Washington, DC: United States Department of Defense and United States Department of Energy, 1977.
Gons, Eric Stephen. *Access Challenges and Implications for Airpower in the Western Pacific*. Santa Monica, CA: Pardee RAND Graduate School, 2010.
"Guided Bomb Unit-12 (GBU-12) Paveway II." Federation of American Scientists Military Analysis Network, 1998. www.fas.org/man/dod-101/sys/smart/gbu-12.htm.
"Guided Bomb Unit-28 (GBU-28): BLU-113 Penetrator." Global Security, 2011. www.globalsecurity.org/military/systems/munitions/gbu-28-specs.htm.
Gulf War Air Power Survey, vol. 5.
Haghshenass. "Iran's Asymmetric Naval Warfare." Washington Institute Policy Focus #87, Sept. 2008.
Hambling, David. "Brawny New Bunker Buster: 'Divine Thunderbolt.'" *Danger Room* (blog), Feb. 4, 2008. www.wired.com/dangerroom/2008/02/bigger-better-b/.
Harel, Amos. "Missile Attack on INS Spear: IDF Probe Faults Navy, Ship's Crew." *Haaretz*, Nov. 8, 2006. www.haaretz.com/print-edition/news/missile-attack-on-ins-spear-idf-probe-faults-navy-ship-s-crew-1.204672.

Harel, Amos. "Soldier Killed, 3 Missing after Navy Vessel Hit off Beirut Coast." *Haaretz*, July 15, 2006. www.haaretz.com/news/soldier-killed-3-missing-after-navy-vessel-hit-off-beirut-coast-1.193112.

Hopper, Craig. "What's Strangling the CH-53K?" *DefenseTech*, Apr. 29, 2010.

Introduction to Naval Weapons Engineering. Federation of American Scientists, 1998. www.fas.org/man/dod-101/navy/docs/es310/syllabus.htm.

Iran's Naval Forces: from Guerrilla Warfare to a Modern Naval Strategy. Washington, DC: U.S. Office of Naval Intelligence, 2009.

"Iran's Nuclear Future: Critical US Policy Choices." RAND, 2009.

"Iran Oil Exports Top 844mn Barrels." PressTV, June 16, 2010. http://edition.presstv.ir/detail/130736.html.

"Israel Boosts Patrols around Naval Gas Fields, Fearing Guerrilla Attacks." *Haaretz*, Nov. 21, 2011. www.haaretz.com/news/diplomacy-defense/israel-boosts-patrols-around-naval-gas-fields-fearing-guerilla-attacks-1.396861.

Johnson. "Iran's Counter-Strike." RAND, Feb. 2010.

Joint Publication 3-01: Countering Air and Missile Threats. Joint Chiefs of Staff, Feb. 5, 2007.

Jones, Seth G. "Striking Iran Is an Option, Not Inevitable." *Christian Science Monitor*, Apr. 11, 2006. www.rand.org/commentary/2006/04/11/CSM.html.

Katz, Yaakov. "Israel Worried Syria Weapons Going to Terrorists." *Jerusalem Post*, Jan. 3, 2012. www.jpost.com/Defense/Article.aspx?id=251944.

Lauden, Mike. "BLU-122 Warhead Program: Precision Strike Technology Symposium." Oct. 19, 2005. www.dtic.mil/ndia/2005psts/lauden.pdf.

Lambeth, Benjamin S. *Air Operations in Israel's War against Hezbollah*. Santa Monica, CA: RAND Project Air Force, 2011.

Lawler, Paul P. "Cost Implications of the Broad Area Maritime Surveillance Unmanned Aircraft System for the Navy Flying Hour Program and Operation and Maintenance Budget." Naval Postgraduate School/DODReports, Dec. 2010.

Lieberthal and Blair. "Smooth Sailing: The World's Shipping Lanes Are Safe." *Foreign Affairs* 86, no. 3 (June 2007): 7–13.

Long, Austin. "Can They?" *Tablet Magazine*, Nov. 18, 2011. www.tabletmag.com/news-and-politics/83631/can-they/.

Majd, Hooman. *The Ayatollah Begs to Differ*. New York: Doubleday 2008.

Matthews, William. "Toward a 10-Year Airship." *DefenseNews*, May 11, 2009.

Matesan and Gay. "El Arish and the Sinai Peninsula Underworld, Egypt." *National Strategy Forum Review* 20, no. 3 (Summer 2011).

McGeorge, Harvey J., II, and Christine C. Ketcham. "Sabotage: A Strategic Tool for Guerrilla Forces." *World Affairs* 146, no. 3 (Winter 1983–1984): 253.

"Ministry of National Infrastructures Fuel and Gas Administration Data Indicate a 15% Decrease in Fuel Oil Consumption during 2010." Israeli Ministry of National Infrastructures Spokesperson's Office, March 2011.

Nasr. "The Implications of Military Confrontation with Iran." *Iran: Assessing US Strategy*. CNAS, Sept. 2008.

"Navy Carrier Battle Groups: The Structure and Availability of the Future Force." United States General Accounting Office Report to Congress, Feb. 1993.

Operation Odyssey Dawn (Libya): Background and Issues for Congress. Congressional Research Service, March 30, 2011.

Perkovich. "Five Scenarios for the Iranian Crisis." 2006.

Preventive Defense Project. "Plan B for Iran: What If Nuclear Diplomacy Fails?" Sept. 2006.

Prospectus, Oil Refineries Limited, section 7-31. www.orl.co.il/financialReports/eng_0011007.pdf.

Raas and Long. "Osirak Redux? Assessing Israeli Capabilities to Destroy Iranian Nuclear Facilities." *International Security* 31, no. 4 (Spring 2007): 7–33.

Rogers. "Iran: Consequences of a War." Oxford Research Group, Feb. 2006.

Rogers. "Military Action against Iran: Impact and Effects." Oxford Research Group, July 2010.
Schlight, John. *A War too Long: The USAF in Southeast Asia, 1961–1975*.
Seelke et al. "Latin America and the Caribbean: Illicit Drug Trafficking and U.S. Counterdrug Programs." Congressional Research Service, Jan. 25, 2011.
"Shahab-3/Zelzal-3." Federation of American Scientists Military Analysis Network, 2008. www.fas.org/programs/ssp/man/militarysumfolder/shahab-3.html.
Shifrinson and Priebe. "A Crude Threat: The Limits of an Iranian Missile Campaign against Saudi Arabian Oil." *International Security* 36, no. 1 (Summer 2011).
Simon. "Contingency Planning Memorandum No. 5: An Israeli Strike on Iran." Council on Foreign Relations, Nov. 2009.
"Small Diameter Bomb/ Small Smart Bomb." GlobalSecurity.org. www.globalsecurity.org/military/systems/munitions/sdb.htm.
Steinberg. "Walking the Tightrope: Israeli Options in Response to Iranian Nuclear Developments." In *Reassessing the Implications of a Nuclear-Armed Iran*, ed. Yaphe and Lutes. Institute for National Strategic Studies (National Defense University), Aug. 2005.
"Taktische Rakete 9M79B,F,K (Gefechtsköpfe)." (Tactical Missile 9M79B,F,K [Warheads]). www.rwd-mb3.de/pages/9m79b.htm.
Talmadge. "Closing Time: Assessing the Iranian Threat to the Strait of Hormuz." *International Security* 33, no. 1 (Summer 2008): 82–117.
Thielmann. "Opening Pandora's Box: Assessing the 'Military Option' for Countering Iran's Nuclear Program." Arms Control Association Issue Brief, June 2011.
"Tor-M1 9M330 Air Defense System." *Defense Update*, 2007. http://defense-update.com/products/t/tor.htm.
Toukan and Cordesman. "Iran, Israel, and the Effects of a Nuclear Conflict in the Middle East." CSIS Burke Chair in Strategy, 2009.
Toukan and Cordesman. "Study on a Possible Israeli Strike on Iran's Nuclear Development Facilities." CSIS Burke Chair in Strategy, 2009.
Udasin, Sharon. "Israel Able to Fulfill Energy Needs—but with Costs." *Jerusalem Post*, Apr. 28, 2011. www.jpost.com/NationalNews/Article.aspx?id=218149.
"United States Marine Corps Weapons and Equipment: KC-130 Hercules." About US Military Marine Corps Fact File. http://usmilitary.about.com/library/milinfo/marinefacts/blhercules.htm.
Wehrey et al. *Saudi-Iranian Relations since the Fall of Saddam*. Santa Monica, CA: RAND, 2009.
"What a Barrel of Crude Oil Makes." Texas Oil and Gas Association. www.txoga.org/articles/308/1/WHAT-A-BARREL-OF-CRUDE-OIL-MAKES.
White. "What Would War with Iran Look Like?" *American Interest*, July–August 2011.

ECONOMIC SECTION

Applebaum, Binyamin. "Its Forecast Dim, Fed Vows to Keep Rates Near Zero." *New York Times*, Aug. 9, 2011. www.nytimes.com/2011/08/10/business/economy/fed-to-hold-rates-exceptionally-low-through-mid-2013.html?pagewanted=all&_r=0.
Asia Trade Hub. "Saudi Arabia: Oil and Gas."www.asiatradehub.com/saudiarabia/oil.asp.
Bandow. "Free Rider: South Korea's Dual Dependence on America." CATO Policy Analysis No. 308, May 1998.
"BEA National Economic Accounts." U.S. Bureau of Economic Analysis, Aug. 12, 2011. www.bea.gov/national/index.htm.
Bradsher, Keith. "As Inflation Climbs, Chinese Policy Makers Face a Problem." *New York Times*, Aug. 9, 2011. www.nytimes.com/2011/08/10/business/global/as-inflation-climbs-chinese-policy-makers-face-a-dilemma.html.

Brito, Dagobert, and Amy Myers Jaffe. "Reducing Vulnerability of the Strait of Hormuz." In *Getting Ready for a Nuclear-Ready Iran*, edited by Sokolski and Clawson, 209–24. Strategic Studies Institute of the U.S. Army War College, 2005.

"Business: Oil Squeeze." *Time*, Feb. 5, 1979. www.time.com/time/magazine/article/0,9171,946222,00.html.

"Chemical Warfare Agents." GlobalSecurity.org, 2011. www.globalsecurity.org/wmd/intro/chem-table.htm.

Clawson, Patrick. "Iran Makes Itself More Vulnerable to Outside Pressure." Washington Institute Policy Watch #1838. www.washingtoninstitute.org/templateC05.php?CID=3391.

Clawson and Henderson. "Reducing Vulnerability to Middle East Energy Shocks." Washington Institute Policy Focus #49, Nov. 2005.

Davis. "Where Has All the Oil Gone?" *Wall Street Journal*, Oct. 6, 2007. http://online.wsj.com/article/SB119162309507450611.html?mod=hpp_us_pageone.

Davis, Dragonette, and Young. Letter to the Editor. *Foreign Affairs* 86, no. 5 (Sept.–Oct. 2007): 194–95.

Davis, Stephen, and John Haltiwanger. "Sectoral Job Creation and Destruction Responses to Oil Price Changes." National Bureau of Economic Research Working Paper 7095, Apr. 1999.

Deputy Director of National Intelligence. "Unclassified Report to Congress on the Acquisition of Technology Relating to Weapons of Mass Destruction and Advanced Conventional Munitions." 2009. www.dni.gov/reports/2009_721_Report.pdf.

DeRosa and Hufbauer. "Normalization of Economic Relations: Consequences for Iran's Economy and the United States." National Foreign Trade Council, Nov. 2008.

Drew. "High Costs Weigh on Troop Debate for Afghan War." *New York Times*, Nov. 14, 2009.

"EIA—Countries—China—Analysis." *China*. Energy Information Administration, July 2010. www.eia.gov/countries/country-data.cfm?fips=CH.

"EIA—Countries—Iran—Analysis." *Iran*. Energy Information Administration, Feb. 2011. www.eia.gov/countries/country-data.cfm?fips=IR.

"EIA—Countries—Saudi Arabia—Analysis." *Saudi Arabia*. Energy Information Administration, Jan. 2011. www.eia.gov/countries/cab.cfm?fips=SA.

"Economic Impact of Transportation." Bureau of Transportation Statistics, accessed Apr. 2012. www.bts.gov/programs/freight_transportation/html/transportation.html.

"Energy Information Administration." *25th Anniversary of the 1973 Oil Embargo*. The Energy Information Administration, 7 Mar. 2007. www.eia.gov/emeu/25opec/anniversary.html.

Gardner, Timothy. "U.S. Seeks Oil Supply Cushion as Iran Sanctions Loom." Reuters, Dec. 14, 2011. www.reuters.com/article/2011/12/14/us-usa-oil-diplomacy-idUSTRE7BD22620111214.

Gholz, Eugene. "Threats to Oil Flows through the Strait of Hormuz: Implications for American Grand Strategy." LBJ School Hormuz Working Group, March 2007.

Habibi, Nader. *GCC States' Import Demand: The Effect of Geopolitics*. Crown Paper #6, 2011.

Hamilton, James. "Understanding Crude Oil Prices." *The Energy Journal, International Association for Energy Economics* 30, no. 2 (2009): 179–206.

Hamilton, James. "What Is an Oil Shock?" National Bureau of Economic Research Working Paper #7755, June 2000.

International Energy Agency. *IEA Response System for Oil Supply Emergencies, 2011*.

Harrison and Cooper. "Selected Options and Costs for a No-Fly Zone over Libya." Center for Strategic and Budgetary Assessments, March 2011.

Henderson, Simon. "OPEC Deliberates: A Saudi Opportunity." Washington Institute Policy Watch #1416. www.washingtoninstitute.org/templateC05.php?CID=2942.

Huntington, Hillard. "Shares, Gaps, and the Economy's Response to Oil Disruptions." *Energy Economics* 26 (2004): 415.

Jimenez-Rodriguez, Rebecca, and Sanchez, Marcelo. "Oil Price Shocks and Real GDP Growth: Empirical Evidence for Some OECD Countries." European Central Bank Working Paper 362, May 2004.

Johnson, Toni. "Expert Roundup: Reducing U.S. Oil Consumption." Council on Foreign Relations, June 11, 2010. www.cfr.org/energyenvironment/reducing-us-oil-consumption/p22413.

Krauss, Clifford. "Saudi Cut in Oil Production Stirs Speculation." *Green: A Blog about Energy and the Environment* (blog), Apr. 22, 2011. http://green.blogs.nytimes.com/2011/04/22/saudi-cut-in-oil-production-stirs-speculation/.

Labonte, Mark. "The Effects of Oil Shocks on the Economy: A Review of the Empirical Evidence." Congressional Research Service, Nov. 15, 2007. http://ncseonline.org/NLE/CRSreports/07Dec/RL31608.pdf.

Litzenberger and Rabinowitz. "Backwardation in Oil Futures Markets: Theory and Empirical Evidence." The Journal of Finance 50, no. 5 (Dec. 1995): 1517–45.

Lieberthal and Blair. "Smooth Sailing: The World's Shipping Lanes Are Safe." *Foreign Affairs* 86, no. 3 (June 2007): 7–13.

Mackey, Peg. "Insight: Catch Me if You Can—Oil Sanctions against Iran." Reuters, March 6, 2012. www.reuters.com/article/2012/03/06/us-iran-oil-sanctions-idUSTRE8250UG20120306.

McClellan, Tom. "Contango Dooms Reason for Strategic Oil Release." McClellan Financial Publications, June 24, 2011. www.mcoscillator.com/learning_center/weekly_chart/contango_dooms_reason_for_strategic_oil_release/.

Nasseri, Ladane. "Iran Parliament Approves Budget Based on $81.5 Crude Oil Price." *Bloomberg*, May 10, 2011. www.bloomberg.com/news/2011-05-10/iran-parliament-approves-budget-based-on-81-5-crude-oil-price.html.

News, CBC. "CBC News in Depth: Oil." CBC, July 18, 2007. www.cbc.ca/news/background/oil/.

Pollack, Kenneth. "The Persian Puzzle: The Conflict between Iran and America." 2004.

Prasad, Eswar, and M. Kose. *Emerging Markets Resilience and Growth Amid Global Turmoil*. Washington, DC: Brookings Institution Press, 2010.

"Potential Impacts of Reductions in Refinery Activity on Northeast Petroleum Product Markets." Energy Information Agency, Feb. 2012. www.eia.gov/analysis/petroleum/nerefining/update/pdf/neprodmkts.pdf.

Robertson, Charles, and Mark Cliffe. "Attacking Iran: The Market Impact of a Surprise Israeli Strike on Its Nuclear Facilities." ING, Jan. 2007. http://media.ft.com/cms/8c72c46c-afac-11db-94ab-0000779e2340.pdf.

Salem, Paul. "The Future of Lebanon." *Foreign Affairs*, Nov.–Dec. 2006.

Scott. *The History of the International Energy Agency*. Vol 2, *Major Policies and Actions of the IEA*. OECD/IEA, 1994. www.iea.org/Textbase/nppdf/free/2-ieahistory.pdf.

"The Shiite Question in Saudi Arabia." Crisis Group Middle East Report No. 45, Sept. 2005

Shifrinson and Priebe. "A Crude Threat: The Limits of an Iranian Missile Campaign aAgainst Saudi Arabian Oil." *International Security* 36, no. 1 (Summer 2011).

Sick, Gary, interviewed by Bernard Gwertzman. "Crisis-Managing U.S.-Iran Relations." Council on Foreign Relations, March 6, 2012. www.cfr.org/iran/crisis-managing-us-iran-relations/p27558.

Smith and Ratnam. "$35B Missile Defense Misses Bullet with Bullet." *Bloomberg*, Aug. 3, 2011.

Stewart, Scott. "Dirty Bombs Revisited: Combating the Hype." STRATFOR, Apr. 22, 2010.

"Strategic Petroleum Reserve Inventory 2005." Strategic Petroleum Reserve, Department of Energy, Aug. 8, 2011. www.spr.doe.gov/dir/dir.html.

Subramanian, Arvind. "The Inevitable Superpower: Why China's Dominance Is a Sure Thing." *Foreign Affairs*, Sept./Oct. 2011.

Talmadge. "Closing Time: Assessing the Iranian Threat to the Strait of Hormuz." *International Security* 33, no. 1 (Summer 2008).

"The Availability and Price of Petroleum and Petroleum Products Produced in Countries Other Than Iran." Energy Information Agency, Feb. 29, 2012. www.eia.gov/analysis/requests/ndaa/.

Toukan and Cordesman. "Iran, Israel, and the Effects of a Nuclear Conflict in the Middle East." CSIS Burke Chair in Strategy, 2009.

Toukan and Cordesman. "Study on a Possible Israeli Strike on Iran's Nuclear Development Facilities." CSIS Burke Chair in Strategy, 2009.

United Nations Development Program. "About Lebanon."www.undp.org.lb/about/AboutLebanon.cfm.

"UP: 2011 West Texas Intermediate Crude Oil (WTI) Prices." *UP: 2011 West Texas Intermediate Crude Oil (WTI) Prices*, Union Pacific Railroad, Aug. 11, 2011. www.uprr.com/customers/surcharge/wti.shtml.

Williams, James L. "OPEC Excess Capacity." 2011. www.energyeconomist.com/a6257783p/opec/capacity/excesscapacity.html.

"World Oil Transit Chokepoints." *EIA—Countries—World Oil Transit Chokepoints*. Energy Information Administration, Jan. 2011. www.eia.gov/countries/regions-topics.cfm?fips=WOTC.

Wehrey et al. *Saudi-Iranian Relations since the Fall of Saddam*. Santa Monica, CA: RAND, 2009.

Wrobel, Sharon. "2006 GDP Growth Tops Forecasts." *Jerusalem Post*, Jan. 1, 2007.

Zhdannikov. "Russian Firm Signs Deal to Fix Iraq-Syria Pipeline." Reuters, March 26, 2008. http://in.reuters.com/article/2008/03/26/russia-iraq-contract-idINL2673766420080326.

Index

About the Authors

Geoffrey Kemp is the director of Regional Strategic Programs at the Center for the National Interest. He has had a long career in academic and research communities and was special assistant to President Reagan and senior director for the Near East and South Asia on the National Security Council staff.

John Allen Gay is assistant editor of the *National Interest* magazine.